STORY SEQUENCE ANALYSIS

STORY SEQUENCE ANALYSIS

A NEW METHOD OF MEASURING MOTIVATION

AND PREDICTING ACHIEVEMENT

By MAGDA B. ARNOLD

 COLUMBIA UNIVERSITY PRESS

NEW YORK AND LONDON   1962

BF
433
A6
A68

This book presents a method of analyzing stories for the purpose of psychological diagnosis. This method was first developed when I was Director of Research and Training in the Psychological Services of the Department of Veterans Affairs in Canada. At that time, shortly after the end of the Second World War, it became imperative to train psychologists working in the psychiatric sections of veterans hospitals in projective techniques. The Rorschach test, of course, offered a well-developed scoring system. Anyone wanting to become proficient at it could go to one of the many workshops offered. The TAT, however, boasted no such advantages, yet it seemed to offer information which was not obtainable from the Rorschach test. It occurred to me then that there should be a way of treating each story as a unit which would reveal specific problems as seen by the storyteller but which would also offer his own particular solution. The method developed in this way proved comparatively easy to teach and easy to learn, for it offered definite rules for abstracting the story import. When each import is abstracted, the sequence of imports reveals the development of the storyteller's thought from story to story and so is easy to interpret in the clinical situation.

Though the interpretations derived from this story sequence analysis intrigued the psychiatrists, they kept insisting that these interpretations were really derived from the clinical record rather than the stories. For this reason, I intended to do research on normal people on the basis of blind analyses before presenting this method to a wider public. The opportunity for such research studies came in 1954 when I came to Loyola University in Chicago. In a series of research studies undertaken together with graduate students, combined with many clinical evaluations of various story sequences, I discovered that this method is as valuable for assessing the motivation of normal people as it is for the clinical diagnosis of mental disturbances. Working with an enthusiastic group of students, I was able to develop a scoring system for assessing positive or negative motivation of normal children and adults. A scoring system which will discriminate between patients with various psychiatric disorders is now being developed and will be presented at a later date.

I gladly acknowledge my debt of gratitude to the members of several seminars I gave on this method, particularly to Sister Helen Gavin, C.S.J., the Reverend H. J. Fagot, S.J., Sister Rosaire, O.P., and Dr. Vasso Vassiliou, who spent a great deal of time on systematizing the scoring and so laid the foundation for the scoring system as it is presented here.

I am grateful also to the Reverend V. V. Herr, S.J., the Chairman of my department, who gave me the opportunity of teaching seminars in this method and who generously gave of his own time in discussing and checking some of the statistical results. Finally, I owe a debt of gratitude to the Reverend J. A. Gasson, S.J., who again, as in previous publications, read the manuscript and helped by his critical suggestions to clarify my thinking and achieve a consistent theoretical position.

The method of story sequence analysis will be found useful for discovering positive and negative motivation in normal people, both through the scoring system and through the clinical evaluation made possible on the basis of the sequence of story imports. This can be a valuable aid in the selection of students for higher institutions of learning or the selection of candidates for responsible positions. Selection based on intelligence alone has a percentage of risk that needs reduction. An additional knowledge of motivation will make it possible to gauge performance in a far more satisfactory manner.

Story sequence analysis thus can be of help in a number of areas where knowledge of prospective levels of performance is useful. I trust what is offered here will be a help not only in Psychology but also in Education and elsewhere.

MAGDA B. ARNOLD

CONTENTS

Part I. THE RATIONALE

1

THE TAT AS A PROJECTIVE METHOD

Since the time Morgan and Murray first published the Thematic Apperception Test (TAT) in 1935 and Murray brought out the final manual in 1943, a great many psychologists have attempted to improve upon Murray's scoring of needs and press, while others were content to use the test merely for clinical diagnosis. According to Murray, a man is likely to reveal his motivation, that is, his needs, wishes, hopes, and fears, while interpreting an ambiguous social situation, such as is portrayed in each of the TAT pictures. In the first version, the instructions were simply to interpret each picture, to guess what went before and what was the final outcome. Increased experience gradually modified the instructions. Now the subject is asked to tell a story about each picture.

This modest beginning has flowered into a vast array of research papers and books. I do not intend to review the many studies that deal with the TAT and other storytelling tests modeled on it. What I do want to discuss is the assumptions upon which work with this test has been based. Wyatt and Veroff (1956) point out that the TAT presupposes three kinds of theory: a theory of fantasy, a theory relating fantasy to individual behavior, and a theory of personality. The theory of personality used by TAT interpreters from Murray to the contributors to a recent symposium (Kagan and Lesser, eds. 1961) has usually been psychoanalytic theory. This proposes that instinctive drives or impulses are the real motivating forces of man which are modified by ego-processes in overt behavior, but reveal themselves in fantasy. This is possible because in fantasy the primary process stemming from these drives is concealed from the ego by various defense mechanisms (projection, identification, etc.). Early TAT workers, particularly, assumed that TAT stories, like fantasy in general, express the storyteller's needs or drives. This theoretical framework seemed validated by Morgan and Murray's report that the material revealed in the TAT of one subject could be verified in five months of psychoanalysis.

Unfortunately for this neat scheme, later research findings did not support it. They looked promising at first: When people were hungry, their TAT stories showed more food themes than when they were sated. But, on further investigation, it was found that the curves indicating the relation between hunger and TAT themes of food and eating were either negatively accelerated or shaped like an inverted U; that is, there was a positive correlation between mild hunger and food imagery, but it often became negative when hunger was prolonged (see Sanford, 1936, 1937; Atkinson and McClelland, 1948; McClelland and Atkinson, 1948; Levine, Chein, and Murphy, 1942; Lazarus *et al.*, 1953). Levine and his co-workers suggested that this curve represents the functioning of the primary process during the first half of the curve, when food is fantasied; while the second leg of the curve reveals the operation of a reality-oriented process which represses such fantasies because they would be unduly disturbing. This explanation might hold for a study like that of Brozek *et al.* (1951), who found that men who had been semi-starved for some time did not reveal excessive food imagery in their TAT.

A similar pattern was found in TAT studies on aggression. Though aggressive themes increased when the storytellers were subjected to annoyance or frustration before the test, they increased principally in the group that scored low on a Manifest

Hostility Scale, while the high scorers tended to have fewer aggressive themes (Hokanson and Gordon, 1958). And, Sanford *et al.* (1943) reported that the number of aggressive themes in the TAT stories of aggressive adolescents was no greater than in the stories of well-adjusted boys. However, Mussen and Naylor (1954) found that aggressive boys told many stories of aggression but few in which aggression was punished. In contrast, well-behaved boys told many stories in which aggression was punished. We may conjecture that aggressive personalities could be distinguished by the way in which they treat aggressive themes in their stories.

Research in achievement motivation (McClelland *et al.*, 1953) shows an even more confused pattern. When a task was given to students with the simple instruction to do it as a favor to a graduate student (relaxed condition), those with high scores on *n* Achievement (derived from TAT stories) did not do as well as those with low *n* Achievement scores. But, when the experimenter described the task as a measure of intellectual ability and urged the students to do their best, high scorers did better than low scorers. The same differences were found in a number of tasks, though these differences were not always significant.

In a group of thirty college men, high *n* Achievement scorers also had higher average college grades during the semester in which the test was taken and in the two succeeding semesters. The correlation coefficient of $+ .51$ was, however, reduced to $+ .39$ when the scores on a verbal and mathematical Scholastic Aptitude Test were partialled out. Other groups of college students showed much lower correlations of *n* Achievement scores with college grades ($+ .05$ and $- .14$, see McClelland *et al.*, 1953, p. 237-41). Lazarus and his co-workers also reported negative or insignificant trends when *n* Achievement was correlated with task performance plus "behavioral evidence of achievement striving" (1961, p. 54). And, Elizabeth French has shown that increased performance can be produced by instructions that arouse not the need for achievement but the affiliative motive (1955).

Moreover, McClelland's *n* Achievement scores of women do not show the same relation to performance as do men's scores. Veroff admits that "obtaining valid achievement motivation scores for women has always been a problem for this apperceptive technique" (1961, p. 102). There is legitimate doubt whether *n* Achievement scores reflect real-life achievement motivation, unless we want to say that women just are not motivated toward achievement. Even the fact that men in high status occupations show higher *n* Achievement scores than men in lower status occupations (Veroff, 1961) is not convincing proof that this score really indicates achievement motivation. It could be that high status men are more articulate or that they are more preoccupied with their work than are low status men—or, for that matter, than women, whether career women or housewives.

A look at McClelland's scoring may clear up some of the mystery. To determine *n* Achievement, McClelland scores each story for unrelated, doubtful and achievement imagery. Unrelated imagery is scored —1, doubtful imagery is scored zero. Achievement imagery is scored +1 when the hero is engaged in competitive activity, is concerned about doing well, and has a unique accomplishment to his credit or shows long-term involvement in a task. Additional scores of +1 are given to the same story for each of the following themes: when there is another reference to achievement (category *TI*); when the story character desires achievement (*n*); when overt or mental activity is directed toward a goal, whether that is successful (*I+*), unsuccessful (*I—*), or doubtful (*I?*); when the character thinks or dreams of success (*Ga+*), or thinks, dreams, or anticipates failure (*Ga—*); when an obstacle to achievement is described, whether that is personal (*Bp*) or external (*Bw*); when positive affect is connected with mastery $(G+)$, or negative affect is connected with failure $(G—)$; when someone aids, helps, encourages the story character (Nup); when achievement becomes the central theme of the story $(AchTh)$ even when that is only described as a daydream. Accordingly, the n Achievement score for a single story may reach $+11$ if the story contains all the above themes and has no unrelated imagery.

From this brief survey of McClelland's scoring, it is clear that the longer the story, the better the chance of a high score. Even expectation of failure is scored under n Achievement $(Ga—)$, so is mere dreaming of success $(Ga+)$, withdrawal on meeting an obstacle (Bw), or despair on incurring failure $(G—)$. In our own studies, such story imports were found in records of low achievers, while high achievers told stories in which failure is overcome, success is achieved by work rather than dreaming, and obstacles are met by resourceful action. It seems likely that McClelland's n Achievement score indicates a preoccupation with the problem of success or failure rather than enduring motivation to achieve excellence. This would explain, for instance, why Veroff's survey (1961) showed that young professional men (but not young unskilled workers) have high n Achievement scores, while older unskilled workers who are increasingly concerned with their livelihood as their families grow eventually reach and even surpass the scores of older professional men who at that time in life are established and need no longer be exclusively preoccupied with their work.

At any rate, all these studies attest that the drives and affects that are assumed to be projected upon the story characters are not a sure guide to the kind of motivation that leads to action in everyday life. As a result of such findings, later theorists began to say that TAT stories could not be called "fantasy" in the accepted (psychoanalytic) sense. Wyatt and Veroff (1956) insisted that a story is an "intentional wide-

awake act of expression" and is neither an instinctual discharge nor the repetition of unconscious patterns. Holt (1961)
pointed out that stories are not like daydreams; when they
are, the storyteller is sick. For Holt, the strength of the TAT
lies in the fact that stories reveal not only primary process
thinking but also defenses and ego-processes. He insists that
stories are not fantasies and claims that we have "gotten away
with calling TAT stories 'fantasies' for so many years *because
nobody checks"* (1961, p. 40, original emphasis).

In accord with these objections, later TAT experts have
argued that the relation between needs and their TAT expression is neither direct nor simple. For Lazarus (1961), needs
and need imagery are positively related only when the need
is not expressed or satisfied in action. If it is adequately expressed in behavior, it will not appear as TAT imagery "except under special circumstances which are not yet clear"
(p. 66). When needs and need imagery occur together, he
postulates low levels of blocked needs; when blocked needs
become very urgent, ego-defenses are brought into play and
prevent fantasy expression because this would only intensify
the disturbance created by the blocked need. In this way,
Lazarus hopes to explain the finding that semi-starved men or
sexually aroused students show no increase of hunger or sex
imagery in their TAT stories (Brozek *et al.,* 1951; Clark,
1952). But it should be noted that Brozek's subjects thought
and talked about food incessantly, fantasied sumptuous din-
ners, even wanted to become cooks or restaurant owners. This
does not suggest reduced food fantasy. What needs to be
explained is why these men did have increased food imagery
all during the day but did not express it in the TAT stories.
Our suggestion that such themes in the TAT indicate preoccupation but not genuine striving might solve the difficulty.
Such preoccupation will be expressed in story themes, provided that the storyteller's convictions do not prevent their

expression; and provided that the theme has not become so familiar through long rumination that the TAT pictures constitute a welcome diversion.

Actually, the storyteller's motivation is illustrated not by the story themes but by the story outcome and the way the story is told. For instance, Lazarus mentioned that strong sexual arousal (measured by the psychogalvanic reflex) produced stories with little sexual imagery while moderate arousal produced stories with extensive imagery, when he instructed his subjects "to tell the most erotic story they could." He gave examples of both types of story. In the first story, which reveals little imagery, the storyteller implies that the young couple give in to their desire out of love and are soon to be married; in the second, that they enjoy an experience in which the girl is encouraged by her mother who wishes she could be in the daughter's place. In the first story, the emphasis is on love and marriage; in the second, on enjoyment of the sex act— which easily accounts for the difference in imagery. Lazarus's conclusion is that the TAT is the end result of the interaction between needs and ego-control processes. For this reason, he thinks it impossible "to make clear inferences about either needs or ego-control processes" from the TAT alone (1961, p. 68).

Among the ego-control processes that are assumed to modify fantasy expression of needs is *anxiety*. McClelland *et al.* (1953) mentioned that "individuals with fairly high (achievement) motivation will fail to express it even in fantasy because of basic anxieties about achieving" (p. 326). And Feshbach (1961) concedes that anxiety, as a result of an approach-avoidance conflict, may result in blocking the expression of approach motivation or may result in stories that combine these motives with expressions of anxiety. Like Lazarus (1961) and Atkinson (1958, 1961), Feshbach insists that we must know the conditions under which a motive is aroused before we could expect a correlation between TAT themes and behavior. Fesh-bach sums up his discussion: "It is by now evident that we should not expect a simple, uniform relationship between 'covert' fantasy expression of a motive and 'overt' behavioral expressions. The proper question is not 'what is the relation-ship?' but rather 'under what conditions would we expect to find a positive, inverse or negligible correlation?'" (1961, p. 137).

This bird's eye view of recent opinions seems to indicate that both the clinical and the research-oriented view of the TAT has profoundly changed since the test was first introduced. Today, clinicians as well as research workers seem agreed that the TAT is not "fantasy" in the sense of "primary process"; that it reveals not only impulses, needs, or affects projected on the character with whom the storyteller identifies but also defensive and adaptive processes. Holt goes so far as to say that "most of the inferences about personality structure that we can draw from the TAT depend on these non-fantasy aspects" (1961, p. 37).

This new emphasis on an organizing, synthetic function of the ego which produces TAT responses (Wyatt, 1958) has led to a renewed preoccupation with the stimulus properties of the TAT pictures (see Murstein, 1961; Kenny, 1961), for it is the picture that provides the stimulus for ego-con-trolled "apperception." This endeavor has its own pitfalls: the problem of determining the "absolute" stimulus value of each TAT picture, of which the question of the "am-biguity" of the picture is a major part. From the first, it was assumed that the stimulus has to be ambiguous to allow re-sponses that will reveal individuality—just as the Rorschach inkblots, for instance, are ambiguous. But inkblots, like fire or clouds, are ambiguous in the sense that they portray noth-ing definite so that a great many things may be seen in them. This is not the ambiguity of TAT pictures. Here, the term seems to mean that a great many stories can be told about pictures that have definite outlines and unmistakably portray people and things. This is not really *stimulus* ambiguity. Rather, it is a difference in the way the stimulus is *used* to create a story.

This brings us to the assumption underlying the scoring methods developed thus far. It is the notion that the story is an aggregate of themes, and these themes must be isolated before scoring is possible. Themes may be categorized in a variety of ways, from Murray's needs and press, Tomkins' vector and level analysis, to Kagan's affect states; but in every case, the scoring is based on isolated parts of the story. This assumption leans on Freud's notion of fantasy, as exemplified by his dream analysis: fantasy images are conceived as the end product of a causal chain stemming from drives aroused by the original traumatic experience. For Freud, every fantasy is a wish fulfillment, an image of the object cathected by the drive. Influenced by Freud, most modern psychologists seem to think of fantasy as a series of personal memories, strung together haphazardly, connected up and cleverly disguised by the superego. For this reason, Tomkins, for instance, suggests that we need a theory of memory to explain how TAT pictures are related to stories (Kagan and Lesser, eds., 1961, p. 312).

This view of the TAT story as a patchwork of personal memories has not changed, despite the changing view of what it is that is expressed in it. At least this is the conclusion that seems to be implied by the unanimous agreement of TAT experts to score each story theme individually. Despite Henry's insistence that "there is no single element in a given TAT record that has any meaning in and of itself" (1961, p. 117), the themes are scored one by one; and the variables supposedly revealed in these themes remain similarly isolated. Veroff (1961), for instance, reports that he found no correlation between *n*

Achievement, *n* Affiliation, *n* Power, in a nationwide survey of a representative sample of 1619 men and women. Since McClelland's system is one of the best worked-out scoring methods, it is not likely that we may expect better success from other systems if they are based on the same assumptions.

If it were true that the themes represent the storyteller's needs, drives, or affects when they are not blocked by ego-processes, and that ego-processes have a similar connection with themes, we should be able to use TAT themes for predicting behavior at least in those cases where fantasy expression is not blocked by ego-defenses. In such cases, the storyteller's actions should duplicate the hero's actions; the storyteller should have the same desires, the same anxieties and inhibitions he ascribes to the hero or, as Piotrowski (1950) and Wyatt and Veroff (1956) would have it, the same affects he ascribes to *all* story characters. Unfortunately for prediction, but perhaps fortunately for this hypothesis, we never can tell whether themes revealed in the TAT accompany behavior or are an alternative to behavior; whether themes missing in the TAT indicate lack of the corresponding need, its blocking by ego-defenses, or its being acted out in reality. It almost seems as if we had to agree with Lazarus, who insists that we will never be able to predict behavior from the TAT alone.

Before we subscribe to such a pessimistic conclusion, we might consider another possibility. Perhaps neither drives nor ego-processes are revealed in story themes. Perhaps motivating tendencies, whatever they are, shape the story *action* and are expressed in the story *outcome*.

Of course, several interpretive techniques are using the outcome in addition to story themes (see McClelland *et al.*, 1953; Eron, 1951; Hartman, 1951; and many others). But surely the outcome is not just another theme like aggression, hostility, affiliation, and the like. The outcome caps the plot, and the plot integrates various themes into a unified whole.

A story is not a collection of themes nor is it a string of memory images. A story is a *creative reorganization* of past sense impressions, a *new product* of human imagination, very different from personal memories recalled in the original sequence and pattern. The story has a meaning which cannot be discovered from the meaning of the individual themes into which it can be analyzed. It is another example of the truism that a structured whole is not the sum of its parts. Whatever score we may assign to such parts, and however we may manipulate or categorize the elements into which we have divided the story, we are disregarding *the story* so long as we deal with themes rather than plot and outcome. If it were possible to score *what the story* is saying, and include *all there is to the story,* we would discover a new dimension in the TAT which might allow very different correlations with behavior.

In this book a method of story analysis is proposed which does just that. Each story is condensed into an import that leaves out incidental details but preserves the kernel—the meat of the story. When all the imports are read in sequence, a picture of the individual emerges that does portray his attitudes, his intentions for action. Every story makes a point, expresses a conviction. It describes an action that may be headed for success or failure, may exemplify cooperation or hostility, may be an attempt to cope with adversity or betray spineless acceptance of whatever may come. Or, the story may speak of hopes and dreams rather than actions and depend on fate or luck to make them come true. In every case, emotions may influence the action, but the outcome is primarily an expression of the storyteller's convictions, garnered from experience and reflection. The plot sets a problem, the outcome solves it. Both the type of problem a man sets himself and the kind of outcome he prefers are characteristic for him. Every story has a moral, though that moral may not indicate very high ethical principles. For instance, the story of a man who tries to rob a bank but is caught and sentenced to a long prison term illustrates the maxim that *crime does not pay*; but the story of a bank robber who through clever planning gets away with the loot and spends the rest of his days in affluence, makes the point that *sometimes it does*. The first storyteller is saying that there are actions that are severely punished and therefore not for him; the man telling the second story is saying that one can get away with violence and dishonesty, if he is clever. This man may never rob a bank, either, but he will expect success to come by luck and tricks where other people expect to achieve it by hard work. The first story could be abstracted into an import that might read: When you try to succeed by violence and dishonesty, you gain nothing but punishment. And the second: You can get by with violence and dishonesty if you are clever enough. The first story reveals positive motivation; the second, negative motives.

I hope to show that it is possible to score such story imports objectively and to arrive at a final score which will indicate a man's positive or negative motivation. Several hundred records scored in this way have shown that positive motivation is found among high achieving elementary, secondary, and college students, among effective teachers, competent executives and well-adjusted Navy men. Negative motivation, in contrast, is found among low achievers, ineffective teachers, naval offenders (see Chapters 10-14). The scoring system presented in the Appendix was derived empirically from records of matched pairs of high and low achievers and was cross-validated on other samples.

This method of scoring the stories depends on a theory of imagination which is discussed more fully in Chapter 2; a theory of motivation which is sketched in Chapter 3; a theory of emotion and action, and a theory of personality which are briefly mentioned in Chapters 2 and 3, but are mapped fully in earlier works (Arnold and Gasson, 1954; Arnold, 1960). Part II (Chapters 4-6) offers a careful description of the way in which imports are formulated and connected into a sequence and gives hints for the clinical evaluation of this sequence. Part III (Chapters 7-9) describes the use of the scoring criteria contained in the Appendix. Finally, Part IV (Chapters 10-14) includes research studies using this scoring system and spells out the implications of our findings for personality theory.

Our method of story sequence analysis, scored according to the criteria given in the Appendix, has several advantages. Since it is the story imports that are scored and not story elements, the score does not depend on the picture on which the story is based. The picture (or description) sets the motif or theme of the story, but the story plot and outcome are provided by the storyteller. Since it is the import that is scored as positive or negative, and the import abstracts the plot and outcome, each picture has the same chance of yielding a positive or negative score. This has been confirmed by statistical investigation (see Chapter 9). For this reason, the "stimulus value" of the picture is irrelevant.

Secondly, the story sequence analysis provides a new dimension in clinical evaluation. It is almost a self-recording portrait of the storyteller which tells its own story without elaborate and often speculative interpretation.

Scoring story imports instead of story themes also equalizes the story length. Whether long or short, every story is reduced to an import which is usually contained in one sentence. Imports make it possible to score and evaluate meager as well as rich records, which is a decided advantage when testing children, low status adults, or mental patients.

Finally, this method reveals positive and negative motivation as expressed in vocational adjustment and achievement. This motivation is stable. In several cases, we have given repeated tests, using different pictures, in intervals up to one year. The positive or negative attitudes revealed in successive sets of stories were similar and obtained similar scores, even though the actual imports were quite different.

2

IMAGINATION AND CREATIVITY

Our notions of fantasy and imagination, like our concepts of motivation, have been decisively influenced by Freud's penchant for systematization. For Freud and his followers, the first psychological activity of the infant consists in fantasy images of wish-fulfilling objects. Fantasy is the oldest form of thought, primary process thinking, which is gradually displaced by secondary process thinking, but is still used whenever wishes are not immediately gratified. As Holt (1961) says, "the more wishes, the more fantasies." The daydream is the prototype of such fantasies, but night dreams and stories also are fantasy products.

Freud emphasized that the hero of a story, like the hero of a daydream, goes through various adventures and is in the center of the plot, while other characters play a clearly subordinate role. Both story and daydream are initiated by personal memories and aim at wish fulfillment. According to Freud, a story is written because "some actual experience which made a strong impression on the writer had stirred up a memory of an earlier experience, generally belonging to childhood which then arouses a wish that finds a fulfillment in the work in question, and in which elements of the recent event and the old memory should be discernible" (Freud, 1953, p. 183).

Freud's preoccupation with the dynamics of action led him to fasten on the wish or need as the moving force that com-

bines childhood impressions and recent memories into a connected story. For him, stories as well as dreams are a mosaic of
reminiscences that have to be disentangled from irrelevant
accretions. This embroidery is the "dreamwork," designed to
hide repressed memories. Freud interpreted the dream through
the dreamer's free associations; the various dream images were
used to recall one memory after another until the original traumatic memory was laid bare. Quite consistently, he suggested
that stories and plays—the products of literary imagination—
could be interpreted according to psychoanalytic principles
which were derived from the analysis of free associations.
Freud's method of interpretation, whether applied to dreams
or stories, depends on the premise that every fantasy product
is made up of memory images that must be tracked down to
their dynamic roots before dream or story will yield its meaning.

On the whole, psychoanalytic interpretations of literature
have been no more successful than the interpretation of TAT
stories on the basis of themes. Whatever the wishes that found
their fulfillment in novels, plays, and stories, there is more to
literary efforts than the needs or drives that may have spawned
them. Fortunately, such interpretations of literature are no
longer in vogue, though similar interpretations of TAT stories
are still to be found among clinical psychologists. Gradually, a
rising dissatisfaction made itself felt with the interpretation of
TAT stories as fantasy attempts at wish fulfillment. Holt (1961)
finally spelled out the differences between TAT stories and
fantasy: A story is an active, continuous, cognitive product,
told verbally with little affect, shows little evidence of primary
process, is easily remembered, has a plot and is "much less
obviously" dictated by wish fulfillment; it engages the storyteller's intelligence and other abilities, does not lead to acting
out, has no obvious self-reference, is relatively public, and deals
with the reality of the stimulus. In all these respects, the story
is different from the daydream.

These differences are obvious once they are stated. The only difficulty is that this distinction leaves the status of stories uncertain. If stories are not fantasy products, what kind of "cognitive products" are they? Stories are obviously different from descriptions and from logical reasoning. They also differ from free associations which are simply a chain of personal memories, as we have demonstrated in an earlier work (Arnold and Gasson, 1954). Though the ingredients could doubtlessly be traced to personal memories, what is important in the finished product is not how scenes and characters resemble something already known but how they differ. It is the novelty of the story that makes it worth reading and remembering. This is the reason why Holt calls it a "cognitive product." But, the only cognitive function besides sense knowledge and memory, and besides reflective knowledge (including conceptual thinking and reasoning) is imagination.

IMAGINATION AND MEMORY IN EVERYDAY LIFE

To solve this problem, let us discuss the interplay of various cognitive functions with action in everyday life. Any action has its origin in something that is known, whether that is an immediate sense impression, a thought, or a memory. What is experienced is next identified by recalling similar situations and their effect on us; this recall may be spontaneous or deliberate. Once something is identified, we imagine what it might do to us and appraise it accordingly as good or bad here and now. Before we decide what to do about it, we imagine possible alternative actions and their consequences and compare them with remembered actions and their success or failure. Whether we are about to write a letter, bake a cake, or calculate the orbit of a rocket, we have to imagine what will happen and imagine what can be done to cope with it. When we have judged one of the alternatives as suitable, we exclude all others from consideration: the impulse to this action is now carried out because no contrary action impulses intervene.* This sequence of perception, appraisal, and action can be traced in every activity, whether strictly psychological like thinking, remembering, listening, or overt like talking, writing, going for a walk, or splitting wood. Sense impressions of every kind have to be appraised as good to know before we turn our attention to the stimulus, before we identify and explore it. Attention is an *impulse to know* that leads us to look at, listen to, or otherwise explore this particular thing. Whatever we do, recall and imagination are active in this sequence from perception to action. Only if both work normally are we able to adapt our actions to the requirements of the here and now.

We can distinguish between *cognitive functions* which mediate sense or reflective knowledge; *estimative functions* that mediate an intuitive, automatic, or a reflective appraisal of things and actions as good, suitable, feasible, or the opposite; and *appetitive functions* which are tendencies to emotional or deliberate actions. Cognitive experiences always lead to an appraisal of what is experienced; and such an appraisal always arouses a tendency to some activity (unless something is appraised as indifferent, in which case it is disregarded).

Sensation, recognition, recall and imagination, understanding, and reasoning are cognitive functions. In man, they are followed both by an immediate, automatic appraisal, and a reflective value judgment. These are estimative functions. The automatic appraisal initiates an emotional tendency toward what is evaluated as good, and away from what is evaluated as bad. We feel drawn toward what we like, we are repelled by what we dislike. Reflective appraisal results in a conscious and deliberate tendency to obtain what we judge is available and worth-while, and to avoid what we judge worthless or undesirable.

* For a detailed discussion and diagram of this sequence, see Arnold, 1960, p. 200f. In actual fact, this sequence occurs in a much shorter time than it takes to describe it.

IMAGINATION IN DREAMS

What distinguishes the dream from waking experience is that during waking we can recall past happenings and so can identify what we encounter, while in dreams we cannot. During waking, every sense impression brings to mind similar situations and their past effects, and so we are able to identify the source of stimulation. We recall (or better, relive) the satisfaction or the annoyance and pain we have experienced from particular things and actions. In this way, we not only know what kind of thing this is but also what it has done to us in the past, and are able to plan effective action.

In dreams, such recall of earlier experiences in their original pattern and sequence is impossible. In an earlier work (1960, Vol. 2), I have shown that recall and imagination seem to be initiated via two different pathways. According to available evidence, the more synapses there are in a neural pathway, the more easily it is blocked during sleep. The hippocampal pathway, activating recall, has many more synapses than the amygdalar pathway which activates imagination, and so will be blocked even in light sleep. In deep sleep, when the amygdalar pathway is blocked also, there are no dreams.

While any cognitive function gives us knowledge (in the sense of experience), it is only when memory recall works together with imagination that this is a knowledge of reality. In dreams, when recall is blocked, we are often caught up in scenes that are impossible as well as improbable in reality. We seem to carry out actions we could not or would not engage in ordinarily, for we cannot recall the necessary conditions and consequences of such actions. Though the imagined scenes and actions are constructed from remembered sense impressions and from earlier judgments and actions, these memories are not recalled in sequence, they are recombined in new patterns and often fantastic structures. Earlier sense impressions are merely the building blocks that are all but unrecognizable in the finished edifice. Since all our memories are available for such restructuring (though not for exact recall), we can reason in dreams, talk, listen to conversation, act, in short, do anything and experience anything fantasy can distill from these memories (including memories of what we have read and thought about). Of course, dream reasoning is often fantastic, just as dream actions are often bizarre, because we cannot check dream judgments and actions against what we know to be true, possible, or expedient.

DIRECTING THE IMAGINATIVE PROCESS

Whether in waking life or during sleep, the imaginative process must be directed in some way. When we are awake, we know what is required for the problem we may encounter and prepare for coping with it. We direct our imagination deliberately to explore possible action alternatives and consider possible consequences. In daydreams, we also direct and control our imagination. But, in daydreams, we use it to explore pleasurable situations and engage in imaginative activities that offer some emotional satisfaction (e.g., a conquering hero dream, or a suffering hero dream). Instead of employing imagination to cope with reality, as we do ordinarily, we use it to indulge our craving for emotional thrills. This is the "wish fulfillment" function of fantasy Freud speaks about. However, imagination far more frequently helps us to cope with reality, and this function Freud does not mention.

In addition to such deliberate control of imagination, there are also imaginative processes that seem to run their appointed course without our direction. The dream is the best but not the only example. In writing a story, for instance, our decision to do so merely supplies the impulse to start imagining, it does not direct the imaginative process. If it did, we would tell a story the way we make a plan: we would start with a situation that poses a problem, and explore step by step what could be done to achieve the desired result. But in telling a story, we have no such deliberate aim. Instead of working out the plot step by logical step, the story "occurs" to us. Novelists often say that the story writes itself, that the characters develop a life of their own that inevitably leads them into the difficulties they encounter or the victories they achieve in the story. Composers have the same experience. Mozart wrote the overture to *Don Giovanni* the night before the first performance of the opera while his wife kept him awake by feeding him punch and telling him fairy stories. Arnold Schönberg tells how he wrote down the whole of his String Quartet No. 2 as he heard it in imagination. It is obvious that such creations required no deliberate guidance, as little as a dream requires it.

Yet, in dreams as well as in stories, there must be some guidance or direction. There must be some active tendency that chooses the images when we do not choose them and combines them into a plot and outcome. Imagination is a cognitive function and as such can only form images or reproduce them; it cannot choose them, as little as the eye can choose what it will see. Something else must, so to speak, guide the brush and sketch the outlines; and that something can only be an appetitive tendency, either deliberate or emotional. Something we like can produce an impulse to imagine what could account for that pleasure, and something we dislike can produce an impulse to imagine what could account for the dislike. During light sleep, when we cannot identify such sense impressions as we may experience, the fact that we like or dislike them (e.g., pleasurable or unpleasant organic changes, light, cold, warmth, pressure, etc.) is enough to initiate dreams that picture corresponding situations (Ayalla, 1957; Beigel, 1960). If the dreamer suffers from discouragement or anxieties in waking life, unpleasant sensations during light sleep will reactivate them. The physiological effects of fear and worry, for instance, interfere with the normal processes of digestion. The resulting sensation of pressure is much like the sensations experienced during anxiety or depression, a feeling as if one were gripped in a vise, smothered by a heavy load. Since these sensations cannot be identified as indigestion, the feeling of oppression will give rise to images that account for it. Before long, these images will be combined in a veritable nightmare plot in which the dreamer sees himself smothered, manhandled, and oppressed.

In this way, our attitudes and emotions set the stage for the dream, but experienced sense impressions are the occasion for the *mise en scène*. The plot and the actors will be scenes and figures that account for the experienced emotions. Consequently, dreams can be correctly interpreted if the dream figures and dream actions are explored to discover their significance *for the dreamer*. Free associations to the dream are not enough; rather, the attitude of the dreamer to the dream figures and their actions is the important clue. There are some dreams so transparent that their meaning is grasped immediately. There is, for instance, the dream of an older professional man who was upset because he was refused by a religious order he wanted to enter. During this period of uncertainty as to what to do next, he dreamed that he was waiting in line at a recruiting center to join up as a buck private because he had been refused a commission in the Engineers. After hours of waiting, he finally left, deciding that he could serve his country better as a civilian consultant. The emotions he experienced in the dream were all genuine: he was annoyed and upset over the refusal, though the dream gave the long wait as the reason. In deciding to serve as civilian consultant, the dreamer proposed a solution that soon afterward occurred to him in reality: to work for what he believed even though he could not become a priest. Thus in dreams as in stories, it is the plot and the outcome that reveal the dreamer's attitude and often, too, the way in which he can or intends to handle his problem.

In telling stories, we also reveal our attitudes and convictions. The picture merely reminds us of various situations: a lover's quarrel, a woman's jealousy, her attempt at seduction—all these are possible story themes for TAT card 4. Which one of these possibilities is chosen depends on the storyteller's dominant attitudes and emotions which now direct the story plot just as the dreamer's emotions direct the dream action. Attitudes are merely impulses to action that have become habitual. These action impulses may be produced by an immediate, intuitive appraisal or by reflective judgments. Whenever these judgments have been made repeatedly and the tendency to a particular action has become habitual, such attitudes (emotional and intellectual) are revived automatically every time a similar situation is encountered. When such an attitude is activated by a TAT picture, the attitude (and not the picture) will initiate a train of images that portray situations and actions to justify the emotion. It is the attitude that guides the plot and dictates the outcome, and the attitude that can be inferred from the story as soon as plot and outcome are combined in the import.

THE ROLE OF IMAGINATION IN PERSONALITY

In telling stories, normal people are not usually talking about themselves in the direct way neurotics and psychotics may do. Knowing that his characters are imaginary, the storyteller can make them act in any way he pleases, though he himself would never act this way. Still, since it is he who is telling the story, he will not be able to keep from saying what he thinks of their actions—for instance, by letting the villain be punished or go scot free. Or, he may indicate his opinion of the characters by the use of revealing adjectives: "lazy bums," "careless workers," which show well enough that they meet failure because of their laziness or carelessness.

Only in the case of a frankly autobiographical story can we assume that it contains actual personal memories and emotions; and there is seldom more than one such story in a TAT record. Most of the time, there is none. In the same way, only dreams that literally repeat an experience (like lying wounded in no man's land or being buried under debris) consist of actual personal memories; and such dreams are practically confined to repetitive dreams of traumatic experiences of a serious kind. Whenever they do occur in this form, we can be certain that the dreamer has not yet overcome his anxiety.

While a strictly autobiographical story allows an inference to the storyteller's past emotions and actions, it is not safe to infer from it his current attitude, unless the general tenor of the story and its outcome justify it. If a young man tells the story of a boy who joins the army because he did not want to go to college, and finally says that the boy did not like the army any better than he likes school or job because he just doesn't like to be ordered about, we can be fairly sure that the storyteller himself feels that way, whether this is his own story or not. The whole tenor of the story betrays a stable attitude toward discipline, whether in school, army, or at work. That the storyteller seems to identify with the young man in the story is not nearly so important as the fact that he describes a negative attitude—unwillingness to submit to any discipline—and gives no indication that he condemns it.

The stories a man tells, like the dreams he has, illustrate problems that occupy him, solutions he is working out, convictions he has achieved. But, both may have an even more important function.

According to Dement (1960) and Dement and Kleitman (1957), dreaming is universal and goes on throughout the night, alternating with dreamless sleep. Indeed, when dreams are prevented by waking the sleeper at the beginning of every dream,* he will be irritable and ill at ease the next day, even though his total hours of sleep remain the same. When the same sleepers are awakened as frequently but during periods of deep sleep rather than dreaming, they wake up fresh and vigorous. We might speculate that interrupted dreams leave a man limp and exhausted because he has not had the help of dreams in working out solutions to the problems that bother him, and so must carry their emotional burden from one day into the next. There is a reason why people are advised to "sleep on it" when they encounter a problem they cannot solve. They may not know that they have tried to find a solution in their dreams. They only know that somehow they see alternatives next day they had not known existed.

The same sort of thing happens in telling a series of stories. In one story after another, a man may go on exploring various alternatives of action and their consequences, under the most diverse circumstances. Or, he may be preoccupied with one problem to such an extent that he talks about it in several stories and explores many possible solutions. In a series of twenty stories, as required when the complete TAT is given, there is an imaginative progression that almost amounts to a monologue about the problems uppermost in the storyteller's mind. If he has no special problems, he will reveal his attitudes to life, as they apply to various situations.

IMAGINATION, CREATIVITY AND THE UNCONSCIOUS

While the term imagination has almost disappeared from our professional vocabulary and the term fantasy has come to mean "primary process" regressive thinking, the notion of creativity has achieved a popularity rivaled only by the bouffant hairdo.

* The beginning of a dream can be observed in the EEG tracing of a sleeping person (see Dement and Kleitman, 1957).

Yet, despite the large number of research articles appearing on the subject, this research has thrown curiously little light on the creative process. Psychologists are not even agreed on the psychological function employed in it, mainly because anything that does not proceed with full reflective awareness is automatically assigned to the unconscious. Though linguistic form suggests that "the unconscious" ought to be a thing or a place, Freud and his followers have always insisted that it is neither.

In that case, what could it be? It is not a function like seeing or hearing or judging or thinking. Is it a way in which these functions work? Sometimes they work consciously, sometimes unconsciously—that might be what is implied in the distinction between a conscious and an unconscious. But in cold fact, all our functions work unconsciously. We are never aware of the way they work, we are aware only of the end product. We do not know how we see, or how we see color. Nor do we know how we move our muscles, how we make an inference, or how we manage to hit upon the right solution of a problem. All we can do consciously is to direct our functions. We can focus on a particular spot and if there is light and we have sight, we see something. We can listen and if there is something to hear and we have hearing, we hear it. So also, we can set ourselves to tell a story, to find a new way of doing or explaining things; or we can look for the solution of a mathematical or scientific problem. If we have enough information and have a feeling for what is required, the remembered facts will fall into a new pattern and we come up with a story, a theory, a new proof. In an earlier work (Arnold and Gasson, 1954), Gasson has suggested that what is called "the unconscious" is really the functioning of the imagination when it is freed from deliberate control. Imagination goes on working in dreams without our guidance and may outrun such guidance during waking. In writing a letter, we may find ourselves skipping a word because our hand has not kept pace with our imagination. So also, the chairman of a meeting when opening a discussion he does not want may pronounce it closed instead of opened. Such slips of tongue or pen are produced by imagining faster than we act. Certainly, the chairman is expressing a wish, as Freud says, but it is not the force of wish or impulse that is pushing the wrong word from the unconscious into the conscious. It is our imagination that maps out what is to be said or done. When imagination is guided not only by deliberate intention but also by some emotional preoccupation, it is more likely that it will lead to unintentional expression.

Creativity also is not the product of a mysterious and forever unknowable "unconscious" but the working of the imagination when it produces something new and original that often may be of great importance. This is not a creation *ex nihilo*. It is a fortunate rearrangement of images that are preserved in memory and may occur in dreams as well as in waking life. The creativity of the artist or scientist may be different in degree but hardly in kind from the imagination all of us use every day. Of course, it is applied to different problems and represents more of a leap into the unknown than, say, the swain's rumination of what to do or say when he dates the girl of his dreams.

In present-day professional writings, the role of imagination in creativity is almost completely neglected. Anne Roe, for instance, well known through her researches on the personality of creative scientists, declares in a recent article, "the creative process involves a scanning or searching through stocks of stored memories" (1961, p. 457). She must know that originality as well as memory is necessary for creative work, but the only hint she gives that something else is required is her statement, "the individual enters a state in which logical thinking is submerged and in which thought is prelogical" (p. 457). The term prelogical,* like the notion of the unconscious, labels but does not explain what goes on in the creative process. Logical thought employs concepts, uses judgments and inferences. Prelogical thought, according to Anne Roe, is "goal-directed . . . preconscious . . . [and employs] appropriate selection and rejection of available connections" (p. 457). This makes creativity a selection of *available* connections—which is exactly what happens in remembering. Though it is true, as discussed before, that we draw on sense memories in creative imagination, we are not bound to their original sequence. Far from being a selection of available connections, the imaginative process forms new connections of striking originality and power when it is truly creative.

Creativity is imagination that is extraordinarily fertile and original, when freed from deliberate control. When imagination is not deliberately controlled, it is guided by man's unwitting action tendencies, his emotions, attitudes, and habitual convictions. When these convictions are too rigid, preventing him from looking for the unexpected, the unconventional, his imagination remains fettered and never blossoms into "creativity."

Whether we call it creativity or creative imagination, the creative process does not work in isolation. A man's initial direction sets it into motion, and his attitudes and emotions guide it. We may be able to measure the extent to which he can come up with something novel, creative, but we still do not know whether he will apply his talent or fritter it away. Today's interest in measuring creativity is reminiscent of the interest in measuring intelligence that was so widespread in the early 1920s. And, as then we had hopes of predicting a man's success or failure in school and even in life by measuring his intelligence, so now our professional hopes seem to be pinned on

---

* The term could just as well or better be "postlogical" or "hypological." "Prelogical" is a humpty-dumpty word.

creativity. Our efforts to measure intelligence have given us reliable measuring instruments—yet, we no longer believe that intelligence tests will allow us to discover the genius or even the extraordinarily successful man, whether in science or industry. Highly intelligent students often perform indifferently in college, and in later life miss the mark altogether. Many a man whose tested intelligence is well below "genius" rating is outstandingly successful both in school and in his later profession.

We are just about to discover that creativity also is not the magic key to outstanding achievement. Personality variables such as intelligence or creativity do not enable us to predict a person's performance or conduct apart from his motivation. Though we might derive separate scores for all these variables, we need to know how to combine them. By themselves, none of the personality variables usually derived from tests can be used for the prediction of achievement or success, either in school or in life. Thus far, psychologists have not succeeded in finding a way of combining such variables for the prediction of future achievement, perhaps because we have gone about it the wrong way. In testing for various characteristics, it is necessary to abstract from a man's activities and break up the natural integration. The integrated pattern is lost for the sake of obtaining scores for the partial factors we believe are contained in it. Would it not be preferable to try for a sample of a man's motives? These, we know, move him to act in distinctive ways. We may then find they reveal creativity, intelligence, aggression, conformity, and any number of other qualities. But, in tapping his motives, we have found the way in which they are combined for action. No longer do we have to be content with disjointed bones in personality analysis. Knowing a man's motives and their hierarchy, we can work with the fleshed skeleton. Thus we will be able, at last, to determine what a person's chances are for achieving excellence.

3

MOTIVES, VALUES, AND ATTITUDES

It is often said that a motive is "aroused" by certain stimuli. In Chapter 1, for instance, we have seen that n Achievement was experimentally aroused by emphasizing that a particular task indicates intelligence, and encouraging the students to try and do well in it. Aggression was aroused by making highly critical or annoying remarks; and the hunger motive was aroused by depriving men of food for several hours. This procedure is based on the assumption that the motive is a need or drive which is aroused by a stimulus or cue, the picture. Atkinson, for instance, suggests that each picture arouses "cognitive expectancies" which can be measured, and represents "fairly standard conditions for the measurement of any human motive" (1958, p. 615).

But, the expectancies aroused by the picture refer to the topic or motif of the picture, not to the story. Even a situation that is completely stereotyped can be the starting point of stories that differ both in plot and outcome. For instance, the picture of a woman at a blackboard and children sitting in rows facing the blackboard will be recognized by anybody who has ever been to school as representing a teacher in front of her class. And yet, when we look at the stories about this picture that can be told by people, we find considerable variations. There may be stories of a good teacher or a poor teacher, of children liking the teacher or detesting her, of liking school or hating it, and any number of variations suggested by school.

In spite of the same "cognitive expectancy," the stories will differ widely and may indicate opposed attitudes. Though the picture is a cue, it is not the cue to a standardized response.

THE MOTIVE

Just as a picture is not a stimulus demanding a particular response, so a motive is not a need or a drive. A need or drive may or may not lead to action. If it does not, how can it be a motive? Surely a motive must really motivate, it must lead to action. A motive could be defined as *a want that leads to action.* When I recognize something as good or bad for me, I want it or want to avoid it, and will take appropriate action as soon as feasible.

Hunger is not necessarily a motive. Hunger is an urge toward food which compels thinking about it, promotes the attempt at getting it, and is accompanied by organic sensations (hunger pangs). It does not become a motive until I decide on action. A man who is on a hunger strike is certainly hungry, but his hunger is not a motive for his refusal to eat. On the other hand, a decision to go to graduate school and work for a Ph.D. establishes a motive even though the student may not be engaged in studying at this particular time (e.g., during Christmas vacation). A motive is neither a need nor a drive nor a stimulus. It is something appraised as good for a particular action. The man on a hunger strike evaluates going without food as good (for the time being) and so refuses to eat. The student appraises the Ph.D. in his specialty as good and decides on the course of action that will lead to it. A motive is active from the moment a man *has decided on the appropriate action* until his goal is accomplished, even though that action may not be continuous. For this reason, a motive need not be "aroused" by a picture before it becomes active.

A motive resembles a set rather than an emotion: once established, it will influence action until the goal has been achieved. When that happens, the motive disappears and cannot be aroused again in this particular form. When hunger has become a motive (i.e., when a man has decided to get something to eat), it remains a motive until he has eaten. As soon as he is satisfied, the motive for eating disappears and cannot be aroused again until either renewed hunger or the appetite for a choice tidbit renews the appraisal and decision for action.

Since motives remain active until the goal is reached, it is possible to discover how they influence a man's thinking as well as his actions. In the last chapter I have tried to show that imagination is the function used in planning action and anticipating its results; and that it is the felt action tendency, stemming from an appraisal, which initiates the imaginative preparation for action and so directs the imaginative process. Now, a motive also stems from the appraisal of something as good or bad, here and now, and includes a tendency to a particular action. The difference between an emotion and a motive lies in the fact that an emotion may or may not lead to action while a motive always does. When emotion leads to action, it *moves* the person toward a goal but not in the same way a motive does.* A motive always includes a tendency to action but this tendency may be deliberate as well as emotional. In the human adult, in fact, it is usually both. A small child may give in to emotion unthinkingly, but an adult usually deliberates and appraises several alternatives for action. He may decide to give in to emotion rather than doing the reasonable thing, but this decision itself is deliberate rather than emotional. Only in the rare cases where emotion is sudden and intense will it lead to action without deliberation (e.g., in panic).

While emotion is the result of a judgment, this could be

* Motive is an ambiguous term. Most contemporary usage in psychology equates it with "motor," what "pushes" us to action. This usage cannot effectively distinguish drive and motive or emotion and motive. We emphasize an older usage in which motive means what "draws" us to action.

called a *sense* judgment because it is immediate, unwitting, intuitive, almost automatic. Before emotion can become a motive, there must be an additional *reflective* evaluation that this is good to have or avoid. In addition, a choice of action is necessary, that is, a decision that action is required and what means are to be used to reach the desired goal. At any particular time, there will be many motives that influence an individual's action. He may have decided to study for the Ph.D., but also to marry his girl and live in a suburb. Both these goals presuppose many intuitive and reflective appraisals: for instance, that the city is noisy; that one gets to know people in the suburbs and can live in a friendly neighborhood; that it is more pleasant there, cleaner, less crowded. All these judgments have combined to bring about the decision to look for a house in the suburbs. As soon as this decision is made, the man has a motive. After he has moved to the suburbs, the motive changes. Instead of wanting to move there, he now wants to stay there—provided his experience confirms his earlier estimate. While the motive remains, and particularly while he is still undecided, every opportunity offered to talk or write about where to live will exercise his imagination. If he tells a story about a young couple getting married, he will explore in it where they might live, in city or country, and sketch the advantages of either as he sees them. If his decision still hangs in the balance, there may be several stories weighing the advantages and disadvantages of either alternative.

Accordingly, stories betray a man's attitudes (both emotional and intellectual) and the way in which they influence him to act: they reveal his motives. And since motives are blueprints for action, it is possible to infer from them what he will do in real life. The problems he sets himself in the stories he tells, he will resolve in real life according to the way in which he evaluates the story solution.

MOTIVES AND VALUES

Our definition of motive as *something appraised as good for a particular action* immediately suggests a connection with value. Dodd (1951), for instance, says: "Let 'a value' be defined as a desideratum, i.e., anything desired or chosen by someone sometime." Now nothing can be a "desideratum" unless it is judged or appraised as good. Kluckhohn's definition is even closer to my definition of motive: "A value is a conception, explicit or implicit, distinctive of an individual or characteristic of a group, of the desirable which influences the selection from available modes, means and ends of action" (1951, p. 395). If value is a conception, somebody must conceive it. For Kluckhohn, it is apparently the social scientist who makes the "scientific abstraction" he calls "value." However, he admits that there is something to which this abstraction applies:

The actor's values are often inchoate, incompletely or inadequately verbalized by him. But implicit values remain "conceptions" in the sense that they are abstract and generalized notions which can be put into words by the observer and then agreed to or dissented to by the actor. [Kluckhohn, 1951, p. 397.]

Apparently, "the desirable" influences action and is then inferred from action by the observer in the form of a value concept. When asked about it, the observed subject (the actor) will agree that this is what has influenced his action or rather that this is what he holds desirable. Most of the time, the actor will agree only that he holds such a value. The action itself may be influenced by many factors, not merely this one value. For instance, a man may refuse the offer of a job in a distant city and decide to remain in his present job, which enables him to live in the country. Life in the country certainly is a value for him, and he will recognize it as such. But, his action may have been influenced just as much by the fact that his wife does not want to leave her relatives or that his children do not want to change their school. These factors were his motives, not just values.

To infer values from actions implies that we expect values to be motives. This silent assumption underlies much of the discussion and research on values in social science. Barton (1961), for example, suggests that values are influenced by the capacity for critical and independent thinking, emotional sensitivity, and philosophical commitments; and, that values (including needs, preferences, and normative standards) in turn determine behavior within the limits of factual knowledge and beliefs about this particular situation. But values as "inchoate, inadequately verbalized" notions of "the desirable" do not immediately result in action. Just as something must be estimated as good before it is desired, so what is desired must be judged as *good for action here and now* before it will motivate. Not every value is a motive. There are values that are recognized as desirable but do not lead to action. A man may consider education valuable but have no desire to continue his own. Often a value may indicate not what a man wants for himself but what, more or less academically, he thinks is good—at least for other people if not for himself. On the other hand, values may become motives. A man who scores high on economic values on the Allport-Vernon scale may have as his main motive earning as much money as possible.

The notion that values are identical with motives seems to have been accepted quite generally. In fact, it could be said with some justice that the experimental study of value has prospered to such an extent in the last few years because it seemed a shortcut to the prediction of action. However, various attempts designed to tap value judgments by questionnaires have not been found particularly useful for such prediction. One of the few studies of values that did provide clues to the occupational choices of students at eleven universities is that of Goldsen *et al.* (1960), in which students were asked to rate a list of abstract criteria as desirable in "the ideal job for me." Those students who ranked "the opportunity to earn a great deal of money" highest, preferred jobs in business, food, restaurant, or hotel occupations. Those ranking creativity highest, preferred occupations in architecture, advertising, and artistic fields; and those ranking "opportunities to be helpful to others" highest, preferred personnel jobs, medicine, and teaching. After an interval of two years, those students who no longer intended to get business jobs were less money-oriented than those who remained interested in business. Those who no longer planned to be teachers were less oriented toward helping people than those who had kept their preference for teaching. This study illustrates the point at issue: when a man is asked what he wants in "the ideal job for me," he makes a choice for action rather than evaluating something apart from action. While this choice is a matter of imagination rather than action as yet, it is closer to a motive than a value. The only difference between this choice for action and the choice implied in a motive is that the decision made implies action at some future time rather than immediate action. But, we have seen that a motive may be active even though there is no immediate action; and a decision made on the basis of an imagined situation does reveal the decisions to be made in reality.

There are other attempts to measure values that employ descriptions of particular situations. The subjects are asked whether they approve or disapprove of an action taken or what they would do in some particular circumstances. A. W. Jones (1941) worked out a set of stories describing concrete situations in which aggrieved economic groups (dispossessed farmers, unemployed workers, etc.) took action against the property of banks, real estate owners, and manufacturers. Union men tended to agree, businessmen to disagree with their action, while middle-class people took an intermediate position. Here also, the men had to make a choice of action which was personalized because of the men's stake in the issues involved.

As for studies that ask people how they would act in certain particular situations, Barton points out that there is a difference between saying you would act courageously or honestly and actually doing so. Still, he recommends this "story" method as having "the closest correspondence to the notion that basic values are those which influence real-life decisions" (1961, p. 45). This again supports the contention that values are important for prediction only when they become motives; and to become motives, a new appraisal and a choice of action is necessary. Values, as such, are closer to interests than to motives. Both values and interests depend on a judgment that something is good, desirable. Interests usually spring from a judgment that this is good to know, while values indicate that something is evaluated as good in any one of a number of aspects under which a man may have considered it. Values include interests but do not include motives. Motives include both interests and values. A value will become a motive when we decide to possess it. Interests become motives when we decide to get to know what we have judged as good to know. Values, like interests and motives, require a deliberate, reflective judgment, in contrast to emotions which follow automatically upon an immediate, almost automatic, estimate.

As Barton implied, stories that recount actions with which we are to agree or disagree do not guarantee that the story action of which we approve will be chosen in reality; that is, that such stories tap motives. It is all too easy to agree with what we know we should do and then do what we really want to do. In the course of our TAT studies, we compared the stories told by a few known high achievers and low achievers with their choices when given a story for each card that had four alternative outcomes. Of these, two were positive (scored

+2 and +1), and two were negative (one scored —1, the other —2).* We found that both high and low achievers consistently chose positive outcomes; but, when asked to tell stories, these low achievers told negative stories. Apparently, people can recognize that one solution is more desirable than another though they would not tell stories describing such solutions when left to their own devices.

One way of forcing the subject to choose alternative outcomes without giving away which of them are desirable and which not, is to give them the Picture Arrangement Test (PAT) developed by Tomkins and Miner (1957). This test employs cards showing three cartoons each, which have to be arranged to form a sequence. One card, for instance, depicts a worker at the bench, a worker hurt, a worker in bed. The sequence chosen is expressed in three short sentences: for example, the man is working; the man gets hurt; the man is in the hospital. This, of course, is not the kind of story we are accustomed to in giving the TAT, nor does the PAT contain achievement themes such as are scored by the McClelland group. Tomkins and Miner do not score themes but compare the arrangement of each plate of three cartoons with the arrangement of the same three cartoons made by others. They argue that arrangements given by most people do not afford information as to the personality of any particular individual; only responses not given by most people can be expected to offer such information. To increase such rare responses in any one record, rare patterns are used as well. For instance, if less than 5 percent of the population tested have the same arrangement in several plates, this pattern is considered rare. Rare patterns are isolated by means of "keys"; and a key is "a characteristic common to the responses on a number of plates" (1957, p. 16). These keys are chosen beforehand by comparing

---

* These are the scores used in our story sequence analysis. They are explained in Chapter 7.

several possible arrangements. For example, when there are more than seven plates in which the arrangement ends up with the hero working rather than not working, this will be a rare pattern according to the "high work" key. Other keys that might show a rare pattern in this case would be the "conformity" and "strong superego" keys.

There are 486 content keys that will yield rare patterns and can be used to explore the personality pattern of the storyteller. After obtaining a profile of rare plates and rare patterns the psychologist must interpret this profile. According to Tomkins and Miner, the psychologist's skill is required to decide on the relationship of the various characteristics so isolated: one characteristic may be subordinate to another, be in conflict with another, or a means to another (e.g., low work may be a means to high aggression or subordinate to it).

Some of these keys can be used for particular purposes. Miner (1960, 1961) has recently obtained correlations up to +.82 between three keys (high work, conformity, strong superego) and rated efficiency in a group of thirty-one, and another group of twenty-three tabulating machine operators. On retest of the first group, the scores proved stable.

The advantage of the PAT method is that it is based on arrangements and outcome rather than on story themes. Its disadvantage, that it prescribes not only the general story theme by showing a picture but limits even plot and outcome by showing two more pictures. In addition, the test depends heavily on intelligence for the interpretation of the cartoons. This is not too serious in practice because the score profile is obtained by comparing the record with the responses obtained from people of the same age, sex, intelligence, occupation, and the like, as the testee. Of course, such subdivisions break up the large normative group (1500 normal, 755 abnormal subjects) into rather small splinter groups.

Though this method does tap preferences for action and

seems one of the more successful attempts to turn a projective technique into an objective method, it is a question whether the advantages gained are worth sacrificing the most important aspect of storytelling tests, namely, the freedom to create one's own plot and outcome. Objective methods are preferable when they save time and do not require special training. The PAT requires about twenty-five minutes for machine scoring per set of twenty-five plates; a record can also be scored by hand (with prepared cards) in about an hour. The interpretation of the profile of "rares" has to be done in addition. This requires considerable skill because there are no rules to indicate how the profile characteristics are to be combined. In comparison, the technique of story sequence analysis requires about twenty minutes for the formulation of ten imports, and another twenty minutes for scoring, once skill has been acquired. The sequence of imports gives an organized picture of the individual's motivation which is immediately available for writing a clinical report. Thus economy of time is added to the advantage of having an organized picture based upon every story told, and so allowing full play to the storyteller's imagination.

Though rare arrangements may tap some of the problems that preoccupy one man and not another, only his spontaneous stories will allow us to discover his dominant problems and the way in which he proposes to solve them; whether he will act constructively and earn success, or negatively, and reap failure. Values will not enable us to make such predictions, whether we study them by means of stories presented to the individual or by means of statements he is asked to endorse. To know that he subscribes to economic rather than aesthetic values is interesting, but does not help us to predict whether this particular person will gravitate toward the most lucrative type of work, and still less whether he will succeed at it. It is not always the man who values money most who manages to amass it. The prediction of success or failure requires a knowledge of a man's motives, that is, those values he has set himself to attain and the way in which he proposes to do it.

MOTIVES AND ATTITUDES

We have distinguished values from motives on the basis of action: values are based on the simple judgment that something is desirable; motives include in addition a choice of action. As long as values are not accompanied by an appraisal for action, they do not influence behavior. When they do, they become motives.

Both values and motives become habitual and develop into attitudes. However, a value that is habitually held as an attitude is not a readiness for action. A motive is, whether it is temporary or has become habitual. Just as values and motives are usually not distinguished, so the two types of attitude connected with them are not held apart. This accounts for a good deal of confusion, both in research and theory. From Allport's definition of attitude as a "mental and neural state of readiness exerting a directive influence upon the individual's response to all objects and situations with which it is related" (1937, p. 810) to Campbell's "operational" definition of social attitude as "a syndrome of response consistency with regard to social objects" (1950, p. 30), it has been assumed that an attitude is a readiness for action. Behavioristic influence has made it plausible to consider verbal reports as a form of action so that the term "response" in these definitions includes both words and actions. But surely, it is possible to report a favorable attitude toward religion, public sanitation, or self-help, and still not do anything about it. These are values that may be habitually held but do not influence action: they have never become motives. If we were willing to distinguish between *evaluative* attitudes (i.e., habitual values) and *motivating* attitudes (i.e., habitual motives), we would realize at once that evaluative attitudes cannot be used to predict action. Without this distinction, even occasional drastic demonstrations have not been able to destroy the illusion that any verbally expressed attitude should allow the prediction of behavior, if only we hit upon the right method of measurement. A long time ago, LaPiere (1934) found that hotels, restaurants, and autocamps accepted Chinese guests in concrete instances though over 90 percent of their managers, when later questioned, said that they would not do so. Yet, research on similar evaluative attitudes is carried on, always in the hope of predicting behavior but never quite managing to do so.

It does not help to distinguish between *verbal* attitudes (either elicited or spontaneous) and *action* attitudes, as Green (1954) does, in an effort at making prediction possible. As an example, Green mentions that a restaurant manager might tell a survey interviewer that he would not serve Negroes (elicited verbal attitude), might mention to friends that he would not do so (spontaneous verbal attitude), and might actually refuse to serve a Negro customer (action attitude). Apart from the fact that it would be difficult to measure these three attitudes separately, it is simply not correct to imply that all verbal attitudes alike are doubtful as predictors of action. True, some verbal attitudes do not predict action; not because they are verbal but because they are evaluative. In contrast, motivating attitudes, also expressed verbally, can and do predict action.

Though all attitudes are habitual tendencies to action (see Chapter 2), evaluative attitudes are habitual tendencies to *evaluate* something positively or negatively, while motivating attitudes are habitual tendencies to *engage in overt action* which is either constructive—positive—or non-constructive—negative. So a man may have developed a tendency to act responsibly, rationally, ethically, while another may habitually act in a selfish, irresponsible manner. One man may act quickly, competently, another may put off action or do it halfheartedly, a third may procrastinate until somebody else finally does what has to be done. All these action tendencies are motivating attitudes and are revealed in stories that have a plot (which describes actions) and an outcome (which shows whether this action is likely to be chosen by the storyteller). Since these attitudes are motivating attitudes, they do predict action, as will be shown in later chapters.

MOTIVATION AND PERSONALITY

With Gasson (1954), we define personality as *the patterned totality of human powers, activities and habits, uniquely organized by the person in the active pursuit of his self-ideal, and revealed in his behavior.* Actions often repeated become habits, just as repeated tendencies to action become attitudes. Each new action is influenced by these attitudes that stem from habits, and in turn reorganizes them. What forms the motive for action is the appraisal of something as good for us and wanting it. Appraising something as good for us here and now arouses the wanting, which is an emotion; appraising it as suitable for a particular action arouses a deliberate action impulse, the intention to attain our objective. Thus emotion influences action, but our deliberate intention initiates and guides it. This intention is the want that leads to action. Motives are ordered into a hierarchy according to what is, by and large, the most important goal. This goal, incorporated in beloved people, important causes, deathless aspirations, attracts us but also demands our devotion, our willingness to live up to the ideal to which we aspire. In this way, the master goal becomes our master motive, the self-ideal that shapes us as we strive toward it.

THE ETHICS OF TAT TESTING

If stories reveal the attitudes a man has formed, the convictions he has made his own, a story-telling test will not reveal anything a shrewd judge of character, given intimate acquaintance over a long time, could not find out about a man. It does, however, make such knowledge available in the space of an hour's testing.

Much has been written in recent years about the ethical problems connected with personality testing. According to Cronbach (1960), virtually all personality tests seek information on areas people usually regard as private. As examples, he mentions tests that assess (or purport to assess) the strength of a man's sexual needs, his attitudes toward authority, or a mother's love for her child. Now, it is one thing to devise questionnaires that demand answers to pointed and intimate questions, and quite another to let a man speak in his own words about imaginary situations he himself devises.

Nobody has the right to demand answers to questions about a man's private life. That is an invasion of privacy. When it comes to projective tests, the answer is not so easy. In spite of the uncertainty expressed in several recent articles whether TAT themes express needs directly (see Chapter 1), all too often the test is still interpreted as if it were certain that they do. Thus the storyteller is credited (?) with desires and emotions he does not recognize in himself. Only because of their theoretical convictions and not because of valid evidence are such interpreters able to insist that these really are the testee's deepest desires which he may conceal even from himself but reveals to the wily psychologist.

This insistence that the psychologist by means of his tests can discover something that is not only private but may be discreditable in a man's own judgment has resulted in the fear of personality tests we find today. It does not help to reassure the testee, telling him that everybody has these needs and desires. He knows quite well that the psychologist would not be interested in his responses if that were literally true. Once we assure him, however, that the test will not discover anything that his acquaintances at work and at play will not find out in time, he may feel differently about it. Perhaps he may not like to be tested even then, but at least he will be assured that the test will not discover anything he does not recognize in himself when it is pointed out.

Now the psychologist may wonder whether a projective test that does not give depth interpretations is worth-while. Is it worth-while to know a man's actual motives, the effort he is willing to put into his work, his positive or negative attitudes to others? Is it worth-while to be able to predict his perform-ance now, when without the test it might take months or years to discover whether he will use his talents to their full extent or do only what is necessary?

It is time to air the whole question of personality testing. In taking a fresh look, we might disperse the misconceptions that have grown up around it. We are psychologists, not seers, and need not pretend to an insight into the innermost core of per-sonality, when all we have to go on is what a man says and does. We should let him speak for himself and do our level best to help him speak clearly.

Part II. THE TECHNIQUE OF STORY SEQUENCE ANALYSIS

4

THE IMPORT AND THE SEQUENCE

Whether TAT pictures, Blacky pictures, or pictures taken from other sources are used, the instructions given are essentially those of Murray (1943), except for the special instruction that narrative should be employed in the stories instead of dialogue or monologue. The number of pictures shown and the time given for each story may have to be changed. Seven minutes has been found ample for both children and adults; with highly literate adults, six minutes may suffice.

Before the first picture is shown, these instructions are given:

This is a test of your creative imagination. You will see thirteen pictures, one after another. As you look at each picture, write as dramatic a story as you can about it. Tell what has led up to the scene shown in the picture and what is happening now. What are the thoughts and feelings of the people in the picture? What will be the outcome?

Since we are interested in your creative imagination, be sure to tell a story with a plot and an outcome. Do not just describe the picture. Try to write a story and not a piece of conversation.

You will have seven minutes for each story. Be sure to write something about each picture. If you can't think of anything for one of the pictures, write that down, too.

Before showing the second picture, the instructions are repeated:

Remember that we are interested in your creative imagination, and be sure to tell a story with a plot and outcome. Tell what has led up to the scene in the picture, what is happening now and how it will end. Write a straight story, not a piece of conversation.

Before the third picture is shown, remind them again of the instructions:

Remember, we want to know what goes on in the picture, what led up to it, what is happening now, and how it will all end. Write a straight story, not a piece of conversation.

After three pictures have been shown, it is not necessary to repeat the instructions unless the tester notices doubt or confusion in the group. In that case, he may want to repeat the third set of instructions again.

It is important to note the sequence in which the pictures are shown. This will be the same sequence in which the stories are told. If the stories are not told in sequence, as shown, the sequence in which the stories are actually told is the one to be used. When fewer than twenty cards are shown, it is often advisable to insert the blank card (No. 16) before the last card to be shown. Stories told to the blank card often give the dominant problem or preoccupation of the storyteller. If another card follows the blank, the storyteller has a chance to recover from the highly personal story he has told in response to the blank card.

My colleagues and I have found the following cards most satisfactory: 1, 2, 3BM, 4MF, 6BM, 7BM, 8BM, 10, 11, 13MF, 14, 16, 20, and show them in this order. While the actual sequence in which they are shown is not too important, we have found that cards 1 and 2 are excellent to start with because most people find it easy to tell stories about these pictures and are put at ease because they are so harmless. When they encounter the more emotional scenes portrayed in cards 3BM and 4MF, they are then less likely to feel threatened.

THE IMPORT

If each story is an imaginative exploration of various problems and their possible solutions, we must try to isolate what it is the storyteller is trying to say. What he says about the picture will reveal his convictions: what could be called the "moral" of the story. When this moral is applied to the storyteller's subjective circumstances, we arrive at the *import* (the meaning or significance) of the story. Once the import of each story is set down in sequence, it becomes possible to follow the storyteller's trend of thought, which reveals his habitual dispositions, the way he evaluates human actions, and the circumstances of man's life. The story import will show how the storyteller thinks people usually act and how he feels they should act; what actions he thinks right and which wrong; what will lead to success, in his opinion, and what to failure; what can be done when danger threatens, and what are the things to strive for. In short, the story imports, taken in sequence, give us a connected statement of the storyteller's principles of action, his motivational pattern. Obviously, this pattern should make it possible for us to gauge how he would react to a situation.

Since the play of imagination is the important factor in a story, it is the action, plot, and outcome that matter, not the picture about which the story is told or even the characters who appear in it. We use the M pictures of Murray's TAT set for both men and women because these pictures are dramatic and lend themselves easily to imaginative exploration. Actually, any general kind of picture could be used. We have obtained as good imports and sequences from pictures found in *Life* and from short descriptive sentences, for instance: "Tell me a story about a boy and a violin." A person who has a rich and fertile imagination can tell good stories about almost anything. However, for those whose imagination is sluggish, pictures illustrating a dramatic situation are a decided help.

In trying to formulate the import of the story, all theoretical preconceptions must be set aside. It is not a question of trying to interpret the story or to guess what particular childhood experience a picture might recall. What is required for an accurate import is to discover what the story is actually saying and formulate the import in such a way that it abstracts from the concrete details of the story and applies to the storyteller's life situation. Whether the storyteller identifies with one of his characters, or with which one he identifies is irrelevant. The import is written from the point of view of the main character without any assumption that in speaking about this character the storyteller speaks necessarily about himself. When in doubt, the sequence usually gives a clue as to which character the import is to describe (see Chapter 5, The hero in the import).

The following stories will illustrate what is meant. They are in a sequence given by a fifteen-year-old boy, an inveterate truant, who tried to avoid trouble by saying he would do what was required without ever doing it.

Record #1

[Card 1] Well, this boy is looking at his violin and trying to think of a way to get out of playing it. His mother wants him to play it and be a good violinist. In the end he will play it as his mother wants, but won't be too good at it.

[Card 2] This girl is going to school because her mother over here wants her to. She would rather do other things but will go to school although she hates it. Finally, she will be old enough to not have to go any more and she will do what she wants. She never was good in school anyway.

[Card 3] This boy is crying 'cause his mother made him do something he didn't want to. He did what his mother wanted, though; probably his homework, but then he couldn't go to a party. He's unhappy, but he did what she wanted.

[Card 4, long pause] Oh, that looks like this guy is pretty angry.

He has had just about enough, feels people or someone is trying to push him around. He's looking at that guy and feels that he will really get him. This girl, his wife, wants to stop him. [Question: "What is the outcome?"] Well, maybe he won't fight this man. I wouldn't.

[Card 5] Oh, that seems like this woman is watching to see that her son does his school work. She thought she would catch him, but he is doing his work, even though he hates it. She gets pretty mad when he doesn't do it, but he will do what his mother wants. Some day he won't have to go to school any more. He might even quit school when he's old enough and get a job.

These are the imports:

1. When a boy is supposed to work, he tries to think of a way to get out of it. Even when he does what he is supposed to do he won't be too good at it.

2. He may go to school because he has to and hate it until he is old enough not to have to go any longer and can do what he wants.

3. When he is forced to do something he doesn't want to do, he may do it but misses out on what he really wants and is unhappy.

4. When he feels that everybody is trying to push him around, he gets pretty angry. He would like to get them but he won't fight, they'll want to stop him.

5. People are always watching to see that he does what he is supposed to do, and they get pretty mad if he doesn't do it. Some day he will be old enough so he won't have to do any longer what people tell him to do.

The import can also be formulated in the second person and read as a monologue. What we aim at in the import is to write a series of statements addressed to nobody in particular—a set of musings that indicate a person's general outlook on life. The imports should not be formulated in such a way that each statement refers directly to the storyteller. Often the storyteller seems to say: "This is how people act or think," not necessarily, "this is what I think or do." This is how the statements would read:

1. When you are supposed to work, you try to think of a way to get out of it. Even when you do what you are supposed to do, you won't be much good at it.

2. You may go to school because you have to and hate it, until you are old enough not to go any longer and can do what you want.

3. When forced to do something you don't want to do and you do it, you miss out on what you really want and are unhappy.

4. When everybody is trying to push you around it is pretty annoying. You would like to get them but they'll stop you, so you won't fight.

5. People are always watching to see that you do what you are supposed to and get pretty mad if you don't. Some day you'll be old enough so you won't have to any longer.

Whatever way the imports are formulated, it is clear that this boy has a problem and is talking about it in every story. He says in effect that he hates school and resents being forced to attend it, being forced to do anything; that he is only waiting until he is old enough so he can do what he wants to do. In the following fifteen stories, it became clear that for this boy growing up means being able to do what he wants to do—and what he wants to do is never what he ought to do. His is a general negative attitude, over and above the transparent school problem. It is brought out in its clearest form in the import to the last TAT story (card 20):

If nobody likes you because you cheat, and you can't fight, it is always possible to get even by crooked means. There will come a time when you'll have everything you want and people will fawn on you, but you won't pay any attention to them.

This import reveals a boy who thinks the easiest way to become accepted by others is to cheat and so become successful.

And, when success is his, he will be able to get back at those who now make his life a burden. Even without a sequence analysis, such a TAT is easy to interpret because the problem is so transparent and is repeated practically in every story. That is the reason why the TAT has been used clinically with fair success while studies with normal groups have been disappointing (see Chapter 1).

However, the fact that the boy is in the habit of lying about school or homework cannot be gleaned easily from the stories though it may be inferred from the imports. In the story, he says again and again that the hero does what he is supposed to do. In the imports, it becomes clear that the boy is trying to think of a way to get out of doing what he is asked to do (1), that he may be forced to do it and hates it (2, 3, 4, 5). We may then infer that he does it only when there is no way out of it—and lying would be one of the more obvious ways out. The reason why there is not a more definite hint that the boy is lying is that the storyteller solves his problems in the stories as he solves them in reality. In real life, the boy tries to evade school and work by saying he is doing what he is supposed to do, that is, by lying. He does exactly the same in the stories.

When the storyteller has no particular problem, an intuitive analysis based on hero identification and childhood dynamics cannot disentangle his problems from the problems of his characters. A sequence analysis, however, may reveal a general negative attitude in spite of a seemingly neutral context. As an example, let us look at the first five TAT stories of a college freshman with a high I.Q.* who barely passed his exams.

Record #2

[Card 1] This boy has probably had some interest in working with his hands. He is looking at the violin with a craftsman's eyes. He takes in the beauty of its finish, the delicate manner in which it has been carved and thinks of possibly making something like

---

* Revealed by a SCAT score falling in the 80th percentile of all freshmen.

this himself. This does not mean that he will become an artist, only that he will probably always appreciate beauty.

[Card 2] The girl with books may be a social worker, going from farm to farm, checking on living conditions. In the picture she has just finished interviewing the couple and the man has gone back to his plowing. From this particular interview the girl has probably discovered that the couple has been fairly successful. This is easily seen by the good condition in which the farmer's body, horse and garden seem to be.

[Card 4] The man is drunk. His wife is trying to calm him down. He probably got drunk in the first place because his wife has nagged at him for not working, not paying bills or something of that nature. He will sleep off his drunkenness in a few hours and probably feel very depressed the next day. However, the next time the world caves in on him, he and his wife will probably stage a repeat performance.

[Card 6] The young man has made his first decision, to join the army. His mother is upset because he is putting off college and going into the cruel world where there are hardships and dangers. When it is time for him to leave, she is very proud because she knows he is doing a brave thing, though it may not be the best thing. Her son has become a man.

[Card 7] This 20-year-old boy is asking his father's advice for the first time since he went to grammar school. The father is doing his best to give a good sound answer so that his son will come back again. He will probably satisfy his son's need and they will be friends again for life. [Cards 3 and 5 were not shown.]

When the imports are read in sequence, it becomes quite clear that the boy's general outlook on life is not constructive even though each story by itself sounds well enough:

1. When a man sees something beautiful, he begins to dream of making something similar. He may not do it but will always appreciate beauty.

2. It is easily seen that people who have land and property are successful,

3. but people without money or job get into a rut and are forced to seek oblivion and escape.

4. Eventually, a boy has to make his own decision. It may not be the best thing but in deciding he becomes a man of whom others can be proud.

7. When a son turns to his father for advice, the father must do his best to give a good, sound answer so he will satisfy his son's need and they can be friends.

These stories reveal a boy without any particular problem but a rather negative attitude to life. In the first story, he seems to say that something will stick when a man is exposed to beauty or culture, even though he is doing nothing about it. In the second and third story, he voices his conviction that success depends on what a man starts out with: if he has money or property, he is bound to succeed; if he has neither, he is condemned to a dreary existence. In the fourth story, he seems to say that a man must have some initiative, but apparently one becomes a man by just making a decision whether it is the right one or not. Finally, in the fifth story, we find him saying that once independent, a man may again turn to his elders for advice; but they must be careful to give the right answer, to "satisfy his need," before they can be friends. This reveals a naïve egoism that is almost childish in a college man.

Any clinician will recognize that attitudes like these do not make for achievement or constructive human relationships. That they do not promote achievement is shown by the fact that this student was referred for counseling because of his low grades. No doubt he will approach the counselor also as someone who has to "satisfy his needs," which will not make for quick or lasting therapeutic success. Without a change of attitude, it is exceedingly doubtful that the boy will get very far in college.

Though the attitudes revealed in the above TAT sequence analysis can be recognized by clinician and counselor as negative—non-constructive—the criterion for what is positive or constructive and what is not has been established empirically.

Our studies have shown that high achievers in elementary and secondary school and in college, good teachers, naval recruits who perform adequately, and better than average executives revealed markedly different attitudes from their fellows whose performance was poor. Let us call the attitudes of the former positive, constructive, those of the latter, negative, non-constructive.

The motivation revealed in the TAT Sequence Analysis is comparatively independent of intelligence (see Chapters 10 and 12). Here it is sufficient to say that high achievers show constructive attitudes whatever their range of intelligence, whereas low achievers of *the same degree* of intelligence show negative attitudes. The following set of five stories, for instance, was told by a freshman in the same college as the low achiever mentioned above. This student had a SCAT score in the twelfth percentile of all freshmen, but had grades in the high eighties at the end of his freshman year:

Record #3

[Card 1] Before the boy begins the violin practice he dreads, he is thinking about the fun he could be having outdoors. Finally he begins to play, and much to his surprise he obtains pleasure from playing the instrument and learns to master the art of playing the violin.

[Card 2] This girl is thinking about one's position in life according to their situation. She is thinking that this man must always remain a farmer since he did not receive educational opportunities or did not take advantage of them. She perhaps then decides to make the best of her educational opportunities in order to advance and better herself.

[Card 4] This man is emotionally disturbed and intends to satisfy his anger by attempting to do something about it by serious action. His wife, however, holds him back and tries to reason with him. After much sound reasoning, the wife calms her husband.

[Card 6] A boy is worried about a particular problem. Since it is a matter which he cannot solve alone, he seeks the advice of a person who is capable of guiding him. The elderly woman listens to his problem and then offers him advice, letting him make his own decisions. The boy considers seriously the facts they have discussed and realizes what he must do.

[Card 7] The boy has taken a drastic step and now wonders if what he has done was the right thing. He confides in an older man in hopes that his step was justifiable. Eventually he realizes that it was his only alternative and he was justified. [Cards 3 and 5 not shown.]

These are the imports:

1. A man may not like the work he has to do but once he starts doing it he will find it fun and become proficient.

2. Thinking about his position in life, he decides to make the best of his educational opportunities so as to advance and better himself.

4. Sometimes it is hard to control one's anger and listen to reason but it can be done.

6. If the problem is serious, one must consult someone with experience and then make his decision.

7. Once the decision is made, one may wonder whether it was the right one. Then the only thing to do is to consult someone who knows, and so realize that it was the only alternative and was justified.

Here the same general situation occurs as was revealed in the low achiever's TAT. This boy also is exposed to some work that is desirable but difficult. But, here the hero achieves success and, even better, finds work fun (card 1). This student realizes that success requires hard work, and work he may dislike in the beginning. He also knows from experience that work done faithfully may in the end prove interesting. There is another problem that occurs in both records, perhaps because both students attended a residential college far from home. It is the problem of having to make independent decisions. Our low achiever seems to think that the making of such a decision is a sign of maturity, while the much less intelligent high achiever realizes that a decision must be reasonable to be mature. He is willing to consult others beforehand, listen to reason, and then make his own choice. If he still doubts whether it was the right decision, he is willing to talk to someone who could be expected to know, and so set his mind at rest.

A third problem that recurs in both sets is the relationship of younger to older people, whether parents or teachers. Our intelligent low achiever seems to think young people have to rebel against the older generation if they want to make independent decisions. When they do consult their elders, it is up to the consultant to give them an answer that satisfies their need, and only if such an answer is forthcoming can they be friends. The not-so-intelligent high achiever, on the other hand, is willing to consult older people when he has a problem and is willing to listen to their advice, though he knows that the decision is his own. A man with such attitudes is sure to work hard at college and listen with an open mind, even though academic work may not come easily. Even more important, he will not be swayed by emotions but will decide what is reasonably required and then do it.

The stories themselves would betray the difference in intelligence between the two students even if we did not know their SCAT scores. Since the TAT was given as a group test in which each student wrote out the stories himself, the wording cannot be the result of awkwardness or timidity in telling stories. The less intelligent high achiever is unsure of his grammar and has a plodding, undistinguished style. The intelligent low achiever writes well and uses words to best advantage. But, as we know, it is not intelligence only that is decisive in school achievement. Given the minimal intelligence that will make it possible to handle the material, achievement seems to depend on the student's willingness to do what is required. It is this motivation, this willingness to apply himself, that is tapped by the sequence analysis.

FORMULATING IMPORT AND SEQUENCE

The import must be formulated in such a way that it is neither a summary nor a statement that is so general that it might apply to anybody, no matter what the circumstances. Let us take the first story of our intelligent low achiever, for instance. Our import for card 1 was as follows: [1.] When a man sees something beautiful, he begins to dream of making something similar. He may not do it but will always appreciate beauty.

Where the story talks about a violin, the import generalizes to *beauty*. Where the story mentions the boy's half-hearted desire to make a violin, the import contracts it into *making something that is beautiful*. Someone not familiar with the method might be tempted to write down a more detailed statement, for instance: "When a boy sees a violin, he begins to dream of making one, too. He may not become an artist but will always appreciate beauty." This is a summary rather than an import; it is so specific that it probably does not apply to the storyteller. He may have no desire to make a violin though he obviously does appreciate beauty and beautiful things. For beginners, there is often the opposite temptation, also. If they try to avoid detail, they fall into the error of making the import so general that it does not apply to anybody. For instance, the same story might be abstracted into this import: "A man may want to imitate what he sees. Though nothing may come of it, he may derive some profit." This version loses the individual note in the story which is the realization that the violin is *beautiful*, and that it is an appreciation of beauty that remains even though the boy may never do more than look at beautiful things. It also implies that sheer imitation is wanted, while the story suggests that the hero wants to make something that is *as beautiful*; he does not want merely to imitate something.

In writing the import, it is advisable to use the actual words of the story whenever a phrase seems significant. For instance, in the second story of the same record, the import says: [2.] "It *is easily seen* that people who have land and property are successful." It could also be formulated as: "When *checking on living conditions,* it *is easily seen* that people with land and property are successful." The quoted phrases are italicized. In both cases, the emphasis is that this is what is found if one cares to make a survey. Similarly, the import for card 6 incorporates a significant phrase: "Eventually, a boy has to make his own decision. *It may not be the best thing* but in deciding he becomes a man of whom others can be proud." And the story import for card 7: "When a son turns to his father for advice, the father must do his best *to give a good sound answer* so he *will satisfy his son's need* and they can *be friends.*"

While nothing must be introduced into the import from outside, it is essential that it should contain all the nuances of the story. For instance, if the import for the above card 6 were to read: "Eventually, a boy has to make his own decision and in doing so he becomes a man," the really important point would be left out. According to the story, the young man has made his first decision. This upsets his mother but also makes her proud, because he is doing a brave thing though it may not be the best thing, and so he becomes a man. Becoming a man is connected in this context with making a decision to face the cruel world, which is a brave thing to do but may not be the best thing under the circumstances, for he could go to college first. Since there is no indication in the story that he ought to join the army (e.g., because his country needs him), the boy seems to imply that the important thing is to make a decision, to do the brave thing, even though that may not be the best thing. This identifies manliness with independent decision and perhaps with bravery, but hardly with reasonableness.

Just as important as formulating the import accurately is to link it whenever possible to what came before and what comes next. This is necessary because a given problem is often explored in several stories. If the story imports are not linked, important clues may be missed. For instance, the second story in the same record carries this import: "It is easily seen that people who have land and property are successful"; followed by the next story import: "but people without money or job get into a rut and are forced to seek oblivion and escape." If the link were missed, the last import might read: "When a man has no job and can't pay his bills, he has troubles at home and seeks oblivion and escape, only to wake up to more troubles. But every time the world caves in on him, he will repeat the performance." Though this import is accurate, it does not convey the meaning of those two stories. In addition, paying attention to the sequence enables us to shorten the second import materially without losing accuracy.

Though it is important to link imports that belong together, it is unwise to force a linkage when the stories obviously refer to quite different trends of thought. For instance, in the record of our less intelligent high achiever we find the following import sequence:

1. A man may not like the work he has to do, but once he starts doing it he will find it fun and become proficient.

2. Thinking about his position in life, he decides to make the best of his educational opportunities so as to advance and better himself.

These two imports obviously belong together and refer to his studies, but the third import starts a new train of thought which is carried on in the next two imports:

4. Sometimes it is hard to control one's anger and listen to reason, but it can be done.

6. If the problem is serious, one must consult someone with experience and then make his decision.

7. Once the decision is made, one may wonder whether it was the right one. Then the only thing to do is to consult someone who knows, and so realize that it was the only alternative and was justified.

If we had tried to link the imports to cards 2 and 4 by sheer force, we could have done it only by adding something to the story, for example:

4. (One may be emotionally disturbed over it and) try to satisfy his anger but calms down after much reasoning.

This would not make much sense. There is no particular reason why the anger mentioned in story 4 should follow from the earlier decision to make the best of one's educational opportunities. Once we recognize that this story starts a new line of thought, we have no difficulty in seeing what is important in this story: that it is hard to control one's anger, and not that one may be emotionally disturbed when angry.

The import with the sequence in which it is imbedded is the backbone of our method of interpretation. The import is objective in the sense that it is abstracted as accurately as possible without adding any kind of interpretation. Formulating the import does not presuppose any theoretical orientation. In fact, particular theoretical convictions interfere with the formulation of correct imports rather seriously. For instance, the notion that the storyteller "identifies" with the hero may lead to all kinds of misinterpretation. Nor can we assume that a mother or father occurring in the story must be the storyteller's own mother or father. At best, we may formulate the import in such a way that a *possible* father-son relationship is described, for instance in the story of our low achiever to card 7: "When a son turns to his father for advice. . . ." Quite likely, the storyteller's own relationship to his father does bear some similarity to the one he describes; but whether it does or not, he obviously approves of it and that is sufficient for our purposes. If there is some conflict in the storyteller's father-son relationship, it will crop up again and again in later stories. Without clinical verification, it is far safer to let the sequence tell the story rather

than prejudge the storyteller's attitude by a premature interpretation.

To keep the import objective, the interpreter must be perceptive enough to catch the fine nuances contained in the
story. This requires practice and, at first, direction and super-
vision. In discussion with others, it is always possible to come
to an agreement as to what is the most precisely formulated
import. For this reason, it is advisable to make the formulation
of imports a group project until considerable facility has been
achieved. Once trained, different investigators formulate imports that are highly reliable and score alike.

It is advisable to formulate the imports before too much is
known about the storyteller. (All our own analyses have been
blind analyses.) This eliminates reading into the stories what
we know from the clinical history and gives us an opportunity
to check the hypotheses we form on the basis of the completed
sequence analysis with other sources of information without
being biased by them. There is only a minimum of factual
information that is necessary: the storyteller's sex, age, profession, marital status, domicile. Beyond that, the only thing
necessary is to formulate the import so that it expresses what
is implied in the story *from the point of view of the storyteller.*
This means suspending judgment, foregoing interpretations
based on some personality theory, however plausible, and simply listening to what the storyteller is saying. Such an attempt
at abstracting the essential meaning of the story is akin to the
effort of the non-directive counselor to get at the "feelings"
behind the client's words without projecting his own. Incidentally, formulating imports is excellent training in the accurate
evaluation of scientific (or any other) literature. Once the student has learned to suspend judgment and listen to what the
writer is saying, he will not make the mistake of reading his
own prejudices into the printed words and jumping to con-
clusions before he has read more than a page.

That the imports form a sequence has been verified over and over in clinical work with this method. Without such a sequence, the storyteller's problems cannot be correctly evaluated even though his general positive or negative motivation can be determined by means of the scoring criteria (Appendix A). It can be stated confidently that such connected sequences occur in the vast majority of records, though the length of each sequence may vary before another trend of thought starts a new sequence. The tester has grasped the method as soon as he can detect the links between the stories so that they fall into a coherent pattern without being forced into it. It has happened repeatedly that a psychologist skilled in this method was able (in a blind analysis) to pinpoint a patient's problems as they had been discussed in months of counseling or psychotherapy (Farrell, 1961; Ennis, 1961).

5

POSITIVE AND NEGATIVE IMPORTS

Since it is the import that counts, the import rather than the story is scored. Only when the import does not seem easily scorable is the scorer advised to go back to the story.

SIGNIFICANCE OF THE IMPORT

In every story, the storyteller says something about a particular situation. This can be generalized to similar situations. The storyteller talks about possible ways of coping with the particular set of circumstances he imagines, and indicates whether the action taken in the story is successful or unsuccessful. When an action is successful, he seems to imply that this is the way to act if you want to achieve success. He may even imply whether the kind of success achieved is desirable or undesirable. The import emphasizes the intention of the storyteller and frees it from incidental embellishments. When that is done, the positive or negative aspect of the story is clearly brought out. A few examples will illustrate what is meant.

Record #4 (Good teacher, age 28, F., I.Q. 120)
[Card 1] Last night, for the last time, Jim heard Dad play his violin. Dad died early this morning. This violin he gave Jim as one last treasure. Now music grows to be a part of his life, as it was of his Dad's. Jim uses his music as a stepping stone to friendliness and cheer, not in a great symphonic orchestra but in his home and in neighborly circles.

Import. If you use the talent you have you can achieve success, not necessarily in a big but in a simple way.

This story shows a realistic recognition that a person's talent may not be great enough to achieve success in a big way. (We remember here that this teacher's I.Q. is 120.) But if she uses her talent constructively, it will brighten her life and that of others. We may expect her to act accordingly in her own life; apparently she is successful in her efforts, for she is rated a good teacher by her pupils. Now let us look at a similar story by an ineffective teacher matched for age and intelligence:

Record #5 (Poor teacher, age 30, F., I.Q. 124)

[Card 1] The boy in this picture is the only son of a musician. His father has lately returned from a concert tour and has left the instrument on the table. Sudden illness followed by unexpected death has left the boy's mother upset and confined to her room. The child has come to gaze at the instrument his father made seem almost alive. It is a link to one he loved and as he is so absorbed in his dream, his one desire is to make the instrument live again. As he dreams, his loneliness fades and he sees his mother's happy smile as he, in years to come, steps into the vacant place of his father. The dream comes true as a result of this moment's searching thought and resolution.

Import. Love for someone you admire may make you want to continue his work and take his place in the world. Your dream comes true as a result of this thought and resolution.

Here we see quite a different attitude. There is a desire for achievement, but neither a recognition that considerable talent is required for the undertaking nor the realization that a great deal of effort must be put into it. The boy in the story dreams, and presto, his dream comes true because of the moment's resolution. It is true that dreams sometimes do lead to achievement. When they do, the first step is a realistic appreciation of what is required; and the next, work and patient effort. In a story, where it is up to the storyteller what situation he will describe, he will express what he thinks about the problem he sets himself and solves in the story. If it does not occur to him in telling the story that dreams must be supplemented by work and effort, it won't occur to him in real life, either.

That this is so is shown by hundreds of records of high achievers in various occupations. Good teachers, high achievers in elementary and secondary schools as well as in college, well-adjusted Navy men, successful executives, all of them do tell stories in which success is achieved by personal effort or initiative, by adapting means to ends. The inadequate or unsuccessful members of these categories, in contrast, do tell stories in which success is achieved as a result of dreams or resolutions without indicating personal effort. It is from the records of these groups of high and low achievers that our notions of positive and negative motivations were derived.

That this difference in attitude is not accidental is illustrated also in the stories given by the two teachers to card 8:

Record #4 (Good teacher)
[Card 8] "Some day I will be a fighter, too," thought Dan. "My battle will be with sickness, disease, cancer." Day by day this desire grew. Dan's big brother died on an operating table. The doctors did their best but Dan knew this disease had the doctors licked. Study, patience, selfless zeal brought Dan his desires and the reality of aiding mankind.

Import. If you cling to your ambition to do good, you may make your desires a reality by study, patience, and selfless zeal.

Record #5 (Poor teacher)
[Card 8] Jack has just finished reading a story of the sea, the days of early sailing vessels, pirates, crude methods of fighting, and the misery of sailors without the proper medical care. The dream grows as he reviews another life, early experiments in science, Louis Pasteur—it grows, seeing now the modern hospital laboratory with its efficient personnel. The light of his eyes shows a will to be a part of that world of testing, to find new and better ways of healing. The dream finds its end in just that hope.

Import. Your dream will find its end in the hope of new and better ways of healing.

Here again, both teachers apparently describe the same goal, but in the one case it is achieved by honest effort, in the other, it remains a bright hope.

Each import states the storyteller's reaction to the whole situation described in the story. For this reason, it is a mistake to dissect either story or import into different "themes" (Murray) or "achievement images" (McClelland). It would be as serious an error if we were to score several different attitudes in one and the same story. The storyteller does not reveal an attitude to women, men, or children, to authority, law enforcement, or crime. He reacts to the total situation by the way in which he speaks about the action of various characters in the story and by the way in which he imagines the consequences of these actions. Whether a man talks about work and achievement or whether he tells stories about people in which work is not mentioned, he always sets himself a problem, the plot, and solves it in his characteristic way in the outcome. For instance, in the stories to card 1 told by the good and poor teachers (records 4 and 5), the death of a loved father is described and both stories express the wish to emulate him. But, the good teacher lets the son be spurred to work and achievement by his love; the poor teacher lets him simply resolve to take the father's place, to become like him and reap his success, without paying the least attention to the effort required to do so. Similarly, in the story about card 8, the good teacher lets the boy be inspired to a life of work and devotion by the suffering of someone he loves, while the poor teacher lets the boy be inspired merely to dream.

IMPORT VERSUS STORY

The constructiveness of an attitude has nothing to do with the merits of a story, either as an imaginative production or as an example of what is right or wrong. For instance, our good teacher tells this story:

Record #4

[Card 3] Blue-black drippings all over the wall—Oh, why did Tom have to duck! Mom's whipping didn't help any. Bill dejectedly wept himself to sleep, head bent over the sofa, the squirt gun alongside of him. In a few hours Dad would be home and the result—Bill would be blue-black, too, for putting ink into his squirt gun.

Import. When something is used for the wrong purpose, things will turn out badly and you must expect punishment.

Compare this with the story of the poor teacher:

Record #5

[Card 3] The youngster in this picture has been caring for his younger brother while his parents were out for the evening. After an hour of romping about he went about the task of settling a not-too-eager young fellow to rest. Then he returned to the living room to pick up the toys. He spied a mechanical airplane at the side of the couch. He bent to pick it up, listlessly ran it back and forth with his hand and dropped off to sleep with his head on the couch and it was there his parents found him.

Import. You may do the job you are asked to do, but you get so tired you fall asleep over it.

Now, on the face of it, the youngster in the second story has done nobly, coping with his little brother, putting him to bed, intending to tidy up. All the same, it is a fact that he starts out well but gets tired and leaves the job half done. We may have much sympathy for the youngster; his fatigue is entirely understandable. But, the storyteller is at liberty to tell any story at all. If he tells a story that ends up with sleep overcoming the hero and justifies it by a plausible explanation, this is something he must know well from his own experience. It may well be that there is a physical reason for the fatigue and exhaustion. We have found that many stories of this type may occur after a debilitating illness, even in records of high achievers. Whatever the reason, it is the fact of fatigue that prevents the story hero from finishing the job, and so is counted as negative. Taken together with the stories in which achievement follows upon dreams and (empty) resolutions, we begin to see why the storyteller of record 5 is a poor teacher, and why, with these attitudes, she would not be successful in another occupation either.

In the good teacher's story to card 3, the boy is mischievous, plays a trick which does more damage than intended, and is promptly punished. The storyteller seems to say that a person had better not use things for a purpose for which they were never meant. While this import is correct (and easily scorable) because the boy is punished for putting ink into his squirt gun, it could also be formulated a little differently: "When you exceed the allowable limits of a joke, something is bound to go wrong, and you'll have to pay for it." Here we take account of the fact that there would have been no objection to water in the squirt gun. Even if Tom had ducked, it would have been harmless. In both cases, the import is positive because an ill-intended action is punished. The second formulation of the import takes care of the objection many a clinical psychologist would voice, that children should not be punished for a harmless joke.

The fact that it is the import, not the story, that is judged positive or negative, also counters the objection that different psychologists may have a different idea of what is positive or negative, based on different notions of what is right or wrong. For the sake of argument, let us take cases where Catholics, say, are expected to have views different from those of non-Catholics; that is, in stories that mention divorce or suicide. Compare, for instance, these two stories about marital disagreements. The first is from a low achiever, the second from a high achiever.

Record #6

[Card 4] John and Mary are having one of their bitter quarrels. But this time is the last. They both realize that living like cat and dog is not worth while and decide to get a divorce and relief from each other.

Import. When people keep quarreling, they'll get tired of it in the end and separate for good.

Record #7

[Card 4] Tom and Milly have had many a bitter quarrel. Looking at Tom, Milly suddenly realizes that the anger she sees in his eyes damages him as much as it hurts her. She knows that goes for both of them and decides that something has to be done. In a calm hour, she talks it over with Tom and finds him willing to cooperate. They still have many ups and downs but with good will on both sides they eventually learn to settle their differences without quarreling.

Import. When people keep quarreling, they damage themselves and hurt each other. With good will on both sides, they can manage to settle their differences without quarreling.

In the first story the import would be negative, whether the remedy decided on is divorce or separation. It is negative because no effort is made to come to any kind of friendly or even reasonable compromise. In the second story, the import is positive just because there is such an effort which leads to success. From the clinical point of view, one may doubt whether it is always possible to save a marriage—but then clinicians do not often come into professional contact with high achievers, or rather with people who have an entirely positive motivation. However, most clinicians would admit that a marriage can be saved when there is good will on both sides, as the second story stipulates. At any rate, whether the story solution is always practicable in reality is not the issue. What matters is the effort made in the story to come to a constructive solution.

Now let us turn to stories dealing with murder and suicide. Here are two such stories given to card 4, the one by a high achiever, the other by a low achiever.

Record #8 (High school sophomore, high achiever)

[Card 4] Sam was a Mormon in Utah. He enjoyed being one and was very faithful to his beliefs even to the extent of having two wives. He married Anne at 28 and Flo at 29. He was the son of a rich rancher and could afford three or four. For three years he was very content, but one day Flo met with another man. Sam just happened to be around at the time, and he overflowed with rage. But he was able to control it. Then the storm broke. For four months Sam trailed her at night. In those four months she had met with twelve men in the same house on Main Street. One night Sam came home with a pistol and he was going to end it all. Quietly he walked towards Flo's room—gun out. Anne saw him, ran to stop him, but he pulled away from her and stepped inside where Flo was dressing. The door slammed and four shots rang out. Anne fearfully opened the door. Both Flo and Sam were dead on the floor. A gun in each hand. Anne lived happily ever after.*

Import. No matter how justified your resentment, giving in to it means the end of both you and the person who wronged you. (Or: If you do something wrong in a spectacular way, a spectacular punishment will follow.)

This is obviously positive, in spite of the fact that the story bristles with actions that are morally wrong (and not only from a Catholic point of view): bigamy, murder, suicide. Compare this with the story told by a low achiever:

Record #9 (High school freshman, low achiever)

[Card 4] After the man had heard what his son had done, he was ready to beat him. The mother, half crazed herself, tried to control her husband, for how well she knew if he started beating him he wouldn't stop. The two policemen had taken the boy away to town in their car. Then they got a report from that station area that the husband had just committed suicide with his wife.

Import. If someone you love goes wrong, you may lose control and end everything. (Or: If a boy gets into trouble, parents may go to extremes in their anger.)

---

* This story, incidentally, was told in an attempt to fake the test with an outrageous plot. In spite of the intent, the story reveals a positive attitude.

Just as obviously, this import is negative, expressing the story meaning that trouble with a son leads to the parents' suicide. If the alternative import is taken, which describes the situation from the boy's point of view, the import is still negative. Even though every clinician would recognize the import from record 8 as positive and the import from record 9 as negative, we do not employ clinical judgment in scoring but use (here as in every other import) the scoring categories that have been derived empirically (see Appendix A and B).

THE HERO IN THE IMPORT

Story 4 in record 9 illustrates another objection that is often met with: From which point of view should the import be written? If it is taken from the parents' point of view, as is the case in the first import, how do we know that this is what the boy meant to say? As the storyteller was a high school boy, he might be expected to look at the situation from the boy's point of view. Usually, the story is told from the point of view of the hero, and the import should be formulated accordingly; in this case, however, the story switches from one character to another, so that this rule is difficult to apply. In most records, the sequence makes it clear if the story does not that the import is to be taken from the point of view of one particular character.

But there are cases where this is not so, and there are others where either import would fit the sequence. In such a case, it literally does not matter which import is chosen because the two imports will be found equally negative or positive if they are formulated accurately. In story 4 of record 9, for instance, the main character is the father—at least in the beginning. Then, the storyteller recounts what the mother is doing, and, finally, the story is told from the point of view of the two policemen. The first import is written from the father's point of view, the second from the son's, yet they are both negative.

It is also possible to formulate imports from the mother's and the policemen's point of view, but they are both less accurate because the essential son-parent relationship is underemphasized. From the mother's point of view, the import would read: "When there is an emergency, you may try to prevent someone you love from losing his self-control, but in the end both of you are lost." And from the policemen's point of view: "When you try coping with one difficulty, there will soon be a greater one to top it." Again, both imports are negative.

STORIES WITHOUT OUTCOME

Every import is either negative or positive. There are no indifferent attitudes as long as any kind of action is described.* Even when there is no outcome, the sequence will often help to infer the import. Consider, for instance, these two stories, told by a young girl, a candidate for a religious order, who left the convent shortly after she took the TAT.

> *Record #10*
> [Card 8] This young man has been called to war. He is thinking about the time when he will be on the battlefield and pictures in his mind some of the incidents which took place many years ago. When some man got shot, the bullet was taken out immediately with a knife. He becomes frightened with the thought but then realizes that times have changed. Now he is ready to go and face the danger bravely in spite of this.
> [Card 11] As you sit and daydream, you picture to yourself many wooded areas. You see areas with trees so tall that you hardly see their tips. You imagine huge rocks. [Cards 9 and 10 were not shown.]

Import 8. You may get frightened thinking of the trials and hardships that are facing you. But you soon realize that times have changed, and you are ready to face bravely today's milder demands;

---

* The only indifferent imports found so far are imports describing rest, e.g., "after work you rest." (See under score *zero,* I.B.1.)

Import 11. but they still seem mountainous whenever you think of them.

Though card 11 has produced a story without outcome—just a description, the picture of a daydream—the import follows easily from the sequence. When the two imports are taken together, we realize that this girl is frightened of the life she has chosen, though she knows that today there are comforts even in the convent that were unknown in earlier generations. Yet whenever she sits and thinks, the demands of this new life loom larger than the tallest trees. No wonder she left the convent.

Even when a card is rejected altogether, it is possible to use the words of this refusal instead of an import. In most cases, they will be found surprisingly apt. For instance, take these stories from the TAT of a teacher considered inadequate by her pupils:

Record #11

[Card 8] Robert was interested in science. He read many scientific books. His recent book was "Undertaker's position." He imagined that he would like to follow the career of an undertaker. In a vision he saw the cutting of veins and pumping of blood. Robert never lived to be an undertaker. He contracted malaria and died.

[Card 9] This picture most probably portrays a hold-up. Perhaps a bank was robbed. The police and bankers defending their rights were shot by the robbers. The FBI took up the case and are now in search of the gangsters.

[Card 10] I have no idea what this picture portrays. It may be spiritism, or revelation of secrets. I don't really know what to write on this one.

These are the imports:

8. You may have interests and dreams, but never achieve your goal because fate makes it impossible.

9. There is no use defending your rights, you'll only get hurt, even though the authorities afterward will step in and search for the trouble-makers.

10. It is all very mysterious, and you don't really know what to do.

All three imports are negative and reveal a general feeling of inadequacy if not hopelessness. The rest of the record is quite similar, with not a single positive import. In general, this teacher seems to expect failure and puts it down to fate or the machinations of others. At best, she depends on the efforts of others to aid her without ever being able to do anything for herself. This attitude finally comes to a head in card 10 which epitomizes her feelings of helplessness. Incidentally, this card is hardly ever rejected—which shows that such a refusal has nothing to do with the card and everything with her state of mind at the moment. Such professed inability to think of a story usually comes in the second half of the sequence, always at the point where the storyteller has reached an impasse and can see no solution to the problem he has pursued in imagination.

INCOMPLETE IMPORTS

Sometimes the import of one story is obviously incomplete and is finished in the next. In that case, both stories are scored positive or both negative, depending on the story that completes the import. Compare, for instance, these two stories:

Record #12 (Good teacher)

[Card 5] Terror clutched the heart of elderly Mrs. Cry as no answer came to her insistent call and knock at her neighbor's door. Old Mrs. Bong, like herself, was a widow and they shared each other's company each day. Mrs. Cry found her neighbor sprawled on the rug near the fireplace. A paralytic stroke ended their life-long friendship. Mrs. Bong never recovered.

[Card 6] "Mother, I tell you this is the opportunity I've been waiting for all these months. You know it was coming. It will mean better pay. It will mean we can pay off the mortgage on the house. It will mean keeping all that is so dear to us. I'll be home weekends." With these words, Robert, Mrs. Wilson's only son, took his leave in answer to the summons as manager of a bigger firm in Glendale, 140 miles out of his village. Though his heart was torn at leaving his mother alone, he knew it was best. And so it was!

These are the imports:

5. Sometimes, a lifelong companionship may suddenly come to an end,

6. but the separation may mean the opportunity to advance. If you act in spite of the pain, it will be the best thing in the end.

Ordinarily, story 5 would be scored as negative, but when it is clear that the main theme is completed in the next story, and the two imports are scored accordingly, it becomes apparent that the combined import is positive.

Some people, apparently in an attempt to tell a good story, prefer to use dialogue. These stories are difficult to score because the outcome is usually implied rather than stated explicitly. For this reason, it is advisable to add to Murray's directions for administration the instruction to tell a straight story with plot and outcome and to omit dialogue.

6

CLINICAL EVALUATION OF THE SEQUENCE ANALYSIS

The storyteller's preoccupation betrays his problems, and the import sequence lets us see them in the correct perspective. The import strips the story of its embellishments and lays bare the kernel of personal truth. The sequence provides the thread that links the imports together and reveals the various alternatives of action available to the storyteller. He can deal with his problem in a positive, constructive way, or in a way that betrays aggression, resignation, anxiety, or despair.

In spite of positive attitudes, a person may not succeed in a particular vocation if he finds it uncongenial for any number of reasons. As mentioned before, positive attitudes will enable a man to succeed provided the work he has chosen is within his range of intelligence. Though positive motivation may be found throughout the whole range of intelligence, it cannot be tested by means of the TAT or similar storytelling tests for the lower grades of intelligence, nor can we give such tests to children who cannot as yet tell a story with plot and outcome. But there are considerations other than intelligence that enter into success in a given occupation. In some highly demanding vocations, like the ministry, or convent life, or the missions, a radical change in the circumstances of a person's life is required, and not everybody who is willing to try will find himself able to go through with it—in spite of positive attitudes that would make for success in less demanding callings. In fact, such arduous vocations may bring out negative attitudes in a person who cannot measure up to them.

For this reason, it is particularly important to devise selection procedures that will discover potential misfits before they enter upon such callings and so will spare them frustration and disappointment. The story sequence analysis seems particularly appropriate for such a purpose. However, it is important in such cases to use a clinical evaluation of the sequence analysis also, because the scores do not tell the whole story. A clinical evaluation makes it possible to discover the special problems and difficulties facing the storyteller so that we may help him solve them, or, if they should make it inadvisable to enter such a vocation, that we may counsel him accordingly. One study (see Chapter 13) was designed to explore the adequacy of the sequence analysis as a test for selecting candidates for religious orders. The following record was obtained in this study and illustrates the fact that a person may be a misfit in the life he has chosen, despite positive attitudes. It is the record of a scholastic in a teaching order who left the order several months after taking the TAT. If the record had been analyzed immediately, his leaving could have been predicted. In this, as in many similar cases, we tried to get in touch with the storyteller as soon as the sequence analysis was completed, to offer counseling. By that time, however, the young man had left the order. These are his stories:

Record #13

[Card 1] Gilbert is not like most boys his age because at ten years old he is blind. When he was just old enough to start school, five years old, he had been playing with a friend next door who was several years his senior. In the course of their play a firecracker had exploded unexpectedly costing his eye. The next two years that followed were exceedingly gloomy and lonesome as he was unable to play with his friends and had nothing to do which interested him. Then his father had brought him home a violin which he didn't want to play. Being forced by his parents to take lessons, he soon discovered that he could produce something beautiful and interesting enough to captivate all of his attention. For the past couple of years now he had been happy and almost completely forgot his blindness for he could now do something which he really loved doing.

[Card 2] Margaret, then sixteen years old, thought that surely she could make her own decisions, but her father thought differently. Like all fathers of that period, he was determined that she should remain in the home. He thought that the place for a girl was home helping her mother and, when old enough, she was to be married and still remain in the home. Margaret had argued with him for many months but to no avail. However, after a year and a half of discussion, her father began to weaken. He saw that her heart was not in what she was doing at home, but it was in the school far away. Therefore, because of her own determination, and because she had in some way convinced him of the good of an education, he let her go to school just as she had always desired.

[Card 3] That morning of July twenty-ninth had been a happy one for Jim. He had awakened all excited, for today was the day of the big race. Since school had let out in May, he had anticipated and practiced for this race. He desired only one thing—to win that race. He lost! He had tried as hard as he could, but one boy was just faster. He had come home tired and discouraged. He told his father about the race and how disappointed he was in merely coming in second for he wanted to win. But his father explained that there were many things better than winning. Jim now realized that he had let the fact that he had not won completely ruin everything.

"After all," he thought, "I did have a lot of fun practicing with the guys and the race had been exciting."

[Card 4] Now he knew for sure. His best friend had betrayed him. He had suspected just a little for the last couple of months that something was phoney about that business deal. Now Thomas knew that he had been cheated of five thousand dollars, almost his entire savings. Hurt and mad he drove with one thought in his mind. There was a gun in the dresser drawer. He wanted to kill that person who once had been his friend. As he was taking out the gun, he met his wife. He had to explain to her what he was doing, not because he wanted to but because he loved her. While explaining to her and looking into her eyes, Tom knew that he would not commit murder. The goodness of his wife and his love for her completely conquered all hurt, all the hate he had just experienced.

[Card 5] That cool gray morning of December tenth she had finally gotten a job. Mary did not mind being a maid, but soon she discovered that her employer was extremely nervous and irritable and was completely obsessed with one idea which she was not able yet to understand. Besides having her clean the house in which he said he and his wife, now dead three months, had lived, he made her close all of the windows in the kitchen, set up a bed in there, and put all his books from the library on the table. He explained that he would remain there a couple of days. Mystified she did all that he asked. He entered the kitchen and she went about the house cleaning. Later that day, smelling a strange odor that appeared to come from the kitchen, she went to investigate and what she found solved all her unspoken questions. Her strange acting employer had committed suicide by gas.

[Card 6] There are times when we must hurt even those whom we love the most, like our own mother. This Alex realized extremely well right at the moment. He had led a life of dissipation and had been extremely unhappy until about six months ago. It was at that time that he had met Father O'Connor, who just yesterday had baptized him. All this was unknown to his mother who disliked, even hated, any mention of anything Catholic. Now as he explained the situation to his mother, he realized how much he hurt her, but even more he realized that he had to do what he had done because it was the only right thing.

[Card 7] At college William had been away from home. Being away from home had given him a feeling of independence. In fact he became so strongly attached to his own freedom that he completely disregarded authority. Now at home again, having been asked to leave college because he had disobeyed almost all existing rules, he found himself speaking with his father. Strangely he found that he even hated the authority of his own father. But as they discussed what type of life he would now have to lead he came to respect the wisdom and experience of his father and found that his dislike for authority, even his own father's, was mitigated. More and more he came to see things with the same logical sense of his father, and he agreed to his mistakes, which he hadn't admitted before and decided to write again to the Dean asking if possible a second chance, explaining that now he felt himself capable of acting properly and realized his faults.

[Card 8] Nathaniel could not play ball. In fact he did not enjoy games as much as the other boys, yet he wanted to be one of a group. After having tried to the utmost of his ability and having failed, he ran to his teacher crying. He asked his teacher why he could not do what the other children were doing, why, when he explained what he felt to them, they never understood. His teacher explained to him that he was not like the other boys, but that he had a most unusual tendency to study and to beauty. He, his teacher explained, was more imaginative, thought like an artist, and in this way was a little different than many boys. His teacher gave him some books to read and said that was where his talent lay. Nathaniel, no longer thinking of his failures but of his capacities, gradually became very happy.

[Card 9] It had been a hard job, one of extreme monotony and little compensation. All week long, day and night, they had been working hard for it is a real job pulling a boat upstream. After long hours of labor and no relaxation they finally received their pay. The only facilities for rest at these times were the many bars. So in they dragged themselves. They got drunk, forgot their jobs, and finally dropped all in a pile in a field near the bars until someone else came to pick them up. This was the life that Bill had been living for the past six months.

[Card 10] He had received his notice. He was in the army. With this news Joe drove home to his young wife. He had to tell her that he was going and yet he hated to. He knew that she had been planning so much that they could do and now that he would be gone it would be impossible. He dreaded getting out of the car and he did so slowly. When he met her, he did not even have to explain, she understood, she read it in his face and in the way he walked. Relieved, he hugged her and didn't even say a word. He marveled how she could give up all she wanted for the love of him.

[Card 12] * Andrew at the age of eighteen had not yet been in a real fight before. Several times he had been angry, but never had he actually hit anyone. His mother had always told him that this

---

* Card 11 was left out but then used by the student as the last card.

was wrong, and he had avoided it. But now he was in a circle of boys who were shouting as another boy continued to pound his hands and arms as he crouched double. Hurt, Andrew suddenly started to fight back and forgot to remember what his mother had always told him. He realized that there are times when even that which appears wrong will be right.

[Card 13] It was back in May that Abernathy had first started to go with Abilene, unknown to his wife. He hadn't meant much at first, but later Abilene had grown upon him and he spent several nights in hotels with her explaining to his wife that he was on business trips. But after the first few months he had become tired of Abilene and his conscience reproached him for his infidelity to his wife. His self-reproach he even came to place upon Abilene so that more and more he came to hate her till finally he murdered her in her bed thus hoping to rid himself of all the trouble, reproaches, and anxiety he had suffered since he had entered on his adventure back in May.

[Card 14] Joe had long desired to go to Paris, having heard and read long stories about the wonderful city. Yet much to his discouragement he did not have the money. He worked long tedious hours in a bank as a teller till he finally saved up enough money to go. Now in Paris as he looked out into the night his desire was fulfilled. Spread out before him was the beautiful city of Paris.

[Card 15] He was up to this time sad and restless. All his friends which he had made and kept for so long were dead, the last of them, J. P. Smith, had just recently died. Julian spent much time doing nothing till one day he decided to visit the cemetery where most of his friends were buried. There, unexplainedly, he came to understand that he could not longer come to know them physically, but yet in a way in prayer he could still be with them. With this realization the lonesomeness he had experienced was gone.

[Card 16] It was a frame, but still he had been thrown in prison. And the Bastille prison is horrible, dark, damp. After many months of nothing to do, sitting in darkness and hardly any sight of human life, he finally despaired. Then he received a note saying that he would soon be set free. He dared not hope, yet he did and slowly it began to capture more and more of him. Then, he, Jean Carlson, victim of a frame, was led into the light. It blinded his eyes, yet he did not mind for it meant freedom.

[Card 17] Pete had no parents, they were dead. He lived with his aunt, but he gradually was getting tired of his life there. Too much school, too much dressing up for "high class" friends. When the circus was in town he went to see it and reveled in its freedom and the many sights and wonders of this new world. He made friends with the caretaker of the huge elephants and when the circus left town Pete went with it.

[Card 18] Ike sat at his desk and shifted positions many times. He didn't know the answer to that question. The last question of the test and he had no idea how to answer it. Large and bold it read: "Explain the main meaning of the 'Hound of Heaven.'" He didn't know; couldn't remember. Slowly he began to dream of a movie he had seen last night of a person who had been chased by the cops for a year after committing murder. The murderer had finally been caught. That's it! He remembered now the poem about God seeking after the soul of a man. Quickly he began writing.

[Card 19] He had given up his business and he spent all of his money on paints. His friends called him crazy, yet he still wanted to paint. Nothing mattered; he had to paint. Year after year he found that his paintings were disregarded and he lived in poverty. Yet it was worth it all for Michael could now view one of his paintings on the wall of the museum.

[Card 20] Raphael joined the gang but he never thought that it would be this bad. Yet here he stood in the dark waiting to kill a man who would soon walk along. The boss had ordered it. Yet should he? When he was told to do it, he was horrified and still he had to do it or be thrown out of the gang. He walked up and down muttering. Then he walked away—he had made his decision.

[Card 11] When he was twenty, Ralph had put all his energy into building the dam. He had spent many hours studying to become an engineer and this had been his first chance to show the profit of his studies. Now, thirty years later, as he looked at this broken wall which had been his dream, he suffered from mixed feelings. He realized that no matter how hard he worked to do something, it was always passing and didn't last long. As a younger man he would not have understood it; now he was older.

These are the imports:

1. If a man has a handicap that prevents him from doing

the things others do, he is lonely and bored until he is forced to take up a particular occupation which he eventually comes to enjoy. Then he can forget his difficulties and be happy.

2. In the end, he can persuade those in authority to let him pursue what he values;

3. and even if he is not first in the race (though he tries hard), others help him to see that the race and the fun of try-ing has been worth the effort.

4. Love helps him to resist temptation and keeps him from doing wrong,

5. but when he loses his love he gives up, and mystifies others by his preparations.

6. There are times when a man has to act according to his conscience even though others feel hurt.

7. But, on considering the punishment inflicted by those in authority, he realizes his mistake and asks for a second chance.

8. Sometimes a man feels isolated because he is different and fails in his efforts to share the interests of his fellows. But, when he asks for advice and is told to develop his own potentialities, he is happy.

9. A job may be so hard that all he can do is slave as long as he can until it is time for rest and relaxation; and then he drops until someone comes to pick him up. This is the life he has been leading the past six months.

10. When a sudden change of plans demands that he leave those he loves, they will make it easy for him by their un-spoken understanding. He marvels how they can give up all they want for love.

12. Though he may have been taught that fighting is wrong, he comes to realize that there are difficulties that can be solved only by fighting.

13. When he finds that what was first a pleasure has become tiresome and a burden on his conscience, he gets rid of it by

impulsive action, hoping to rid himself of the troubles, reproaches, and anxiety he has suffered for months.

14. He wants to go to fabled distant places, and works long
and hard until he can finally do so.

15. He is lonesome for his friends, but suddenly, unexplainedly, he comes to understand that he can still be with
them;

16. though he is in despair, alone and imprisoned in a place
where he does not belong, he is told that he would soon be set
free. The newly given freedom may blind his eyes, but he is
glad to be free.

17. A man who is out of his element is not happy, and
finally finds his happiness by joining those who are his own
kind, foot-loose and fancy-free.

18. He may not be able to solve his problem immediately,
and so he dreams the time away; but, by chance, his dream gives
him the clue to the solution.

19. If he is true to his own inner feelings and pursues his
bent, success will be his, no matter how hard the road.

20. A man must not allow himself to be misled by others and
must make his own decision to do what is right—and act accordingly.

11. Still, it is hard to see the work and achievement of years
of youthful enthusiasm go for nothing. But being older now,
he understands that the fruits of one's work are never per-
manent.

It is quite clear from this sequence analysis that this young
man wants to leave the Order. He says that his life in the
Order, once pleasant, has become burdensome, his love for it is
gone (4, 5, 13) and that he believes he is following his best
judgment in leaving (6, 19, 20). He is certain that those he is
leaving will make it easy for him by their sympathy (10), even
though his giving up mystifies them (5). He in turn is marveling
how they can give up so much to follow their conviction (10).

He is unhappy because he is among people who do not share his intellectual and artistic interests (8, 15, 16, 17) though he had hoped he could eventually persuade his superiors to let him pursue them (2), even if he should not come out on top (3). He wants to rejoin his friends who are his own kind (15, 17); but he also wants to be untrammeled and fancy-free (16, 17), travel and see the world (14, 17). He is willing to take determined action to be free (12, 13) because his situation has caused him trouble, self-reproaches, and anxiety for months (13). He finds the work too hard and has been exhausted for months (9). He is at a loss for a solution but finally the right answer occurs to him (18). He is certain he will succeed in his plan (19) if he does not listen to others, makes his own decision, and acts accordingly (20). All the same, he is sorry to see the work and enthusiasm of years go for nothing, though he consoles himself with the thought that nothing lasts for ever (11). Most of these imports are positive (see Appendix B).

This sequence analysis demonstrates that positive imports do not necessarily mean that a man will be happy in his life situation. Positive attitudes cannot guarantee either success or contentment in the vocation a man has chosen. For this reason, the scoring should always be supplemented by a clinical evaluation of the sequence analysis if the test is to be used for screening.

The sequence analysis is helpful when evaluated clinically, not only for vocational problems but for the diagnosis of the difficulty that has brought a patient to seek psychological or psychiatric help. Though the TAT has been used for this purpose for many years, the sequence analysis adds a dimension that is lacking with the usual methods of interpretation. From the sequence of imports we see at a glance whether we are dealing with a positively motivated person who is temporarily in difficulties, or with someone whose difficulties are so serious that they make it impossible for him to function adequately in everyday life. As an illustration, let us consider a set of TAT stories given by a patient in a psychiatric hospital, diagnosed as suffering from a personality disorder.*

Record #14

[Card 1] This young fellow's mother wants him to take the violin lessons. Now this young fellow he doesn't intend to do this because he doesn't like it. So he's just sitting there, thinking how he would like to bounce his mother on the head with the violin. So the outcome of the story is that he ends up by taking his violin lessons because his father steps in, and he wouldn't dare bounce his father on the head with the violin. Your poor hand will be sore from writing.

[Card 2] This is a farm in Switzerland. This young girl is very— I'd say anxious to study school, and she lives on the farm, and all she had to do was to learn how to help on the farm, but she doesn't want to do this, she wants to go to school. So her family won't have anything to do with her, she is an outcast, the black sheep of the family, but the outcome of the story is that she goes to school anyway, and her family accepts her, and they live happily ever after.

[Card 3] This young girl has just committed suicide. Her boy friend called her up and told her that he had another girl friend and told how much he loved this other girl friend, and that he didn't love her anymore. So she took her father's forty-five and shot herself in the head. That's all I can think about this story. You are sure it's good enough?

[Card 4] Well, this is a story about the coal fields, coal mines in Pennsylvania and the workers are on strike for better wages. So the boss is bringing in these Chicago roughnecks, and he's going to teach these peasants a lesson. So this guy is going to go out and fight these roughnecks, and his wife doesn't want him to go, so she is trying to stop him. Of course, the man is stronger than the woman. So, he goes anyway. But it turns out that the boss changes his mind, and so he doesn't have to fight the roughnecks, so he goes back to his wife, gets higher wages, and lives happily ever after.

* The stories in this record were recounted by the patient and taken down verbatim by the psychologist.

[Card 5] Can I skip? This woman opens the door and then she sees her daughter sitting on the couch with her boy friend, and they were kissing, but she didn't like that because the girl was very young. So she sends the boy home and puts her daughter to bed without supper [laughs].

[Card 6] This young fellow, he comes home from the army, and he had a dishonorable discharge, and his mother didn't like it very well, so he is trying to talk her into liking it, into taking him back home. She's thinking about it, but says no. So he leaves without pursuing the thought any further.

[Card 7] This guy and his father are talking about marital problems—got that?—this one fellow hasn't gotten along with his wife so well, so he is talking to his father about it, and his father says, "Go home and talk your problems over with your wife, and everything will turn out swell."

[Card 8] This guy is thinking about what happened when he was young. He had appendix trouble—appendicitis—and is imagining how it looked when the doctors took his appendix out. Now, let me see . . . but everything turned out all right, and he's glad it's over.

[Card 9] Hm . . . Hm [laughs]. These are a group of hoboes, and they just got off a train, and they are laying down to get some sleep. Now this fellow right in the middle is an FBI agent, and he thinks how to catch these fellows in the act of wrong. But the only trouble is that the hoboes are watching him very carefully, trying to catch him doing . . . you know get some information from him . . . so the outcome is he gets killed, the hoboes killed him, and they went on doing their wrong.

[Card 10] This woman is very rich, she's getting up in years and is afraid of becoming old and losing her beauty, so she's going to marry this guy who's kissing her on her cheek and get a little out of life before it's too late. Now this guy marries her for money and she knows it, but she doesn't care because all she wants is a little joy, so he marries her, poisons her, and gets all the money. Did you think that was good?

[Card 11] I don't see anything in this one.

[Card 12] This guy is a hypnotist [sighs], and he's going to hypnotize this other guy and get him to rob a bank for him. So he hypnotizes this guy, and he goes out and tries to rob a bank, but he gets caught. The cops wake him up, but he couldn't tell them anything because when he woke up he didn't remember anything. So the guy who hypnotized him didn't get caught.

[Card 13] Oh, another murder! [laughs]. This guy has killed his wife, and he is a student at one of the leading universities, married, no children, very ignorant [laughs]. He is trying his best to learn his stuff and gain some good grades, but his wife kept nagging at him to take her out to have some fun. So she got to a point where he couldn't take it anymore, so he killed her.

[Card 14] This is a good one. This guy wants to be a space traveler, so one night he was looking up to the stars to see which one he's going to travel to. But he doesn't travel to any one of them because he couldn't meet the requirement of a space traveler.

[Card 15] I can't see anything on this one. I haven't the slightest idea what to say on this guy.

[Card 16] This is another space story. This guy, he's a complete failure, but his father is very rich and is kind of head of the United Space Ways, so this fellow gets his rocket ship that his father give him for his birthday and travels to a distant planet to find fame and fortune. While he is on this planet, he meets a young girl who has encountered this terrible beast and she looks just like this girl back home. He helps her from this terrible beast and talks to her via mental telepathy, and she tells him to go back home and try harder and become something. So he did.

[Card 17] This muscle-bound guy is an acrobat, and he's thinking of climbing the rope to get on a high trapeze, but, not to his knowledge, the fellow he works with envies him a great deal and cuts the rope so he'll kill his buddy, and the people would talk about him instead.

[Card 18] This guy is in a fight. He takes this girl out that belongs to the other fellow, and the other fellow comes in to where they are and starts this fight. Fortunately this fellow is very strong and tough and knocks the living stuffings out of this other guy and he wins the fight and the girl.

[Card 19] Gee, I just can't think on this of anything either.

[Card 20] This guy is thinking about his recent argument with his girl friend. He is not sure what he should do, whether he would make up with her or just forget about her. Chances are she would just forget about him anyway. So he just forgets about her.

The sequence analysis for record 14:

1. When you are supposed to work, you'd like to hit those who give the orders; but if they are powerful, you have to do what they ask.

2. Even when you want to do something useful (study), they may protest, and you become the black sheep of the family; but if you do it anyway, they'll accept you, and you'll live happily ever after.

3. But, when those you love reject you for someone else, that is the end for you.

4. Sometimes you have to fight those in power to protect your livelihood, contrary to the advice of weak people. You can get what you want by force, and sometimes even the threat of force is sufficient.

5. But, if people have power over you, they'll make you behave and punish you if you don't.

6. If you get a disgraceful punishment, you may try and talk your family into taking you back; but if they won't, you don't pursue the thought any further.

7. When you don't get along with your family, people advise you to talk it over with them and everything will turn out swell;

8. you can still remember past difficulties where everything turned out all right.

9. You, the outlaw, can be cleverer than the law and destroy those who are waiting for you to make a wrong move so they can catch you.

10. What does it matter that you have to pay in the end? Life is short and you want to get something out of it before it's too late. Isn't that good?

11. You can't see anything

12. but to influence somebody else so he gets for you what you want; and if you do it right, he won't be able to tell on you, and you won't get caught.

13. When you are trying to get somewhere and people keep

nagging at you to be kind to them, you get to a point where you can't take it any more and shut them up for good.

14. Of course, you may aim too high and fail because you don't have what it takes,

15. but you don't have the slightest idea what (that is).

16. So you go to outlandish places, supported by others, only to be told in the end to go back home and try harder and become something. And you do,

17. but people are envious and set traps for you so they will become famous.

18. So, you move in on the other guy if you are strong enough and win the fight and the prize.

19. You can't think of anything

20. except recent arguments, and wonder whether to make up or forget about the other guy. Chances are he would not stand by you, so you just forget about him.

This 19-year-old boy is preoccupied almost exclusively with getting the better of other people (2, 4, 6, 7, 9, 18, 20), though he acknowledges that those in power can make him behave (1, 5). If he can't fight, he tries to get what he wants through others (12) without the slightest regard for their wishes. On the contrary, he shuts them up for good if they become insistent (13).

This young man has a history of stealing automobiles, running away from home, being aggressive and belligerent toward police, teachers, and the like, since the age of fourteen. He is tall, handsome, well-developed, and has an air of breezy self-confidence and casual unconcern. His verbal I.Q. is 110, performance I.Q. is 86. In the hospital, he was aggressive, peevish when angered, and resistant. From the sequence analysis, it appears that this air of casual unconcern is a deep-seated attitude, which does not promise well for the future. We can understand why it was decided that psychotherapy would be unprofitable, and he was referred to a custodial institution.

There is no sign of any thought disorder either in psychiatric interviews or in the TAT.

Though this record can be scored according to our scoring criteria (see Appendix B), several of the imports are more negative than the scores indicate (particularly, imports 1, 2, 6, 12, 13, 17, 18). We are now preparing a set of scoring criteria usable for the diagnosis of psychiatric disorders, to be published at some future date (see Vassiliou, 1962). Record 14 when scored according to these new criteria is clearly that of a psychopath.

The sequence analysis can also provide valuable clues to factors that may impair a man's effectiveness. The following record is that of an executive whose work motivation is overshadowed by his private problem:

Record #15
[Card 1] The boy is dejected for he had planned to spend the afternoon playing baseball with the neighborhood gang. The violin is not to his liking but the desire of his parents for something they wanted. The practice session on the violin will be done, but not with the enthusiasm of a musical prodigy.

[Card 2] This is a scene of "Agricultural America." The family has grown up, the daughter is on her way to school to get the education never acquired by the parents. The work at the farm, representing the needs of the family, goes on. The daughter will eventually marry and live in a city; the parents will continue to be on the farm.

[Card 3] A dejected girl has just had a "lover's quarrel," and is suffering the pangs of a broken heart. In the spirit of romance, everything will turn out for the best.

[Card 4] The unwanted quarrel. The woman is attempting to prevent a fight between two men for the attention and affection of a woman. The fight will take place, and the woman goes to the other man.

[Card 6] The grandmother has just refused the request of her grandson for a loan of money. There is a tense feeling of animosity between the two. However, the subject is closed as far as the grandmother is concerned. The grandson is quite bitter. The result, no money and the tense feeling will continue.

[Card 7] A son is seeking the sage advice of his father. The father, an immigrant, the son, a natural-born American. The advice will not be taken, for the father still retains the thinking of the old country. This is the point at which the son leaves the close ties of old-line family and actually starts his life in the melting pot of American culture. His success will be mediocre for his thoughts are confused between the old and the new lines of thought.

[Card 8] The boy, an idealist with a trend for the fine arts, was injured during a revolution or clash of the classes. The sight of the blood, death and destruction—during this formative period of his life—will have a lasting impression on his future. He is and will be convinced that the world needs cultural aspects to overcome the brutality of mankind.

[Card 14] A man contemplating the culmination of his dreams. He is looking forward and planning in a dreamy way the fulfillment of his course of action. The future looks favorable but as far away as the stars. He is ambitious, and his goal high and far. If he does not yield to the complacency of life, he will be an outstanding success.

[Card 17] A circus aerialist. A muscular body and the face of a gargoyle, the mind of a dreamer. He has elected the life of the flying trapeze since, in this, his face is not seen; the symmetry and the perfection of the high wire and trapeze are his only ways of attaining his goal. As yet, he still aspires for his goal and performs to the plaudits of the crowd. His goal will never be achieved, but he will spend his life within the atmosphere of his dreams.

[Card 19] A child's portrait of his home during a severe winter storm. The ghosts—his outlet for the unknown fears—are all around the house. The lighted windows of the house portray his faith or strength in the home, his only proven saver. After the storm abates, the house will stand, affirming his faith that the home is indestructible.

These are the imports:

1. A boy may do what his parents have wished on him but without enthusiasm, for he has other plans.

2. Children go their own way in life while parents continue their old ways.

3. There are quarrels, but everything eventually turns out for the best.

4. Though quarrels are not wanted, they may lead to fighting; and the fight may be lost.

6. The older generation may refuse what the younger one wants and tension and animosity remain between the two.

7. Though a man may not take the advice of his people, who still retain the thinking of the old country, his success will be mediocre, for his thoughts are confused between the old and the new.

8. The unfortunate impressions a man gains during his formative years have a lasting influence on his future and make him want culture and refinement.

14. So, he dreams of the fulfillment of his ambitions, and his dreams will come true if he does not yield to the complacency of life.

17. He has elected a profession in which his deficiencies will not be noticed. His goal may never be achieved, but he will spend his life in the atmosphere of his dreams.

19. Though his fears are pressing him hard, he can keep them at bay safe in his home and affirm his faith in something indestructible.

Obviously, this man suffers from the disabilities often found among second generation immigrants. He cannot go the way his parents mapped out for him, yet he is not able to shake off his childhood impressions and strike out for himself. His emotions are engaged in the struggle so that he cannot find a solution. His negative attitudes, however, are not the result of this struggle; rather, he cannot find a solution because his attitudes remain negative. He insists that his childhood experiences doom him to mediocrity (7, 8), but the high achievers we have tested say in their imports that adverse circumstances can be overcome. Only low achievers blame failure on childhood impressions, lack of love, etc. This storyteller gave seven stories (from cards 1 to 8) that consistently develop the theme

of conflict between the generations. When there is such a
dominant theme, it should be brought out in the imports. They
should be formulated rather more specifically by retaining
the original phrasing as much as possible (e.g., in import 7.,
". . . his people who 'still retain the thinking of the old country' "). This will help alert the examiner to the clinical problems revealed in the sequence analysis. Even if no clinical
evaluation is intended, it is advisable to formulate the imports
as accurately as possible because they may help to evaluate
the quantitative score.

In this particular case, for instance, the unresolved conflict between the old and the new takes up a disproportionate
share of the story imports. It is altogether possible that this
man's work motivation may be more positive than these imports suggest. This seems likely from the imports that speak
directly about work (1, 2). Some positive work motivation is
needed to enable the storyteller to function in an executive
position; but apparently, the conflict still alive in his attitudes prevents him from forging ahead.

Not only does the sequence analysis pinpoint the dominant
problem in a way that is not equaled by other methods of
interpretation; this method also reveals the patients' preoccupation with conflicts and difficulties that can usually be
uncovered only after weeks and months of therapy. One clinical
psychologist (Vassiliou, 1961) has been able to spot suicidal
intentions which the patient did not admit until many therapy
hours later. I myself have on occasion warned the referring
psychiatrist of an impending suicide (after a blind TAT analysis) only to be told that the patient had already attempted it.
In some cases, the sequence analysis revealed an incipient schizo-
phrenic break which occurred months or years afterwards
(Vassiliou, 1962); in still other cases, the sequence analysis revealed positive attitudes in hospitalized depressive or schizo-
phrenic patients, indicating an early remission.

Part III. QUANTITATIVE SCORING

7

USING THE SCORING CRITERIA

The scoring criteria have been derived empirically from studies extending over the last seven years. The first of these studies was one by Snider (1954), who found that records of high achievers could be reliably distinguished from records of low achievers. In an attempt to verify these findings, Brown (1953) repeated the study and reported similar results. The next step was taken by McCandlish (1958), who tried to develop a scoring system that would allow a more objective assessment. He used the thirteen story records of forty high school seniors from Chicago that had been collected by Snider, and of forty St. Louis high school seniors collected by Brown. These eighty boys were matched in pairs on the basis of I.Q., A.C.E. score, age, and socio-economic background. One member of each pair had school grades that put him in the upper third of his class during the past six semesters; the other had grades that put him in the lowest third during the past six semesters. Twenty of these pairs (ten from Chicago, ten from St. Louis) were selected for preliminary inspection. On this basis, merely by comparing the records of both members of each pair, sixteen out of twenty pairs were correctly placed; that is, in sixteen pairs, McCandlish was able to tell which member of the pair was a high achiever and which was the low achiever.

In an attempt to make this assessment more objective, McCandlish now scored as *plus* imports that were found in records of high achievers but not in those of low achievers, and as *minus* imports found in records of low achievers but not in those of high achievers. These positive and negative imports could be fitted into a few categories which were then used to score the TAT sequence analyses of the remaining group of forty boys. Their records were scrambled, so that the scorer could identify neither the pairs nor the individuals. Thirty boys were given predominantly negative scores, and so were correctly designated as low achievers. Twenty-nine boys had positive scores for most of their stories and so could be correctly identified as high achievers. The remaining record had been given predominantly negative scores, but was that of a high achiever. On reexamining the record, McCandlish found that this boy had a schizoid, withdrawn personality and told stories that were rather bizarre and had definitely negative imports. Seemingly, his high intelligence and his withdrawal from social contacts made it possible for him to achieve good grades despite negative motivation in social situations. From the knowledge of TAT imports we have gained since then, we would suspect that this boy might have been preschizophrenic, but unfortunately we have not been able to verify this guess or even to discover where he is now.

In the next few studies a similar plan was followed: a few high achievers and their matched low-achieving fellows were first selected and their TAT records examined for positive and negative imports on the basis of the categories established thus far; distinctive imports found in this preliminary examination were added to the scoring categories which were now used to score the remaining records. These studies will be reported in detail in Chapters 10-13. Eventually, the criteria derived from all these studies were combined, ordered into categories (from I to IV), headings (A., B., C., etc.), subheadings (1., 2., 3., etc.) and divisions (a., b., c., etc.). In a few subheadings, further divisions (i., ii., etc.) were necessary. This combined list of scoring criteria will be found in Appendix A.

It deserves special mention that all the sequence analyses from which the scoring criteria were developed were "blind" analyses of normal people. For the preliminary scoring of a few pairs, the only information available to the scorer was that one member of the pair, X, was a high achiever, the other member, Y, was a low achiever. When the rest of each set of records was scored, this information was not available. Since the records were scrambled, the scorer did not even know which records formed a pair. The fact that the middle range of motivation was excluded by matching the extreme high and low achievers is important in explaining the extremely good match obtained by experienced scorers. At the same time, this match cannot be achieved merely by inspection of the TAT records. Without the sequence analyses, even experienced TAT scorers did no better than chance matching.

The undoubted success of intuitive TAT interpretations in clinical settings seems to contradict such a result. But, TAT stories of neurotics and psychotics are very easy to interpret because their intense preoccupation with their problems (in the case of neurotics) or their confusion in thinking (in the case of psychotics) is so transparent. Interpreting such records on the basis of a sequence analysis is even easier. It is almost as easy to score the imports of extreme high achievers, even without well worked-out scoring criteria. The imports that are difficult to score are derived from stories of people whose motivation is neither consistently positive nor strongly negative. These stories are often ambiguous because the storyteller tries to hedge or tries to convince himself that his negative attitudes are really justified. It is for these middle-range imports that the scoring criteria must be as concise and complete as possible. As soon as we have to score the whole range of motivation in a given group without excluding the middle range, we need well-defined scoring categories.

Since it is the import that is to be scored and not the story, it is imperative to formulate the import in such a way that it includes story aspects that are needed for scoring. If that is not done, the scorer will have to look up the original story, which means considerable delay. The beginner should start by *scoring* at least twenty sequence analyses that have been done by experts. In this way, he will familiarize himself with the scoring categories before he ever tries to abstract an import. It is true that perceptive clinicians may be able to formulate acceptable imports even without knowing the scoring categories, but they will find that it is difficult to score such imports without going back to the original story. For an import that is correctly derived from the story and which at the same time can be scored without resort to the story, the tester must know his scoring categories and has to remember which story situations are important for scoring. After the sequence analysis is completed, each import should be scored *by consulting the scoring categories,* at least until the scorer is so familiar with them that he can remember the main category, the headings, and the main subdivisions. These categories and headings are ordered according to their importance for scoring, so that the scorer will soon begin to recall the most important, category I, and recall the various situations covered by it; gradually, the others will fall into place.

If in spite of every effort the import does not seem to fit into any scoring category, the story should be reread and pondered. A seemingly unscorable import is usually the result of neglecting important story details to emphasize the sequence (see record 13, card 4). When this happens, it is best to go back to the story and reformulate the import in such a way that it continues the sequence and includes everything necessary for scoring. If both these conditions cannot be met, the import

must include the omitted story details even though this formulation does not seem to fit the sequence as well as the first.
When this is done, it will often be found that the new version
gives a new twist to the sequence, which is actually more accurate than the shorter import. (See record 16, Chapter 8,
second versus first sequence analysis.)

There are four scoring categories: I. Achievement, success,
happiness, active effort (or lack of it); II. Right and wrong;
III. Human relationships; IV. Reaction to adversity. These
include all the imports likely to be contained in stories.

*Category I. Achievement, success, happiness, active effort
(or lack of it),* includes success and failure in its widest sense.
It includes not only financial success, or success in work and
effort of every kind, but also happiness and other kinds of
favorable outcome. Similarly, lack of success includes failure
of every kind: failure in business or profession, but also unhappiness, any kind of unfavorable outcome. The one condition
to be met is a goal contemplated or reached, no matter how
vague the goal or how ineffective the means. This category
also includes active effort of every kind that does not lead
to success or failure and has no antecedents that would fit into
one of the other categories. But if, for instance, there is some
disappointment or loss that is successfully overcome, the score
will be found under Category IV., Reaction to adversity.

Category II. Right and wrong, includes well-intentioned,
reasonable, constructive or responsible action and its opposite:
ill-intentioned, impulsive, harmful, destructive, or irresponsible action. It also includes actions that carry out duties and
obligations, or the omission of such actions. Intentions as well
as actions are included, and so are the consequences of such
intentions and actions. Stories can be scored under this category when not success or failure but *the ethical significance of
an action or its personal consequences are the theme.*

Category III. Human relationships, is intended to cover all stories that describe actions and attitudes concerning other people and things, when these actions or attitudes cannot be readily found under the previous two categories. Since the imports are always written from the point of view of the dominant story character (subject to the demands of the sequence), it is possible to distinguish the influence of other characters on the hero, and the influence of the hero on other story characters. Accordingly, these two kinds of relationship are separated into two different subheadings.

Category IV. Reaction to adversity, includes the main possible reactions to various different kinds of adversity. Loss, harm, terror, separation, disappointment, difficulties, all require some attempt to cope with adversity. The only kind of adversity that is excluded is failure, which will be found under *Category I. E. Consequences of success (failure).* Adversity may be overcome or not overcome; it may simply be accepted; or there may be a statement that adversity is the outcome of some event or personal action. Whatever the adversity, reactions to it, as abstracted in the import, should be scored under the various subheadings of this category.

Every category with its various subdivisions is designed merely to indicate the general lines that should be followed in scoring. Once the category is determined, the conditions of action as stated in the import should be looked up under the various headings and subheadings of this category. Each category contains headings, subheadings, and the like, under four possible scores; from very positive to extremely negative: $+2$, $+1$, -1 and -2. In general, $+2$ is scored when the import describes overt and positive action; $+1$ indicates activity that may not be overt (e.g., planning, positive attitudes) or is not very positive (e.g., there is failure along the way but success is reached eventually). Lack of positive action is indicated by -1 (e.g., success is the result of passive dependence on others; failure comes because nobody helps or advises) while —2 indicates frankly negative, impulsive, or malicious actions or attitudes (e.g., failure leads to desperate action; success comes in spite of refusal to take reasonable advice; wrongdoing succeeds). This progression will be found in all categories. It was not deliberately planned but was gradually revealed as hundreds of stories were scored.

While it is impossible to provide a subheading for every import that can be found in stories, the scoring criteria should make it possible to locate any import at least within the category and heading. Even if no subheading is found into which it fits, it should be easy to see by comparison with the listed subheadings what score should be assigned to such an import. This will make it possible to implement the categories with additional subheadings without loss of precision in scoring. Obviously, it is impossible to give a set of scoring criteria that is complete in every last detail. The best we can hope for is to provide a guide to correct scoring and leave it to future studies to fill the gaps gradually. However, most imports derived from stories of normal people can be easily found, some of them under several categories or headings, which increases the chances of locating a given import quickly.

The scoring categories and headings are listed in order of their importance for scoring stories that have plot and outcome. In determining the score, the import is first examined to see whether it indicates success or failure of any kind. If it does, the import is scored under Category I. If an import does not contain some hint of success or failure, or if the failure mentioned is punishment for some ill-intentioned action, we go on to the next category, *II. Right and wrong.* If the import fits here, we will find that it concerns ethical implications of actions. It does not matter whether the action is merely unacceptable for social reasons or is considered wrong from a strictly ethical or religious point of view. Such imports are concerned with reward or recognition for a well-intentioned action (rather than with successful achievement) and punishment for an ill-intentioned action (rather than failure or lack of achievement). While Category I embraces the imports indicating a goal and ways and means of achieving it, Category II is meant for imports that speak about the ethical aspect of action. This category also covers imports that indicate intentions, attitudes, and emotions in their ethical aspects.

When an import is neither concerned with a goal and means of achieving it nor with the right or wrong of action, it may fit into *Category III. Human relationships.* These are imports that describe some confrontation of person with person or of person with his environment. There is no question of success or of the ethical aspect of action; rather, the effect of one person on another or of human relationships as such is talked about. For instance, a story telling about a son taking leave of his mother to go to war has no goal, nor could the action be taken as either right or wrong. It certainly is a well-intentioned, reasonable action; but that is not the aspect the storyteller seems to be concerned with. What he seems to be saying is that a man must part from his family if his country requires it. This import is scored +2 under Category III (Human relationships) A. (Good relations), 4.a ("sacrificed for a higher motive, e.g., God, country, etc.)."

If the story should go on and say that the son is killed and the mother is grief-stricken and inconsolable, the import might read: "Leave-taking is hard, but it is harder to have those we love never come back; nothing can console us for that." This import would be scored —2 under Category IV (Reaction to adversity) A.4 (Adversity cannot be overcome; action is) e. (incomplete and has no outcome). This import illustrates how important it is to take the complete story into account in the import. Though the ending seems sometimes not important for the sequence, it is important for scoring. Without the ending, the sequence may actually be pushed in the wrong direction and become quite misleading. In most cases, it will be found that the import that includes the meaning of the whole story will also be the import that provides the best link to the story before, and the story after it.

Let us now go back to the examples of story sequences given in earlier chapters and try to score them. The import for card 1, record 1, is:

1. When a boy is supposed to work, he tries to think of a way to get out of it. Even when he does what he is supposed to do, he won't be too good at it.

This import deals with work, and so falls into Category I. Work is a means to achievement or success and will be found under heading B. (Means taken toward goal). Here we find under score —1 two subheadings that might apply: 4. (Low achievement, no achievement, or unhappiness are caused by extraneous factors), c. (lack of ability, aptitude, opportunities), and also, 6. (Negative attitude toward work), b. (done under constraint). The import does suggest that there is little achievement because the boy "isn't too good at it." This seems to mean that he has no aptitude for this particular work (violin-playing in the story). Accordingly, the correct score will be —1, I.B.4.c. If the import had said in the second sentence, "finally he does what he is supposed to do because he is made to do it," we would also score —1, but under the second alternative, I.B.6.b. To make checking easier, the minus or plus score is always complemented by giving the category, heading, subheading, and the like.

This is the next import:

2. He may go to school because he has to, and hate it, until he is old enough not to have to go any longer and can do what he wants.

Now "going to school" is a means to achievement for the child, just as working is for the adult. This might indicate that we would find the import under I.B. (Means taken toward goal).

But, in this import, we find no hint of success or failure. However, under score —2, we find imports from subheading 5 on that talk about means toward the goal, but have nothing to say about reaching it. Subheading 6.a., for instance, reads: *work is distasteful, harmful, degrading.* This would apply, but does not take in the import as a whole. The second half of the import implies that the boy is waiting "until he is old enough not to have to go any longer and can do what he wants." Apparently, he expects a future in which he can do what he wants to do. In other words, his only goal is to do what he wants to do, without discipline of any kind. This amounts to having no goal in the proper sense of the term, or at least no goal that imposes its own discipline. Accordingly, the heading A. (Goals, purposes) under score —2, subheading 6. (No goal) would apply even better. But, in both cases, the import would be scored —2, whether we score the import under Means or under Goals.

The next import says:

3. When he is forced to do something he doesn't want to do, he misses out on what he really wants to do and is unhappy.

Here we have the same theme we have met in the first two imports: the boy is not able to do what he wants to do. So he does what he is supposed to do and is unhappy. Since unhappiness is a kind of failure, and the import is again concerned with some active effort, we look it up under I.B. (Means taken toward goal). Under score —2, we find subheading 3. (Despite active effort, failure follows in the form of) d. (disappointment, unhappiness). We could also find this import under heading D. (Influence of others on personal success, achievement, etc.) in Category I. Under score —2, we find our import under subheading 2. (Through the fault of others, positive action results in . . . unhappiness) e. (when obeying legitimate commands). This actually is the more accurate scoring, though it is noteworthy that both alternatives will give the score of —2.

The import to card 4 reads:

4. When he feels that everybody is trying to push him around, he gets pretty angry. He would like to get them, but he won't fight, they'll want to stop him.

This is a "reaction to adversity"—our Category IV—namely, to people pushing the boy around. His reaction is a wish to fight —but he won't because people want to stop him. This would seem to fit under score —2, Category IV.A.4. (Adversity cannot be overcome; action is) c. (hindered). It could also be argued that the boy contemplates doing something wrong ("to get them"), but this intention is not carried out because others will want to stop him. This would fit under score —2, II.B.1. (Wrong intentions are not carried out because) b. (something or somebody interferes). That the intention of the story character can be called a wrong intention is shown by the way the story is told: he "*feels* people or someone is trying to push him around." There is no indication that people are actually pushing him around, or why they should do so. Since the story really reports a feeling and the consequent anger of the story character, it would be possible to score the import also under Category III (Human relationships) F. (Attitudes toward people and things, etc.). Here we find under score —2 a subheading 1. (Negative attitudes toward others), a. (others are troublesome, malicious, self-seeking). This is not as accurate a fit, because the last part of the import is more or less disregarded, but it is permissible, because the man's anger and impotent wish to fight is part and parcel of the same negative attitude to others. We note again that whatever the category and subheading chosen, all three alternatives provide the same strongly negative score.

The last import in the series reads:

5. People are always watching to see that he does what he is supposed to do, and they get pretty mad if he doesn't do it. Some day he will be old enough so he won't have to do any longer what people tell him to do.

There is a sameness about these imports that is typical for people who have problems and land in a mental health clinic. Again the boy says that he is looking forward to the day when he won't have to do any longer what people tell him to do— and, by implication, that he will be able to do what he wants when that happy day arrives. The fact that "people get mad" if he does not do what he is supposed to do is not taken as a punishment for doing something wrong but merely as an annoyance, a difficulty. The boy in the story is looking forward to the day when this difficulty will be over, when he will be old enough to do what he wants. This can be considered an expectation of or a wish for an eventual good outcome. Accordingly, this import will be found under score —2, IV.A.5. (Adversity leads to undesirable actions or attitudes) d. (has no outcome, but good outcome is wished for).

Now we will similarly score the imports of record 2, but without explaining in detail why they are scored under particular scoring categories. We will let the scoring speak for itself.

Record #2 (see Chapter 4)

1. When a man sees something beautiful, he begins to dream of making something similar. He may not do it but will always appreciate beauty.

This import really says: Dreaming will produce something desirable even without ever trying to translate the dream into reality. What is produced is an appreciation of beauty, which is a kind of achievement. This import will be found under score —2, Category I.B.2. (Success despite ineffective means) d. (despite dreaming instead of active effort).

2. It can easily be seen that people who have land and property are successful [Score —1, I.B.1. (Success because of extraneous factors) c. (possessions)].

4. (Card 3 not shown) but people without money or job get into a rut and are forced to seek oblivion and escape [Score —2, IV.3. (Adversity is not overcome but evaded) a. (by escape)].

6. (Card 5 not shown) Eventually, a boy has to make his own decision. It may not be the best thing, but in deciding he becomes a man of whom others can be proud.

Here the emphasis is on the decision rather than what is decided. The decision itself, even though it may not be the right one, proves manliness. Because of the decision, others can be proud. The achieving of manliness may be called success; thus the import is found under score —1, I.A.3. (Success follows action for extraneous motives) d. (for self-centered motives). Since it is the decision that matters and not its reasonableness or its content, and the decision is something to be proud of, the motive can be called self-centered.

7. When a son turns to his father for advice, the father must do his best to give a good sound answer *so he will satisfy his son's need* and they can be friends. [Score —2, III.A.1.f. (Good relations are established or maintained for selfish reasons)].

This sequence of a low achieving college freshman is strongly negative. Now let us score the sequence of the matching high achiever who is lower in tested intelligence than is his low achieving fellow. Both these sequences were discussed in Chapter 4.

Record #3

1. A man may not like the work he has to do but once he starts doing it he will find it fun and become proficient. [Score +2, I.B.1. (Success comes through active effort) a. (through personal effort, work)].

2. Thinking of his position in life, he decides to make the

best of his educational opportunities so as to advance and better himself. [Score +1, I.A. (Goals, purposes) 4. (Imports appreciating immaterial values, e.g., education)].

4. Sometimes it is hard to control one's anger and listen to reason but it can be done. [Score +2, III.C. (Influence of others) 4. (Reasonable advice is desirable) b. (it is not asked for but is heeded)].

This import could also be formulated differently so as to fit the sequence better: "Then he can persuade others to see reason and calm them down." This import is also scored +2 and would be found under III.E.1. (Exerting positive influence on others; one is successful in) b. (persuading others to be reasonable).

6. If the problem is serious, one must consult someone with experience and then make his decision. [Score +2, I.D.1. (Success follows upon positive reasonable action) b. (actively seeking professional help for problems that need it)].

The "success" here is the decision successfully arrived at.

7. Once the decision is made, one may wonder whether it was the right one. Then the only thing to do is to consult someone who knows, and so realize that it was the only alternative and was justified. [Score +2, I.D.1.b. as above].

Obviously, this sequence is as positive as the earlier one was negative. The reader should now try to score the imports given in Chapter 6. The correct scoring for these records (4 to 16) will be found in Appendix B.

8

SCORING DIFFICULTIES

Though years of work have convinced us that the imports collected in the sequence analysis can be reliably scored, there is no doubt that every beginner will encounter difficulties and experience doubts that may threaten to discourage him. I will attempt to deal here with some of the more frequent perplexities scorers have encountered.

Perhaps the most frequent cause of difficult and unreliable scoring is inaccuracy in formulating the import. Unless the whole story is taken into account, the import will be defective, will prejudice the sequence, and will create difficulties in scoring. To illustrate this point, let us consider the following set of stories. This record was obtained from a student who was an extreme low achiever. When the sequence analysis was done originally, the scoring criteria had not been worked out sufficiently. Thus, the scoring was done on the basis of a few principles rather than the present fairly exhaustive set of categories. This also resulted in a formulation of imports that were less precise than is desirable for reliable scoring.

Record #16.

[Card 1] Steven Young is eleven years old, the son of an English couple who reside in Glasgow. Steven's ambition in life is to play in a great orchestra like his father. Steven was doing his homework when his father returned home and placed his violin on the table before him while he went to get his material to clean it. Steven begins to dream of the day when he would also be in the large orchestra—blending his music with the sounds of the other instruments. Years go by and he practices daily for many hours. Upon the death of his father, Steven is now twenty-nine, he is given the opportunity to replace his father in the ensemble. A dream has come true and the following night Steven is seen for the first time playing his cello for the symphony.

[Card 2] Isabel is a school teacher at Mojave elementary school in Danville, Ohio. This is her first year teaching. She has to wait for a bus at sunrise daily in order to be on time for class. She wishes it wasn't so murky and humid now, even at this early hour. She figures that if it is hot now, it is going to be terrible in class all day and the students will be troublesome. The other woman is her friend who rides into town with Isabel frequently from the country. Her friend tries to relax and catch some more sleep, but the bus is now seen by Isabel in the distance. It won't be long now until it comes and she begins another hectic day of work. That evening she returned exhausted and hungry.

[Card 3] Bobby Gene Smith is the youngest of a family of six, five boys and a girl. He lives in Oildale with his family. It is early afternoon and he is playing with his two brothers. Bobby is seen as he was supposed to have been shot. You notice his gun on the floor by his left foot. The family often does things together like this rather than play with the neighbors and they enjoy it. Bobby will rise in a few moments and shoot back—knowing that the game will continue endlessly and harmlessly until his mother calls for dinner.

[Card 4] Jack Mills is a mental patient. He has been taking treatment for some time and doesn't seem to be responding. On this particular day while at the clinic he went into a rage and opened and closed cabinets, doors, jars, etc., around the office. Doing so quite violently. He is pictured as caught by a photographer for a city paper, being talked to by a nurse who is attempting to delay him while help comes. This is the major break in his mind and he will be sent to the State hospital until he is properly adjusted.

[Card 5] This is Mary Grove. She is the neighbor of Susan Wells and is coming over to Susan's house for a chat. Mary had heard of the renovation of the house and seems surprised as she enters to see the work finished so soon. Mary and Susan exchange views and ideas. Mary returned home convinced that she, too, should do her house over on similar lines.

[Card 6] Jack Ward and his mother are seen as he tells her of the death of his wife's baby prematurely. Jack seems rightly disturbed but his mother has the "I told you so" look on her face. She had frequently warned him that allowing his wife to work would have bad consequences especially in her pregnant state. Sorrowfully Jack tried to explain the reason and his mother begins to join in his sorrow and they embrace. As Jack leaves, she tells him to send his wife over to stay a few days.

[Card 7] The scene is in the court room and Mr. Lawson on the left (the lawyer) is explaining to his client that the situation does not appear good concerning his suit against the company he works for. Jim Sutherland was injured while leaving work one day and he is suing for damages incurred at the time. Since he was off duty and leaving the grounds the company refuses to pay. The testimony of the client is next and the lawyer is briefing him on necessary points which should be in it in view of previous testimonies given. A long legal battle is in the making, but Jim is sure he will win. The trial will take at least two weeks and both sides refuse to give ground. When it is over, Jim Sutherland is awarded the suit on the grounds that he was injured by carelessness on the part of the ground crew of the plant in not cleaning up.

[Card 8] Joe Miles is recalling his wartime adventures. He fought on German soil, and he was the victim of a poison plot. He remembers the emergency operation on the battlefield and how close he was to death. It is easy to look back now as he enters his home in Michigan for the first time since his discharge from the army. He had given up hope of recovery then, but he looks back in happiness as he glances around the house—the one that he was never to see again.

[Card 9] Jed Smith and the men at his office took a day off to go hunting. Because they rose early to get started and had walked for great distances, they were tired by early afternoon. All grouped together for a rest in a meadow. They slept for about two hours and then they rose to continue their hunt for the ducks. After having had success in early evening, they all got together for the return trip home and arrived home happy at their successes, but tired from their trip.

[Card 10] Mary Ackers and Jack Cunningham had been going together for about eleven months. On this particular evening on their way to a dinner dance, they had gotten into an argument over the time when they would be married. Jack had told Mary the wedding would have to wait until certain business deals came through. The discussion had continued while they danced and Mary had mentioned to Jack that they must be married within a month or they would break up. She laid it on the line—an either/or deal. Jack assured her that a month would be fine and the dancing took a livelier beat as the happy couple put new life into it.

[Card 11] While herding cattle in Mexico, two from the herd had wandered off. After the herder spotted them, he chased them, but they headed for the canyon. When they reached the waterfall and the small bridge, the two animals stopped because of fright and would not cross. It is at this point that the laborer who was on foot caught up with them and was able to coax them to turn about, and they retracked their steps to the rest of the herd.

[Card 12] Bob Murphy was a patient in the New Jersey Clinic for nervous people. He had tried almost all means and the doctors to find stability of mind because his business had been suffering from his inattention. He finally decided to have a doctor at the hospital hypnotize him. The doctor volunteered and Bob went through with the experiment. As a result of the treatment, he found peace and quiet and was able to put his entire attention to his business affairs.

[Card 13] The Duncan couple had been married for three and a half years. They lived in a small three-room apartment in Brooklyn. During the winter, Mrs. Duncan began to suffer a heart ailment. One night she had a heart attack with intensity when she was in the bath. Her husband discovered her and carried her to her bed, but he found she was dead within a few minutes. Struck with terror and sadness, he staggered to the phone to call the undertakers and then collapsed on the couch in tears.

[Card 14] It was early morning and the sound of thunder coupled with flashes of lightning awoke Jacob Anderson. Arising from bed he went to the window to observe the storm. Heavy rain crashed to the earth and soon the land was filling with water. After carefully checking the shutters on the house and all the equipment in the yard to insure against damage, Jake returned to bed and went to sleep assured and with ears ringing from the sounds of thunder.

[Card 15] Michael O'Riley was a fan of Edgar Allan Poe. He

had read almost all he had written except for a few stories. One day he happened to be browsing in a library and came to the section of Poe's works. Glancing over the selections, he pulled "Murders in the Rue Morgue" from the shelf, knowing he had not read this selection. Upon opening the cover he noticed this strange and grotesque figure on the page adjacent to the title page. Intrigued, he began reading the story and becoming enthralled in it. Before he realized the time, he had finished the story. Hurriedly replacing the book on the shelf, he left the library so as to be home in time for supper.

[Card 16] There was a couple in New Orleans who had invited a large list of people to dinner. As the date approached, the wife prepared the house and meals with great care. When the hour was near for the arrival of the guests, the phone rang. One couple was unable to come. Another couple called to say problems had come up and they couldn't come either. Hesitantly, she called her husband to ask him to invite a few people there at work to replace the other couples. Her husband, however, had already left the office. Then the doorbell rang and she knew guests were arriving. After seating the guests in the parlor, she quickly removed four places at the table only to find her scheme of decorating was ruined. Hastily she moved things around to make the setup better. More guests arrived, until all had come but her husband—who came in last. It was his usual job to serve cocktails, etc., to the guests, but she had done this too. By the time that the dinner time came, she was exhausted and unable to eat because of all the excitement. After the guests left she didn't bother to clean up, but went to bed exhausted and nervous.

[Card 17] Bart Mason was a prisoner at the State prison for grand larceny. After three years he was put on the auto repair crew and later switched to handling of material which went out of the prison. It was on this job that he came in contact with great amounts of rope. One day he placed some rope at a certain spot near the walls. He waited for the proper time to throw the rope over the wall and then after having taken off his colored clothes to prevent being spotted as easily against the cream-colored walls, he climbed the rope to the other side of the wall, only to drop into the waiting nets of the prison guards who had seen him. Back to the prison he went, this time to solitary confinement.

[Card 18] Tim O'Rourke liked the taste of any type of liquor.

On this particular day he tried, it seemed, to taste them all and as a result he was more drunk than usual. Seeing that his customer was past the safe stage, yet knowing he wasn't apt to leave on his own, the bartender came up to Tim after several warnings and grabbed him. He asked one of the other customers to drive Tim home and he did.

[Card 19] Irene Orsini is in the third grade. During art class the teacher asked the class to draw a picture of a house during a snowstorm. After thinking along these lines for a long time, Irene began to draw until she completely covered the page with clouds, snow, and smoke. That day she took home the drawing and gave it to her mother, explaining what it was. After commending her child, Irene's mother framed the work and placed it on the wall above the child's bed. It was very good for a first attempt at art.

[Card 20] Every Thursday night that the local team is in town, Tom Rush goes out to see them play baseball. On this particular night, the team lost a close one to their arch rivals—chiefly, Tom thought, because of poor umpires. After the game was over, he went to a bar for a drink and then waited on the corner in the cold fog for the bus. Over and over in his mind went the key plays of the game. When the bus came, he got on and continued thinking of it although to a lesser degree. When he reached home and his wife asked him how it went, all he said was, "We'll get there next time."

This is the original sequence analysis with the original scoring:

1. Through hard work a man can achieve his ambition. [+2]

2. But when working conditions are difficult, he winds up exhausted and hungry,   [—2]

3. but if he belongs to a closely knit group, he can recreate with them until duty calls again.   [+1]

4. If a man does not respond to limited treatment, he will be sent to a place for special care until he is adjusted.   [+1]

5. But if he exchanges views with another and sees how well that person has done, he can resolve to make some changes too,   [+1]

6. for by explaining his problem, one can get understanding and help   [+1]

7. in his fight for what is his right and so justice will pre-
vail. [+1]

8. And so one may later look happily back on a time when
he had given up hope and recall how others helped to save
him, [—1]

9. for those who persist until the goal is won will be happy
with their success even though the effort involved is tir-
ing; [+1]

10. for it is procrastination that creates friction whereas a
definite decision puts new life into things. [—1]

11. Those who get out of line may persist until they face a
great and frightening obstacle, and then they can be coaxed
back with the others. [+1]

12. A man may not be able to achieve the peace of mind he
needs until he willingly places himself under the direction of
another, [—2]

13. for, despite one's efforts, a man can suffer a sudden loss
and be left alone in sadness, [—2]

14. but if a man can foresee possible trouble, he can fore-
stall it and thus rest easily. [+2]

15. When a man's interest carries him away, he will have to
move fast to get back where he belongs, [+1]

16. and last minute changes in one's plans may require so
much energy that he cannot enjoy the results of his work. [—2]

17. If a man tries to escape just punishment, he will wind
up worse off than before, [+2]

18. and if he gives his appetites free rein, others will have
to take charge of him. [+1]

19. But if a man tries hard and accomplishes something on
his own, others will praise his initial efforts, [+1]

20. and even should he not succeed the first time because
of a bad break, others will have faith in him that he can succeed
in time. [+1]

The final score of this sequence analysis is +7, as scored
originally. When we attempt to score it according to our set

of scoring criteria, we notice first of all that several imports, notably *3, 6, 10,* and *15* can only be scored after rereading the story. This not only delays scoring but usually means that the import is not precise. In fact, imports *1, 3, 7,* and *9* are downright misleading. If our scoring criteria had been organized at the time, import *6* could have been formulated more correctly because the tester would have realized that the story describes a reaction to adversity and is not just talking about "problems." As it stands, this import is formulated in such a way that it prejudices import *7* and so results in an incorrect score. The first import is formulated incorrectly because at that time we had not discovered that the notion of a "dream coming true" because of external circumstances (in this case, the father's death) is invariably negative. On rereading the story, it becomes clear that the only reference to work is the bald statement that he "practices daily for many hours." Everything else in the story (which is quite lengthy) is concerned with the great dream of taking his father's place, which eventually comes true upon the father's death. We attempted to rescore the imports, as they stand, without rereading the stories except where absolutely necessary for scoring. These are the new scores, with the old scores in brackets.

1.	+2, I.B.1.a.	[+2]		*12.*	−1, I.B.1.e.	
2.	−1, I.B.6.a.	[−2]			*or* I.D.2.a.	[−2]
3.	+1, I.B.5.b.	[+1]		*13.*	−2, IV.A.5.b.	[−2]
4.	+1, III.E.1.b.	[+1]		*14.*	+2, IV.A.1.a.	[+2]
5.	−1, III.C.3.b.	[+1]		*15.*	−1, I.B.6.d.	[+1]
6.	−1, IV.A.4.c.	[+1]		*16.*	−2, I.E.4.a.	[−2]
7.	+2, II.A.3.a.	[+1]		*17.*	−1, II.C.3.b.	[+2]
8.	−2, IV.A.7.c.	[−1]		*18.*	−1, III.C.3.c.	[+1]
9.	+1, I.B.1.d.	[+1]		*19.*	+2, I.B.1.b.	
10.	−1, I.B.2.f.	[−1]			*or* +2, I.B.4.c.	[+1]
11.	−1, III.C.2.b.	[+1]		*20.*	−1, I.E.2.b.	[+1]

The final score of the same sequence analysis, when scored according to our fully developed scoring criteria instead of on the basis of a few principles now becomes —5 instead of +7 and so enables us to say that this is a low achiever. To show that a sequence analysis can be formulated which is both accurate and easily scored when the imports are abstracted with a knowledge of the scoring categories, we will give the full sequence of imports worked out in this way:

1. When given the means to achieve your perfection, you can dream of the day it will be reached. After years of regular practice, an opportunity will come that will make your dream come true.   [—1, I.B.1.a. or 2.b.]

2. But the work required is hard and exhausting and is made more difficult by unfavorable circumstances.   [—1, I.B.6.a.]

3. In the afternoon, you seem to be almost dead, but this is just a game of pretend you play with the Brothers; you are alive enough when you are called to dinner.   [—1, III.E. 2.a.]

4. If you do not respond as you should you may be given more radical treatment until you become adjusted.

[+1, III.E.1.b.]

5. So you talk things over with others. Seeing the improvement they have achieved, you become convinced that you should reorganize your life along the same lines.

[—1, III.C.3.b.]

6. When others are unsympathetic about your difficulties, you try to explain the reason and they will understand and help,   [—1, IV.A.4.b.]

7. for if you should come to harm accidentally, they will be liable for any damages that occur while you are their responsibility.   [—1, II.A.5.a.]

8. You recall how difficult things had been and how everything turned out well after you had almost given up hope.

[—2, IV.A.7.b.]

9. Even for fun and recreation you have to put in a lot of effort until you are exhausted; and when you finally get what you set out for, you are tired from your exertions. [—2, I.B.7.a.]

10. Sometimes you make up your mind to a course of action for which you think you have good reason, but give in to others' wishes as soon as they put on pressure. [—2, III.C.1.a.ii.]

11. For if you persist in your course of action in spite of attempts to bring you into line, there comes a point where you are afraid of going on and they can easily coax you back.

[—1, III.C.2.b.]

12. When you have tried everything in vain to find stability of mind, you may find it by artificial means which you try as a last chance. [—2, IV.A.2.a.]

13. When catastrophe strikes unexpectedly, you are struck with terror and collapse, [—2, IV.A.4.b.]

14. but when you have sufficient warning and there is time to secure yourself against damage, you can rest easily despite the uproar. [+1, IV.A.1.a.]

15. Sometimes, though, time slips by when you are intent on your own fun and you have to hurry [—1, I.B.6.d.]

16. to get done what you have to do, if you want to be in time for dinner. Even if everything goes well, you can't enjoy it and droop from exhaustion. [—2, I.E.4.a.]

17. There is no use trying to escape from the prison you are in, you'll only find things harder afterwards. [—1, II.C.3.b.]

18. But if you are incapable of doing your share, others will take care of you. [—1, III.C.3.c.]

19. And if you try hard to follow instructions, they will commend even your first attempt at mastery. [—1, I.D.5.a.]

20. But if you fail, perhaps because of biased bosses, you can still hope to get there next time. [—1, I.E.2.b.]

All these imports can be scored on the basis of our scoring categories without recourse to the stories. Also, these imports form a sequence that is more consistent than the original sequence and can be more easily interpreted. This seems to be a boy who finds the work he is doing (and even his recreation!) so exhausting that he does not even enjoy the small successes that come his way (*2, 9, 16*). He is always hungry and ready for dinner (*2, 3, 15, 16*) despite his exhaustion; in fact, sometimes his exhaustion seems to be a game of pretend he plays with the Brothers who run the school (*3*) though at other times he is so rushed that he cannot enjoy his food. He realizes that he is not adjusting as he should (*4*), wants to do better (*5*) but depends on others for understanding, help, and sympathy (*6, 7, 18, 19, 20*). He cannot stand up for himself but gives in to others' insistence or coaxing (*10, 11*), mostly out of fear (*11*). He hopes to find stability of mind by some extraordinary means (*12*), for he easily panics (*13*) and has to have time to adjust himself to difficulties (*14*). So he resigns himself and sees that it is useless to escape from the institution which is a prison to him (*17*); the best he can do is to follow instructions. If he shows at least the beginnings of mastery, he will be commended (*19*). Even though he may not succeed, there is always a next time (*20*).

No wonder this boy is a low achiever; in fact, he is third lowest in his group. When scored according to our criteria, this new sequence shows a final score of —21, as compared with a score of —5 for the old sequence. It would seem very likely that this continuous exhaustion mentioned in the stories coupled with the preoccupation with food indicates some organic upset, but thus far we have not been able to verify this guess.

SCORING OF DIALOGUE STORIES

We have mentioned before that stories written in dialogue are very difficult to score and may even be unscorable because the dialogue, though containing a "punch" line, usually provides no outcome. For this reason, we recommend that the testees should be warned not to use dialogue. However, even with such warnings, there may be a few dialogue stories among the narratives. When they occur only occasionally, they usually can be scored without too much difficulty. The following sequence of three stories will illustrate this. It also illustrates how the sequence guides the import and that the import, not the story, determines the scoring.

Record #17

[Card 18] "Yellow and cowardly" was the description of Jim. He bragged about his money and daring ventures to everyone. He bragged about never being caught. He was too smart for the police. He told everybody. One day in a dive Jim started talking to a guy he had never seen before. He started bragging and he kept going at it, stronger and stronger. Finally his bragging took the form of actually confessing to several crimes recently committed. At this a guy came up from behind and nabbed him. "We're cops," he said. "You're under arrest. We're very pleased that you have a big mouth!"

[Card 19] The colony had just come to America. They decided to build homes near the seashore. One settler advised against it, saying that the storms would tear their homes apart. The others didn't listen. The single settler built his home into and around a hole in the ground. When it was finished, it was only half sticking above ground. The others built ordinary homes. When the storms of the sea came, the huge waves and winds washed their houses away. Only the settler's was saved. He had built a large house so he took in the survivors and later helped them rebuild homes like his.

[Card 20] Myron was a dope addict. He was a heavy advocate of opium. But tonight his supply ran out and he had to have a fix before eleven o'clock. He called up Sam, his peddler, and wanted some more opium. Sam was sick but he said he would send his son with the stuff. He told him to meet him at the corner of Sixth and Main at ten o'clock. Sixth and Main at ten. Myron waited under the street light. The whole street was dark except for the light. Soon he heard steps. He saw nothing. It was dark. Finally a voice said, "Are you Myron?" "Yes," he answered, "have you got the stuff?" "Yah, where's the money?"

Sam Jr. grabbed the money and walked away. Myron took the package, broke the seal, cracked a vial and jabbed the glass vial into his arm. It was crude, but it brought relief. He floated back to his home.

These are the imports:

18. When a man brags about his evil deeds, his big mouth will be his undoing. [+2, II.A.1.a.]

19. If he won't listen to good advice, he will pay for his foolishness and have to depend on his wiser neighbor to get him out of his difficulties. [+2, III.C.4.c.]

20. And if he is a slave to his own appetites, he has to pay the price, suffer pain and inconvenience, and is at the mercy of those who pander to his vices. [+2, II.B.2.a.]

In these three stories, the boy (college student, high achiever) says that bragging, refusing advice, and addiction lead to harm and make a man helplessly dependent on the good nature of others. But without story 19, the import to story 20 would be difficult to abstract. Story 20 has not only dialogue but an outcome that is taken from the story character's point of view rather than from the storyteller's. This is the kind of story that leads to serious misinterpretation if the interpreter is convinced that the storyteller always identifies with the hero. Even when imports are made the basis of scoring, it would be difficult to realize without import *19* that the point of the story is the state of abject helplessness that results from addiction or any kind of vice. The beginner might think that this could be scored under score —1, III.C.3. (Blind dependence on others) a. (help from others saves from despair). But, this scoring would neglect the fact that no despair is indicated in the story, and that the dependence on others is brought about by the man's addiction. The beginner might also be tempted to score the import —1 under IV.A.1. (Adversity is overcome through external circumstances) a. (through other people or things). But, distress brought about by a man's own actions is not adversity but the consequence of his own behavior. *It should never be scored under adversity.*

Careful attention to the story will help in putting the proper emphasis on the fact of addiction in the import: "If he is a slave to his appetites. . . ." That this is the actual import seems confirmed by story 19 which also speaks of such dependence, this time as the result of refusing reasonable advice. In both cases, this dependence is the outcome of the story character's own actions. The storyteller seems to say that the price of acting unreasonably and lacking emotional control is harm and dependence. The ease with which the import can be abstracted from the narrative (story 19) as against the difficulty of abstracting the correct import in story 20 where the narrator uses dialogue and tells the story from the point of view of the hero serves to emphasize our warning that stories must have an outcome and should not employ dialogue.

DECEPTIVE STORIES

Some stories must be scored negative though at first glance the import seems highly positive. These are the "phony" stories, stories which profess high-flown ideals that turn out to be nothing but empty clichés. Usually, such stories can be recognized only when reading the complete sequence, though a scorer who is alert to subtle nuances may spot them almost immediately. Often, the first couple of stories in such a record are genuinely positive, but as they go on, their insincere, pretentious, and deceptive content is gradually revealed more and more clearly. The following set is one of many we have found among low achievers in high school and college and among teachers rated ineffective by their pupils.

Record #18. (F., age 20, I.Q. 108)

[Card 1] The young boy sat gazing at his violin. Why did he have to practice that old thing anyway? He could be out with the other boys at the ball park or at the swimming hole. But Mama had made it quite clear that he was to practice for one whole hour. And so it was; Mama kept up her persistence and the little boy grew to enjoy his practice. It wasn't a struggle any longer. As time went on the little boy became a big boy and music and his violin were the most important things in his life. After his first private recital, the young man was approached by a well-dressed gentleman. Would he consider becoming a professional violinist? Would he like to play at concerts? Yes, this young man had hidden talents. Talents given to him by the Almighty. Thanks to the foresight and loving guidance of his mother, the young man made a success with his musical knowledge in the cultural world. Practice makes perfect and perseverance means assured success, if not in one way, then in another.

[Card 2] Mary wanted to go to school, but Mama thought differently. Why couldn't she be content to stay home and marry a good farmer like her Pa? Couldn't Mama see that times were changing? Couldn't she see that farming wasn't as necessary as in times before? And Daddy, too; he couldn't seem to make a decision. Dad was a hard-working, loving, devoted father. He saw and longed for his wife to understand Mary. Mary loved her parents very much, and she despised anything that hurt them. Yet, she had her life to live too and she had had the education to realize the importance of a higher education. The decision was made—Mary left her home to find a job which would yield enough for her education. After four years of hard study and work, Mary graduated from college. These years had been full of heartbreaks and trials. She had written to her family once a week, never missing once. She had prayed for help. Then she went home—Mama and Daddy were there to meet her and proud as proud could be. Wasn't it all so wonderful!

[Card 3] It was just another sad story in the annals of life. The news had come by telephone—Edward Doe—killed in action. Why did it have to be Eddie? God has His own way in these things. What was Jane to do? Eight years previous, Eddie's and Jane's parents had been killed in an auto accident. Eddie had raised Jane and given her all the affection and love he could to make his little sister happy. Now it was all over—she had no one. As time passed, the wound in her broken heart healed. Slowly but surely she conquered her loneliness and gave herself to loving and helping others who, like herself, had no family. She was happy, but she had known love and what it was like to be loved. There was still a void in her life. Providence had planned it all—within the year Jane met a wonderful devoted young man—love was once again in her life. These two would raise a family and give love to all!

[Card 4] Who was it that Jim really loved? Was it Jean or Ann? The divided heart of a man is an awful sight to see. The torture of a double love clearly penetrated his actions. His eyes were filled with the torture of—no decision. Can you realize the feeling of a man who has just found out that his first wife is alive—and he, believing her dead, had married again. What are his thoughts? What can he do? Who can he see? Father Malony always was a big help in his life. Jim took the next train to the neighboring town. Within the week, Jim was back. His very gait gave the appearance of relief and satisfaction. He always had loved Ann and he knew it deep down. She was the one he chose. Jean had no trouble finding another mate and she really didn't care anyway. Thank God he had given him the initial push to Father Malony.

[Card 6] Grandma stood rigid, gazing at space. I knew she'd act this way—the mention of a Catholic would set her on pins and needles. I didn't care anymore. I knew there was something in this Catholic philosophy that answered a lot of problems in my life. I knew that there was and is a God and an afterlife. I felt that Christ had formed the Church and I've read up on the history. What harm was there? She believed in God. I took instructions and on Holy Saturday I was baptized. My life became a joy, even the sufferings, for I knew of the afterlife and the Beatific Vision. After years of faithful prayer, Grandma once again accepted me with all her love and goodness. She had seen grace work in a man. She had seen what wonders it accomplished. It was my greatest joy to see and hear her call for a priest on her deathbed!

[Card 7] Mr. James had told Tom that this life consists of a few basic principles—loving God, neighbor and self. Doing these to the best of your ability was fulfilling life's purpose. But Tom's ears were deaf to the words of this wise old friend. He wanted the world and all its thrills and pleasures. He didn't want any obligations and he cared little whether he stepped on the toes of his fellow men. As for self—he loved himself too much. As for God; there's time for Him when he was old and feeble like Mr. James. The world had a bite worse than its bark and Tom came tumbling down from his pinnacle of dreams. Down, down to the plain of basic reality. Down to the wise proverb of his old friend and teacher. He, too, must pass these wise words on to the younger generation—to the imprudent youth. And so, he devoted the rest of his life guiding and counseling the young on facts he had proven by living. No teacher teaches like experience.

[Card 8] The window was opened to let in enough light for the doctor to see for the incision. There were no anesthetics in those days, the man was given a bottle of whiskey and knocked himself out. The frightened young rascal who accidentally shot the man had eluded all search. The man was laid on an open cot and the incision made. The bullet out, the wound was sewed up with a plain needle and thread. Black at that! Paul thought this old story over, wasn't medicine wonderful? That doctor knew enough to cut out that bullet and sew up the man. He saved that man's life! Paul knew then and there that he was going to be a doctor. He was going to help people in pain and save lives. He wanted to be a doctor more than ever now that he had seen the movie of the first uses of medicine and operation.

[Card 11] It was dark, very dark. One could feel the earthly figure of the devil hovering overhead. The slime green of the slinky figure could almost be felt slowly twining around the neck and waist. The path was narrow and straight and steep. A deep ravine on each side made the path appear even narrower. Was it worth it? Was there perfect happiness on the top of this climb? Look up [down?] to the plain of comfort, it's only a little way off. On and on the figure plodded, slowly, surely, taking every safeguard, fighting every obstacle, fleeing every temptation. Man's life is just this, an ever ascending struggle on the path to true happiness. It is sad to see men riding the "highways" instead of crawling the path. Happiness lies in God alone—He is Love.

[Card 12] Isn't hypnotism something weird? The young man just wanted to try it once. Just to see what it is like. Have you ever had a bad dream from which you would swear that it was real? That's what it felt like, only you knew it was real and you didn't know what your body had done in your mind's absence. Mr. Jones was a good man anyway and the young lad went away satisfied that he had been hypnotized and knew what it felt like. Mr. Jones was very good, so no qualms of conscience bothered the lad. He was fully satisfied.

[Card 14] All I could see was a figure of a man in the window.

My heart began to beat faster and faster. I didn't make a move, but lay as still as I could in my bed. He began to open the window, slowly, ever so slowly. Could I scream? No! Don't move! Then he began to climb in. I knew it wouldn't do any good to scream—no one was around for miles. Why didn't I lock that window? Why did I volunteer to stay home tonight? My God, my God, help me! He began to come towards me. I'm sure he could hear my heavy breathing. . . . All of a sudden I screamed at the top of my lungs! "You ought to scream—couldn't you leave at least one door open?" It was my brother Bill. I had locked all the doors and hadn't heard him knocking. That's the last time I'll ever leave my bedroom window unlocked!

[Card 16] "Say, there's Sister Placida!" "How are you? How are things down there? It's been so long since I've seen you! How do you like my new habit? It's much whiter than the old ones down there! And it never tears, it lasts for eternity you know! And look at my new headpiece! Isn't it just beautiful? Everyone looks so stunning in it—it glimmers so! Angel Gabriel announced your coming this morning—I got so excited! Did you have a long trip? Isn't it wonderful up here? It sure is wonderful that you and I can get together like this. I know you'll enjoy your stay in Heaven. We just love it!"

[Card 20] There we were—five minutes before the wedding and the best man had leaned against a white-boiled frosted cake! Black and white go nice together—but not on a black tux. What could we do? Send Jonnie home for Daddy's old suit? No time. How about running down the street for Grandpa's? No, it's too old. Ahem! Father, do you happen to have a black overcoat? The wedding was just beautiful and the best man was there with a black jacket to match his pants. Wasn't it just perfect that Father Smith was the same size as he? And so obliging.

These are the imports:

1. When you are set to work at something you dislike, others' persistence keeps you at it and you gradually come to enjoy it. Through the foresight and recognition of others you become a success.   [+1, I.D.1.d.]

2. But times are changing and you insist on work that affords you an education. In the end, others will rejoice with you as

they see that your education is complete.   [+2, I.D.1.d.]

3. Sometimes Providence takes away what you value most. In the course of time, you conquer your loneliness and *give yourself to loving others* until Providence so plans that once again you find a special love to fill the void.   [—1, IV.A.8.]

4. But when your first love revives you may be unable to make a decision until Providence gives you a push to seek help from just the right person; then you are relieved that you can return to your first love, for the second doesn't care any-way.   [—2, IV.A.3.b.]

6. When you follow the call of your conscience and are ostracized, *years of prayer* will bring others to accept you again and even join you in the end.   [—1, II.A.4.b.]

7. But sometimes when you ignore the advice of others and go ahead regardless, you come to see that they were right; *then you devote the rest of your life to counseling others, warning them.*   [—1, II.A.2.a]

8. When you consider the profession you covet, and *how wonderful it is even in the crudest environment* you are con-vinced that this is the vocation for you.   [—1, III.F.2.a.]

11. But the difficulty of getting to the top makes you wonder if it is worth it, when comfort is just a little way off, though you plod on. *Man's whole life is just one ever ascending strug-gle,* and happiness lies only in God.   [—2, III.F.2.a.]

12. You just wanted to try something weird once, but it feels like a bad dream you could swear was real. But the person who initiated you was very good, so you have no qualms and are fully satisfied.   [—1, II.A.2.a. or I.B.8.b.]

14. And when you get frightened because somebody is com-ing, you find out that there is no reason for the fright and you could have prevented it by being more circumspect—which you will be next time.   [—2, IV.A.1.b.]

16. You can still look forward to your eternal reward which will satisfy every earthly wish;   [—2, I.B.1.e.]

20. for if something should happen to stain your wedding garment, there is always an obliging priest around who will see that you appear as you should.   [—1, IV.A.1.a.]

In this sequence, only the two first imports are scored plus. For anyone familiar with our scoring, even these two sound suspicious. Certainly, the first import fits into category I.D.1.d. under a score of +1: *Success comes upon positive action undertaken at the legitimate command or influence of another.* At the same time, in spite of the fact that the boy "grew to enjoy his practice," the main emphasis is on the "foresight and guidance" of the boy's mother and the fortunate discovery of his talent by the well-dressed gentleman. This is the reason we did not score the story +2 under I.D.1.e (Yielding to legitimate pressure but also doing work that is interesting). When parents merely ask the boy in the story to practice, and from there on the boy not only enjoys the violin (though not necessarily the practice) but sets his own goal, we simply score +2 under I.B.1.a (success comes through personal effort, work). In the import quoted above, it is not the boy who eventually makes the task his own but the mother who keeps guiding him, which is hinted at by the final comment in the story, that "perseverance means assured success, if not in one way, then in another." Apparently, it is the mother's persistence rather than the boy's which earns success.

The second import is still positive. It fits without difficulty into Category I.D.1.d (Insisting on the right to determine one's own course of action and acting accordingly) under score +2. The same score will be found under Category III.C.1.d.ii. which adds to the above statement: *this is accepted after some time but without anger or persisting conflict.* The last comment in the story, however, should alert us: "Wasn't it all so wonderful!" The third import is easily recognized as negative, though the statement in the story that "you conquer your loneliness and give yourself to loving others" could be taken for positive action. This import is "phony" in our sense of the term: to *give* yourself to loving others already implies an essential passivity. The last part of the import finally reveals that this affection for others is merely a stopgap: all along Providence has planned to replace what it has taken away, without the slightest effort on the girl's part. From now on, almost every story has a twist that marks it as counterfeit: "years of prayer" (card 6); "the rest of her life" she is going to counsel and warn the young (card 7). In her story to card 8, she thinks the profession she has chosen is "just wonderful" even in the crudest environment; in 11, however, she decides that "man's whole life is just one ever ascending struggle" and is ready to try something new to relieve the drudgery (12). Knowing that this is not something that everybody would approve, she reassures herself with the irrelevant observation that those who initiated her into this new experience are "very good, so you have no qualms." Finally, she tries to assure herself that despite everything, her eternal reward is secure; and that, she thinks, will satisfy every earthly wish (16) and so everything is going to be all right in the end (20). While the first eight stories make a valiant attempt at being all sweetness and light, the last four give away her fear that all is not right within herself. The easy optimism of the last two cards deceives no one.

This record is instructive in that it demonstrates that we must be alive to fake positive imports. Not that this fake is deliberate. Undoubtedly, this girl is deceived in her appraisal of herself and the attitudes she holds. But, it is important to recognize this self-deception and appraise it correctly. There are some records of low achievers that carry the easy optimism of the last two stories through most of the imports. We have called such stories "Pollyanna stories" and find that once attention is drawn to them, they are rather easy to recognize. All these stories can be scored in the usual way, except that we must be extra vigilant not to score them higher than they deserve.

STORIES FOR CARD 2

There is one kind of story import that often gives rise to scoring difficulties. It is the story of a farm girl who leaves home and parents because she wants an education. This is a typical story told by high achievers and is usually scored +2 under Category I.D.1.d (Success follows upon insisting upon one's right to determine his own course of action and doing so). (It can also be found with the same score under III.C.1.d.) For students and teachers, this is almost a stock theme. But not every story of this kind can be scored positive. Compare, for instance, the following two stories; the first is told by a low achiever, the second is told by a high achiever.

[Card 2] Sue's desire for an education has led her to ask to go away from the farm. The mother has talked it over with her but has left the decision to Sue. Sue knows she owes her parents much and does not like to grieve them. However, she is going on to study.

Import: You know you owe others much and you do not like to grieve them, but you will do what you desire.

[Card 2] Elaine is looking her rejection of farm-life to her mother who stands by undecided, not knowing whether to approve or blame. Elaine's hard-working farmer father gave her every opportunity for an education in the hope that she would love life on the modern farm and teach others to love it. Her final decision is to seek success away from the farm.

Import: After you have been prepared, you may decide to reject the way your elders planned for you and seek success elsewhere.

At first glance, the stories seem much alike. But the difference in tone is revealed in the import. In the first story, it is the girl's *desire* that decides the issue. There is no indication of what she is going to do with the education she intends to seek. She mentions the fact that she owes her parents much and does not like to grieve them—yet does so without further explanation. This points the way to the score of —1 under I.D.4.a. (Decision to follow own course in life puts burdens on others). In contrast, the second story emphasizes the fact that the education is to be used *to seek success.* Incidentally, the girl in the story dislikes the farm; but the emphasis is not on this dislike or the implied liking of city life but on striving for success. It is scored +1 under III.C.4.a (deciding on choosing one's own work, etc.) and also under I.D.1.f.ii.

For good measure, here are two more stories with the same theme, again scored very differently. The first is the story of a high achiever, the second that of a low achiever.

[Card 2] A family living on the farm where work was always plentiful. The daughter learned how to read and would rather study than work. Mother wants the daughter to do the farm chores assigned. With the training she received from her parents the girl performs her tasks but reads whenever she can and thus educates herself and becomes quite a renowned personage.

Import: If you do what you are asked to do you can still pursue your own interests in your spare time and become quite a personage.

[Card 2] In early spring Laura's father always had to work doubly hard and her mother lost some of the beauty with each passing year. But Laura just couldn't let all their troubles come between her and her books. She just wouldn't end up a farmer's daughter, she thought, as she turned away.

Import: But you just won't let anything, not even the troubles of your loved ones, come between you and what you want most.

Here the problem is really self-education served by an abiding interest in books. In the first story, the conflict between duty and interest is solved by doing what is required and then reading when possible. In the second story, the girl's interest in books overrides all considerations of duty and affection. The first story earns a score of +2, I.B.1.b. while the second story earns a score of —2, III.A.2.b.iii (Good relations are broken by independent action, for selfish reasons). In the first story, the girl achieves success, she "becomes quite a personage," through active effort and adequate means, through personal initiative, which justifies the score of +2. In the second story, there is no indication of success or active effort, which makes scoring under Category I. impossible. Though good relations are not formally broken, the fact of turning away from the troubles of her family surely means a virtual break, which justifies the score of —2. The break is produced by selfish reasons: the girl is not motivated by a thirst for education but merely by the wish to become something other than a "farmer's daughter."

Perhaps enough has been said to show that scoring cannot be done in a routine manner. But, if the import is correctly abstracted and the scorer is sensitive to the nuances of the story, it can be scored reliably and, after some practice, quickly.

9

THE MOTIVATION INDEX (M.I.)

Scoring the import of a story as strongly positive (+2), slightly positive (+1), unscorable (0), slightly negative (—1), and strongly negative (—2) has the advantage of reminding the scorer continually of the significance of his scores. With such scoring, he is never allowed to forget that he is dealing with positive, constructive imports versus non-constructive, negative ones.

THE INTENSITY SCALE

These scores from +2 through zero to —2 represent a five-point scale which measures the direction and intensity of motivation. Fagot (1961) has found that the scores +2, +1, —1, —2 may be converted into normal deviate scores without any gain in precision. (Zero scores were not frequent enough to be included in the normalizing process.) This was done on a group of records from 252 subjects consisting of twelve stories each. The converted scores were found to correlate almost perfectly (r .97) with the raw scores using the weightings +2 through —2.* Of course, it is well known that any system which normalizes the weights may tend by its very nature to obscure desired individual differences. Consequently, there seems to be no advantage to using the more complicated system of finding scores by normal deviate weights when the simpler system of

* Since each response score from +2 to —2 may be considered a rating, this corresponds exactly to the procedure used by Likert in defining his method of summated ratings (see Edwards, 1957, pp. 149-71).

integral weights, as used in our scoring system, shows a high correlation—unless and until further studies provide evidence to the contrary.

In this intensity scale, a score of zero means that no motivation is revealed, either because the story was not completed or because the storyteller gave a description rather than a story, which is unscorable by this method. Let us call these scores of individual stories the *intensity score*.

If stories are omitted in a record or are unscorable, we must decide whether the missing stories could perhaps not be written or completed for lack of time, as can happen when the test is given in one session with only five or six minutes allowed per story. If a story is omitted because of lack of time, we have a choice of asking the subject to write out the omitted stories after the session and adding them at the end of the record, because that is where they now fit in the sequence; or, of calculating the value of the final score by using the number of stories actually given as divisor.

If a story is unscorable because it contains simply a statement, for example, "This is a man and woman talking," it is assigned a zero. But, if there are more than two such stories in a 12-story record, or more than three such stories in a 20-story record, the record should be discarded for purposes of motivation research with normal people, though it may give valuable clinical pointers. Such stories are never given by normal adults and only rarely by children of normal intelligence who are eight years and over. Even younger children can tell stories with a plot and outcome.* Descriptions without plot or outcome may be given by disturbed psychotics and so have diagnostic significance.

---

* It is well known that a child can describe a picture long before he can tell a story about it. If a record contains more than two descriptions (instead of stories) despite the instructions to tell a story with plot and outcome, it can be reasonably assumed that the individual is *unable* to tell a story, whether that is the result of some psychiatric disturbance or lack of intelligence. In either case, it is impossible to gauge his motivation by a type of analysis that depends on story plot and outcome.

Most stories are scorable, if not by themselves, then in conjunction with the story before or the story after (see Chapter 5, records 10, 11). Every attempt should be made to give a negative or positive score according to the scoring criteria. To assign a zero without strictest necessity will reduce the reliability of our final score, for it reduces the number of measurements we have made in a given record.*

We do not recommend to use fewer than ten TAT cards or show fewer than ten pictures from other sources. There is a progression in thought from one story to another which requires several stories. It may happen, for instance, that a person starts out with stories that give positive though conventional imports and only gradually reveals a negative attitude as he comes to grips with his own problems. Another person may start out with stories that explore several solutions to his particular problem—some positive, some negative—until, toward the end of the sequence, the basic positive orientation prevails.

THE CONSISTENCY SCORE

Since Fagot's study has shown that the integrally weighted scores can be legitimately added and subtracted, we may add the plus and minus scores in a record algebraically and use this sum as the final score. This score indicates how many more positive than negative scores a record contains, and vice versa. If he were completely consistent in his motivation, an individual would reveal only positive or only negative attitudes, and all of them in the same strength. In a 20-story sequence, his final score would be $+40$ if his motivation were strongly positive, and -40 if his motivation were strongly negative. In contrast, a man whose motivation is so inconsistent that he is just as likely to reveal negative as positive attitudes in a story, and reveal the one in the same strength as the other, would have

* There is only one indifferent type of import (Score o, I.B.1) which is abstracted from actual stories but amounts almost to a description, e.g., "after work, you rest." It is found equally among low and high achievers and so indicates neither negative nor positive motivation.

a final score of zero because the positive and negative intensity scores would cancel out.

Between these two extremes, there are various degrees of consistency. A man may tell stories most of which have a positive import, but there may be some that are negative. His final score will be anywhere from $+1$ to somewhere near $+40$. Another may reveal rather negative attitudes, but here and there he adds a constructive outcome to the story. His final score will be anywhere from -1 to somewhere close to -40, depending on the individual imports. Apparently, the final score is a measure of the consistency with which the individual reveals either positive or negative attitudes. Since he cannot reveal what he does not have, this score represents simply the consistency of his motivating attitudes, or the consistency of his motivation. Let us, then, call the final score his *consistency score*. If a storyteller reveals imports whose positive and negative scores cancel out, he has zero consistency, neither definitely positive nor definitely negative motivation.

To say that two people have the same consistency score does not necessarily mean that their pattern of intensity scores is the same. One man may have only extreme intensity scores, for example, five scores of $+2$ and seven scores of -2 in a 12-story record, with a final score of -4; while another has only mild intensity scores, for example, four scores of $+1$ and eight scores of -1, which also add up to a final score of -4. Since the weights have been shown to be equal for practical purposes, we can say that both of the subjects have the same degree of negative motivation, or the same degree of consistency in a negative direction. Of course, this score may indicate, as in the first example, a man who has motivating attitudes that reveal rather intense convictions of a self-seeking, antisocial kind, perhaps with a few positive attitudes toward adversity. Or, it may indicate, as in the second example, a man who is much less intense in his negative motivation and also shows a very few equally mild positive attitudes. The consistency score indicates both the direction and the consistency of motivation; accordingly, a story sequence will obtain the same consistency score whether there is strong negativity with relatively few negative scores, or mild negativity with many negative scores and relatively few strongly positive scores. It is the clinical evaluation which will distinguish between these different types of motivation (see Chapter 15).

Our consistency scale has a zero point, the point at which the storyteller has no consistency at all, where positive and negative intensity scores cancel out. It has an upper limit, the highest number of units that can be obtained with a given number of stories: with a 20-story sequence, this will be 40 units, corresponding to a consistency score of +40. The scale has a lower limit as well, the lowest number of units that can be obtained with the same number of stories. In a 20-story sequence, this will equal a consistency score of —40. Since we use story sequences of various lengths, we actually have a number of consistency scales, each with its own number of units as determined by the number of stories used. Obviously, it is impossible to compare the consistency score obtained by one individual with that obtained by another who has perhaps told only half the number of stories. One man may obtain a consistency score of +20 for a 20-story sequence, another may obtain the same score of +20 for a 10-story sequence. The first man has obtained only half the possible units on his scale in the positive direction, while the second has obtained all the units that were obtainable because his scale is limited to 20 units in the positive and 20 units in the negative direction.

THE MOTIVATION INDEX (M.I.)

To make the two scores even roughly comparable, we must use a linear transformation which will not change the nature of the raw scores but will give us their equivalent in units of the two different scales. We can transform the raw scores into a proportion, the ratio of actual scale units obtained over the maximum units obtainable and express it in decimals. With 20 stories, the final (consistency) score can range from —40 to +40, which means a total range of 80 units. When the final (consistency) score is —40, we have arrived at the lower limit of the total range; with such a score, the individual has not obtained any of the units obtainable on this scale. If his score is —39, he has obtained 1/80 of the total possible units. Transformed into a decimal, this will be .0125. To facilitate calculations, we multiply the values for each possible ratio (units obtained over units obtainable) by 200. This gives us 100 as the arbitrary zero point for consistency, that is, the point at which an individual obtains half the possible units on this scale. All negative consistency scores will give index values below 100, all positive consistency scores will give values above 100, up to the scale limit of 200. Thus, all index values below 100 indicate negative motivation of increasing consistency as they approach zero. All index values above 100 indicate positive motivation of increasing consistency as the upper limit of this continuum is reached, namely, an index value of 200.

The formula for calculating the index value for any score in a 20-story record is

$$\frac{n}{80} \, 200$$

where n is the *number of units* of the total scale *actually obtained;* this number can be derived from the final (consistency) score. Since it is the story import that is scored and not the picture about which the story is told, this formula can be used for any set of 20 consecutive stories—whether TAT cards or other pictures are used or whether stories are elicited by a verbal description (e.g., "tell me a story about a boy and a violin")—provided only that they are told spontaneously and in sequence and are scored according to our criteria.

It is a simple matter now to calculate the index values of the final score for records containing 10 stories (range 40 units, from —20 to +20), 11 stories (range 44 units, from —22 to +22); in fact, for records containing any number of stories.* The midpoint will always be 100, indicating complete inconsistency, while the lower end of the scale will be at zero and the upper limit at 200. These values represent an index based on the proportion of scale units obtained against the total number of scale units obtainable. This index is the Motivation Index (M.I.). The two tables on the next two pages make it possible to find the M.I. for any final (consistency) score derived from sequences of 10, 11, 12, 13, 14, 15, 16, and 20 stories. The M.I. for sequences from 17 to 19 stories has not been calculated, because there is no advantage to be gained from shortening the test by two or three stories. Shorter sequences than 10 stories should not be used for psychological reasons, as has been explained earlier in this chapter. For this reason, we have not calculated the M.I. for records based on fewer than 10 stories. If, however, it should seem desirable to employ sequences longer than those for which the M.I. has been calculated, it can be found according to the formula

$$\frac{n^o}{n^p}\ 200$$

where n^o is the number of units obtained (derived from the final score) and n^p is the number of units obtainable or possible. The number of possible units is 80 for a 20-story sequence, 76 for a 19-story sequence, 72 for an 18-story sequence, and the like; that is, four times the number of stories used.

To use the tables, locate the number of stories on which the test is based (in the horizontal column at the top in the table

---

* This is not to say that motivation indices based on sequences of different length are perfectly transformable. However, studies done with such sequences justify the confidence that such a measure is at least roughly comparable. At present, this is all that can be claimed for the relationship of indices based on sequences of different length. Further studies on this relationship are projected for the immediate future.

TABLE 1. *Transformation of* NEGATIVE SCORES *into M.I. (Motivation Index)*

Final score	20	16	15	14	13	12	11	10
				Total stories in record				
—40	0							
—39	3							
—38	5							
—37	8							
—36	10							
—35	13							
—34	15							
—33	18							
—32	20	0						
—31	23	3						
—30	25	6	0					
—29	28	9	3					
—28	30	13	7	0				
—27	33	16	10	4				
—26	35	19	13	7	0			
—25	38	22	17	11	4			
—24	40	25	20	14	8	0		
—23	43	28	23	18	12	4		
—22	45	31	27	21	15	8	0	
—21	48	35	30	25	19	13	5	
—20	50	38	33	29	23	17	9	0
—19	53	41	37	32	27	21	14	5
—18	55	44	40	36	31	25	18	10
—17	58	47	43	39	35	29	23	15
—16	60	50	47	43	38	33	27	20
—15	63	53	50	46	42	38	32	25
—14	65	56	53	50	46	42	36	30
—13	68	59	57	54	50	46	41	35
—12	70	63	60	57	54	50	45	40
—11	73	66	63	61	58	54	50	45
—10	75	69	67	64	62	58	55	50
— 9	78	72	70	68	65	63	59	55
— 8	80	75	73	71	69	67	64	60
— 7	83	78	77	75	73	71	68	65
— 6	85	81	80	79	77	75	73	70
— 5	88	84	83	82	81	79	77	75
— 4	90	88	87	86	85	83	82	80
— 3	93	91	90	89	88	88	86	85
— 2	95	94	93	93	92	92	91	90
— 1	98	97	97	96	96	96	95	95
0	100	100	100	100	100	100	100	100

TABLE 2. *Transformation of* POSITIVE SCORES *into M. I. (Motivation Index)*

Final score	Total stories in record							
	20	16	15	14	13	12	11	10
0	100	100	100	100	100	100	100	100
+ 1	103	103	103	104	104	104	105	105
+ 2	105	106	107	107	108	108	109	110
+ 3	108	109	110	111	112	113	114	115
+ 4	110	113	113	114	115	117	118	120
+ 5	113	116	117	118	119	121	123	125
+ 6	115	119	120	121	123	125	127	130
+ 7	118	122	123	125	127	129	132	135
+ 8	120	125	127	129	131	133	136	140
+ 9	123	128	130	132	135	138	141	145
+10	125	131	133	136	138	142	145	150
+11	128	135	137	139	142	146	150	155
+12	130	138	140	143	146	150	155	160
+13	133	141	143	146	150	154	159	165
+14	135	144	147	150	154	158	164	170
+15	138	147	150	154	158	163	168	175
+16	140	150	153	157	162	167	173	180
+17	143	153	157	161	165	171	177	185
+18	145	156	160	164	169	175	182	190
+19	148	159	163	168	173	179	186	195
+20	150	163	167	171	177	183	191	200
+21	153	166	170	175	181	188	195	
+22	155	169	173	179	185	192	200	
+23	158	172	177	182	188	196		
+24	160	175	180	186	192	200		
+25	163	178	183	189	196			
+26	165	181	187	193	200			
+27	168	184	190	196				
+28	170	188	193	200				
+29	173	191	197					
+30	175	194	200					
+31	178	197						
+32	180	200						
+33	183							
+34	185							
+35	188							
+36	190							
+37	193							
+38	195							
+39	198							
+40	200							

of positive scores if the final score is positive, or in the table of negative scores if the final score is negative). Next, look up the *final score* obtained for each record (i.e., the algebraic sum of all plus and minus scores in the record) in the first vertical column at the left, and read off the M.I. where the chosen horizontal and vertical columns intersect.

A few examples will illustrate the use of the tables. TAT record 16 (see Appendix B) has a final score of —22 in a 20-story sequence. We look up the score under column 20 of negative scores and find an M.I. of 45, which means consistently negative motivation. Record 13, a 12-story sequence, has a final score of +21 which is found under column 12 of positive scores and gives an M.I. of 188, extremely consistent positive motivation. Record 14, with a final score of —36, yields an M.I. of 10; and record 15, with a final score of —25, yields an M.I. of 38. Both are 20-story sequences and consequently the M.I. is read from column 20 of negative scores.

Since the M.I. is a ratio between the number of units actually obtained and the maximum units possible on a given consistency scale, it is in principle roughly comparable even though the final scores of the records (consistency scores) may be derived from story sequences of different length. True, the units are of different lengths when expressed in M.I. values, but each unit is the smallest obtainable proportion of the total units possible in each scale. We are not saying an M.I. of 150, for instance, when obtained from a 20-story sequence, is measured in the same absolute units as the same index obtained from a 12-story sequence. But we are saying that it indicates the same ratio of obtained to obtainable units.

To work out the M.I. from standard scores would take many years of research because it would involve a careful sampling not only on the basis of sex, age, intelligence, geographic distribution, socio-economic level and the like, but especially on the basis of achievement or effectiveness in life. When obtained, these scores would allow us to compare the consistency of a testee in his positive or negative motivation with the consistency found in a normative population. There is a reasonable doubt, however, whether this additional comparison would offer a worthwhile return for the labor required. Since it was felt that the measures here recommended could be profitably used for both research and application, it was decided not to delay the presentation of this work for the lengthy period necessary to develop a Motivation Index from standard scores.

RELIABILITY OF MOTIVATION INDEX

Since every story is scored by reference to the same scoring criteria, and since the import derived from the story is scored and not the picture about which the story is told, it stands to reason that every "item" in the test must be equal to every other "item." This has been shown to be the case by H. J. Fagot (1961) who found that the two positive and two negative scores were evenly distributed among all the cards used in a sample of 252 records of twelve stories each. For this investigation, Fagot used the records of 99 teachers (Burkard's data, see Chapter 10), 100 college students (Garvin's data, see Chapter 12) and 53 seventh-grade children (see Chapter 12). In addition, the units of our "intensity scale" are equal for all practical purposes, as mentioned at the beginning of this chapter.

Since the "items" measured by our intensity scale are equivalent, even one story should theoretically give us a correct picture of the storyteller's intensity and direction of motivation if he were completely consistent and our scoring were completely reliable. Unfortunately, not many of us are so completely consistent in our positive attitudes that we would always tell stories with highly positive import. On the other hand, it is fortunate that there are still fewer people who have such strong (and such strongly entrenched) negative attitudes that they would reveal them in every story they tell. We can consider each story as a sample of the storyteller's motivating attitudes, his habitual motivation. Our intensity score is a measurement of this motivation. By demanding several stories, we are in fact applying repeated measurements.

Given perfect scorer reliability, the consistency of these measurements would be a direct indication of the storyteller's motivational consistency. Burkard (see Chapter 10) found 97 and 94 percent agreement between herself and two other scorers in scoring 1,200 stories; Petrauskas (see Chapter 11) found 80 percent and 82 percent agreement between himself and two other scorers in scoring 780 stories. Using the more exact scoring criteria we have worked out since then should improve scorer reliability further. This makes it likely that most of the variance from one story to the other is not a variance in scoring but in the consistency with which the storyteller expresses either positive or negative attitudes. Thus a split-half reliability coefficient (odd *versus* even numbered stories) would not reveal the reliability of the test items (for all our "items" are equal by definition) but the consistency of the storyteller's motivation.

That the consistency score is actually a measurement of the storyteller's consistency and not of the reliability of the "items" is shown by two sets of correlations. Burkard's group of matched pairs of effective and ineffective teachers (see Chapter 10) had high consistency scores, the good teachers in a positive, the poor teachers in a negative direction. After rescoring 99 records (one had been lost) on the basis of the improved scoring criteria (Appendix A), we found a correlation of r .86 between the odd and the even numbered stories. In comparison, the records of a group of children which ranged in consistency scores from zero to extreme consistency in both a negative and positive direction (see Chapter 12) had a split-half reliability (odd against even numbered stories) of r .79. In Burkard's group, the midrange of consistency scores had been excluded by the device of matching a highly effective with an extremely ineffective teacher in each pair. In this group, it would be fairly safe to restrict the test to 6 instead of 12 stories, for the first half of the sequence analysis (6 stories) had a correlation of r .86 with the second half (6 stories). In contrast, the correlation of the first half of the sequence analysis with the second half dropped to r .61 in the group of children.

To gauge a storyteller's consistency, we must make repeated measurements; in other words, we must ask him to tell several stories. Instead of measuring various dimensions of the quality we want to measure, as we do in intelligence tests and in most personality tests, we are actually taking many measures of one and the same dimension, which is the storyteller's motivation, positive or negative. Highly consistent people will reveal essentially the same type of motivation in every sample and so show high "reliability"; as do, for instance, the good and poor teachers. But in a group that represents the whole range of consistency, we have to take quite a few samples before we can be sure that we can strike an average that will fairly represent the individual's degree of consistency.

For our purposes, there is an optimum number of samples we can take. We must have enough stories so that further samples will neither significantly increase nor decrease the final score. Ideally, there should come a point where additional stories would not change the M.I. even for inconsistent storytellers. While we may not reach this ideal point, we can compromise on an optimal number. Too few stories may give a spurious measure of consistency, while too many stories will extend the testing time and exhaust the storyteller without materially improving our consistency score.

Thus far, we have found high correlations with the outside criterion when using 11-, 12-, 13-, and 20-story sequences. While the Motivation Index allows for a direct comparison between records containing the same number of stories, it does not give exact equivalents for sequences of different lengths. We are now instituting a program designed to explore the relation between sets of stories of different lengths and also their relation to the outside criterion. When these studies are completed, it will be possible to indicate the reliability of the Motivation Index for sets of stories of varying length. In the meantime, publication of this new method of story interpretation seemed justified because it does afford an exact way of diagnosing positive or negative motivation and of comparing the motivation cf different individuals when the number of stories is kept constant.

Part IV. RESEARCH STUDIES

10

MOTIVATION AND TEACHER EFFICIENCY

Chapter 7 mentions that the first studies using the method of story sequence analysis for the prediction of performance were designed to spot large differences by comparing subjects scoring high on an outside criterion with those scoring low on it. In this way, high achievers among high school students were correctly distinguished from their low achieving fellows.

After Snider, Brown, and McCandlish had shown that such a discrimination could be successfully achieved with high school students, Burkard (1958) attempted to discriminate between effective and ineffective teachers on the basis of the sequence analysis. Obviously, the difficulties of such a project are great because it is not at all certain that we know how to define teaching effectiveness and how to rate teachers so as to have a valid and reliable outside criterion.

Everybody would agree that we want good teachers. They are needed today in greater numbers than ever before. Yet, we do not know what personality characteristics distinguish good from poor teachers, nor do we know how to select men and women who will become good teachers or how to help ineffective teachers to become effective. Many studies have increased our knowledge of teachers' qualities, both good and poor; they have discovered what kind of teachers are wanted by administrators, by supervisors, by pupils; they have measured factors that may contribute to good teaching. But, we cannot say that the problem of what makes a good teacher has been solved. Indeed, Ryans (1953), who has published several studies on teacher characteristics, says: "Few, if any, statistically reliable findings have been reported that help to answer the question, 'What are effective teachers like'" (p. 379); and Getzels (1955), working in the same area, says: "It is a peculiar circumstance that, despite the critical importance of the problem and a half-century of prodigious research effort, very little is known for certain about the nature, measurement and prediction of teacher effectiveness" (p. 427).

Anyone attempting to isolate the characteristics of good teachers must have some notion as to how to measure good teaching and how to measure the personality characteristics that will distinguish good from poor teachers. A teacher's effectiveness may be *rated* by the administrator, the supervisor, or the pupils; or it may be *inferred* from his success in bringing about changes of various kinds in the pupils. All these criteria have been used. In some studies, both administrators and supervisors agreed in their ratings of teacher efficiency. There was even more consistency among the thousands of pupils who rated their teachers. Yet, in the studies reported so far, these criteria did not lead to a valid distinction of the personality characteristics of good and poor, effective and ineffective teachers. Ryans claims that the validity of our opinions about teaching cannot be readily tested because there is little understanding and no adequate measurement technique of teacher effectiveness. In spite of these failures, it is safe to say that the differences are there. If they have not been discovered, perhaps the devices used to measure effectiveness in teaching or the personality variables selected for measurement have not been adequate.

In her doctoral dissertation, Burkard (1958) attacked the problem from a new angle. For her criterion of teacher effectiveness, she accepted the rating of teachers by pupils, which has been shown to be both consistent and reliable,* as sufficient.

---

* See Amatora (1954); Beecher (1949); Bryan (1937); Bush (1954); Davis (1924); Hart (1934); Tiedeman (1942); Witty (1950).

But, in measuring the personality characteristics of good and poor teachers, she departed from the usual techniques. Neither personality inventories nor attitude scales seemed to be particularly useful, because they do not give a measure of the teacher's motivation; yet it is this area that seems to be decisive for success in teaching. The TAT sequence analysis provided the required measure of motivation.

Burkard used the Diagnostic Teacher Rating Scale Form A, developed by M. Amatora (1950), as her rating instrument for teacher efficiency. The scale consists of a short form called the Area Scale which includes seven divsions: (1) liking the teacher; (2) teacher's ability to explain; (3) kindness, friendliness and understanding; (4) fairness in grading; (5) discipline; (6) amount of work required; (7) liking for lesson. The pupils rate the teacher on each area on a five-point scale. Following this is a diagnostic check list consisting of 49 scaled statements, arranged in seven intra-scales of seven items each. These items are scaled in turn, so that their value extends from highest to lowest, with the fourth item at the midpoint.

In a preliminary study, Burkard tested the scale developed for elementary school pupils as to its validity for secondary school students. One hundred forty-six high school students were asked to rank 34 characteristics of teachers in the order of their importance. Half of these items were taken from Amatora's Diagnostic Teacher Rating Scale Form A, the other half from other rating scales which had been prepared specially for high school students. Of the 17 items taken from Amatora's scale, the 13 that seemed of top importance to these high school students were ranked in the upper half of the list. Included in these 13 items were all of the broad items of the Area Scale. Thus, Amatora's scale seemed to be adequate for both high school students and elementary school pupils and was used exclusively. This facilitated the comparison of teacher ratings.

The teachers were drawn from fourteen schools staffed by a Catholic community of Sisters in four Midwestern states. To avoid bias, only those schools were chosen where the teaching staff decided to participate as a group. Because of the placement methods used in this community of Sisters, any teacher may be stationed at any of their schools. No factor other than availability and need determined which teachers belonged to the faculties of the participating schools.

The sample consisted of 300 teachers, of whom 150 were teaching in grades four through eight, and 150 in grades nine through twelve. These teachers ranged in age from 20 to 68 years and had from one to forty-eight years of teaching experience. The median age of the elementary group was 41.5, of the secondary school group, 47.5.

TESTING THE TEACHERS

Since preliminary studies had shown that it is not necessary to use 20 cards to arrive at a motivational pattern, 12 cards were used (1, 2, 3BM, 4, 5, 6BM, 7BM, 8BM, 9BM, 10, 16, 11, in that order). Since the sequence analysis is based on the scoring of story imports which contain plot and outcome, it is desirable to have the stories short and to the point without the irrelevant elaboration and even disorganization that often is the result of asking someone to *tell* a story. For this reason, the TAT was given as a group test, with groups ranging from two to twenty-three, according to circumstances. The cards were numbered and displayed in the above order. The teachers wrote the stories in two sessions, each session varying according to individual needs from 55 to 95 minutes. The standard directions of Murray were given with emphasis on writing a story that contains a plot and an outcome. Each teacher was asked to write age, number of years of teaching experience, and highest degree on the face sheet. The papers were identified only by a number drawn by the teacher.

THE INTELLIGENCE TEST

To see whether more intelligent teachers were rated more favorably by their pupils, the Otis Intelligence Test was given to the 300 teachers. The median Gamma I.Q. of this sample was found to be 109.5.* The median of the grade school group was 108.2, while that of the high school group was 110.6. In the group of high school teachers, there was a significant correlation between I.Q. and the pupil ratings to question 2 (How clearly can your teacher explain things?) of .44 ± .09, and between I.Q. and question 6 (Does your teacher give the right amount of work to do?) of .33 ± .09 (significant on the 1 percent level). No correlation was found between pupil ratings and teachers' I.Q. in the group of elementary teachers, though the I.Q.'s of the high-rated group were consistently somewhat higher. It was also found that the younger teachers made significantly higher intelligence scores than the older teachers, both in grade and secondary schools. This difference may be attributed at least partly to the fact that the younger teachers were more "test wise" than the older teachers, for many of whom this was the first experience with any kind of test. It was also found that there was a tendency for the pupils to rate younger teachers higher, but this tendency was not statistically significant.

RATING OF TEACHERS BY PUPILS

The rating scale was given to each class in its own classroom. The teacher first informed the class that someone was coming to give them a questionnaire and assured them that nobody would know how they answered it. Each child received the number by which the teacher would be known; this number was written on the questionnaire. The teacher divided her

---

* Gamma I.Q.'s above 100 are generally lower than I.Q.'s derived from other measures. This is particularly true on the higher levels. The highest possible I.Q. on the Otis Test is 138.

class into thirds according to school grades, and gave each pupil one of three code letters which would indicate to the experimenter (but not to the children) in which third a pupil ranked.

The second part of the scale, the Diagnostic Check List, was answered first. The pupils marked each one of the 49 items they considered true of their teacher. In the fourth and fifth grades, the scale was read aloud; in all grades, any words that seemed difficult were explained. After the 49 items were checked, the pupils were told to arrange the seven areas of the Area Scale in the order in which they thought their teacher was "good in them." After this preliminary ranking, they had a fairly clear understanding of what each area implied and were now ready to answer Part I of the scale, the Area Scale, which was the only part to be used. This scale consists of the seven questions mentioned above. The instructions asked each pupil to rate his or her teacher from 1 to 5. For each question, he had to compare the teacher with all the other teachers he had ever had. If the teacher is the best he ever had, he was instructed to put a ring around number 5; if the worst, to put a ring around 1; if the teacher is just about in the middle, to put a ring around number 3; and so on. The finished sheets were put in an envelope, sealed, and taken by one of the children to the principal's office to be added to the questionnaires from all the other classes. In this way, complete anonymity of teachers and students was preserved.

In both grade and secondary school there was a much closer relationship between question 1—"How well do you like this teacher?"—and questions 2, 3, and 7, than there was between question 1 and the other three questions. This seems to show that the teacher's kindness and friendliness (3), the way she taught her lessons (7), and her ability to explain (2) had more bearing on the children's liking for her than her fairness in marking (4), her discipline (5) and the amount of work she gave (6). This was particularly true in high school. Since questions 4 and 6 were difficult to interpret because different schools have different customs of grading and assigning work, Burkard decided to use only the remaining five questions as basis for rating the teachers' effectiveness.

TECHNIQUE OF MATCHED PAIRS

In comparing the sequence analysis scores and the ratings, several problems had to be solved. In the first place, both intelligence and age seemed to be a factor in the ratings. Second, it was important to isolate differences between good and poor teachers that were significant enough to show up easily. To make such differences visible, Burkard decided to select two samples of 50 teachers each, who were paired on the basis of intelligence test scores and age; the one sample to be selected from the highest third of all teachers rated high by their pupils, and the other sample to consist of teachers in the lowest third of the group rated low by their pupils.

In addition to age and intelligence, several other factors were considered in the pairing of the samples. To offset differences in rating between pupils from different schools, the pairs were, whenever possible, taken from the same school or at least from the same type of school (same size, location, population). All pairs came from the same grade group and, in high schools, from the same subject or kind of subject. The high and low samples thus appeared to be as alike as possible in the controlled variables and as different as possible in the independent variable to be used as outside criterion: Pupils' ratings.

CRITERIA FOR SCORING OF SEQUENCE ANALYSIS

Since this was one of the first studies that attempted to *score* the sequence analysis for positive or negative attitudes, it was important to work out adequate scoring criteria. It was not immediately certain that the scoring criteria developed by Mc-

Candlish for high school students would be appropriate for teachers.

Ten high-rated teachers and their low-rated paired match from the group of secondary teachers were compared for their story imports. It was soon found that a certain constructive attitude was running through the sequence analyses of the high-rated group, while the low-rated group had attitudes that could be clearly distinguished from their constructive counterparts. On the basis of these differences, two opposing classes of possible imports were built up; one represented the attitudes of the high-rated group, and the other, those of the low-rated group. The former imports were scored as plus, the latter as minus. The areas in which these attitudes could be scored were tentatively set up as follows: Success, Failure, Loss, Duties and obligations, and Relations with other people. It is interesting that these categories were substantially the same as those incorporated in our final set of scoring criteria, though every study attempted to find more adequate categories. The only improvement we were able to make was to combine Burkard's two categories (Success, Failure) into one (*Category I. Achievement, success, happiness, active effort* [*or lack of it*]) and to broaden her category of *Loss* into a general category of *Reaction to adversity;* a similar broadening accounts for the change of Burkard's category of *Duties and obligations* into our *Category II. Right and wrong.*

On the basis of these criteria tentatively set up in each scoring area, Burkard undertook a trial test to see whether the same criteria would hold for elementary school teachers. Twenty records were selected at random from this group, without identifying either the ratings or the pairs. This attempt at prediction from the scoring criteria derived from the high school teachers' records was only partly successful. Though the same positive or negative attitudes were revealed in this group, the criteria were not clearly enough defined to make it possible to recognize such an attitude in every import or every sequence.

For this reason, this group was examined for the kind of statements that would characterize a positive or negative attitude, in the same way as the first sample of twenty records of high school teachers had been examined. The additional definitions of imports were now combined with the criteria derived from the high school group and constituted the scoring standard. This set of categorized statements was thus derived from 40 cases, 20 of which were elementary and 20 secondary school teachers. It is included in the scoring criteria given in the Appendix and need not be repeated here.

The sequence analyses of the remaining 60 teachers (30 matched pairs) were now scored according to these criteria. The teachers were not identified as to pairs or ratings. The number of plus signs in each sequence analysis were added and represented the final score.* Above a score of 6, a teacher was judged to be in the high-rated group because she had more plus than minus signs in the sequence of 12 stories; below this score, she was judged to be in the low-rated group. Only two teachers were assigned to the wrong group. When their sequence analyses were reexamined, it was found that they contained errors in imports. As soon as these were corrected, the two records plainly fell into the groups to which they actually belonged. The range of TAT scores was 8 to 12 for the high-rated group, 0 to 4 for the low-rated group. There were no scores between 4 and 8, for the middle range (200 teachers) had been excluded.

Two other examiners trained in this method of analysis and scoring, now scored the 100 sample protocols independently,

---

* Since the negative scores are always the obverse of the positive scores, they were disregarded to simplify the scoring. For instance, a record with 10 imports scored plus would have 2 imports scored minus out of the total of 12 imports. A record with 5 plus-imports would have 7 minus-imports. This method of scoring is convenient but narrows the range of possible scores. To preserve the total range, a scoring system was eventually worked out which uses the algebraic sum of scores, as described in Chapter 9.

and accurately placed every teacher into the high- or low-rated group in which she actually belonged. When the scoring on the 1,200 different stories was compared, judge *A* and judge *I* (*Investigator*) agreed in 97.2 percent of stories; judges *A* and *B* in 94.3 percent of stories; and judges *B* and *I* in 96.6 percent of stories (all significant beyond the 0.1 percent level of confidence).

To see which questions in the rating scale were most significant for the selection of teachers revealing positive attitudes in their story imports, Burkard now computed phi coefficients. The two TAT categories used were the number of teachers with low TAT scores from 0 to 4 and the number of teachers with high scores from 8 to 12. The ratings were dichotomized at the 50th percentile. Table I shows these correlations for the elementary and secondary school teachers rated by their pupils. The phi coefficients ranged from .37 to .96, all significant beyond the 1 percent level.* The lowest correlations of TAT scores were obtained with question 4 (fairness in marking) and question 6 (amount of work given), which justifies the decision of omitting these questions in combining the ratings. The only

TABLE 3. *Relationships (Phi coefficients) between TAT scores and ratings on the seven questions of the scale*

N	Level	Questions of rating scale						
		1	2	3	4	5	6	7
50	Elementary	.96	.85	.92	.69	.88	.68	.96
50	Secondary	.96	.81	.77	.41	.73	.37	.78

All coefficients are significant beyond the 1 percent level.

Questions: 1. How well do you like your teacher?
2. How clearly can your teacher explain things?
3. How kind, friendly, and understanding is your teacher?

* Burkard points out that phi coefficients are restricted in size and are, therefore, lower than Pearson's r's; and that the phi coefficients in this study are further reduced by the use of Yates' correction for continuity and thus may be considered conservative estimates.

4. How fair is your teacher in grading?
5. How well does your teacher keep order with the children?
6. Does your teacher give the right amount of work to do?
7. How well do you like the lessons taught by this teacher?

question that correlates highly with TAT scores both for secondary and elementary school pupils is question 1 (How well do you like your teacher?) which has a phi coefficient of .96. All other questions show a drop in correlation from elementary to high school students. Apparently, for the high school students, the teacher's ability to explain (2), the students' liking for lessons (7), the teacher's kindness and understanding (3), and the discipline she insisted on (5) played a progressively smaller role in judging her a good teacher; while it is safe to say that the better the teacher, the better she is liked.

It could be argued, of course, that the causal relation is the reverse: that the better a teacher is liked, the more highly do students rate her teaching. Accordingly, the positive attitudes of high-rated teachers as revealed in the TAT scores would distinguish the teachers who are best liked. But for one thing, the only way a teacher can make school interesting for children is to teach well. Sheer personal liking may stimulate interest in the classes she teaches, but such liking would never survive consistent boredom with the subject matter. Since positive attitudes as revealed in story imports also distinguish those who are successful in other types of jobs, whether they are students, Navy men, executives, or members of a religious order (see Chapters 11 to 14), sheer liking cannot be the explanation of achievement in these areas. People with positive motivation may also be well liked, but they seem to be well liked because they have constructive attitudes; they do not have such attitudes because they are well liked.

11

PERSONALITY DIFFERENCES BETWEEN OFFENDERS AND NON-OFFENDERS

Once it had been found that differences in personality, specifically differences in motivation, allow a correct prediction of high and low achievement among high school students, and of good and poor teaching among elementary and secondary school teachers, it seemed advisable to leave the area of student and teacher performance and see whether the same test would also indicate motivation that is unrelated to school achievement.

In his doctoral dissertation, Petrauskas (1958) proposed to investigate the motivational characteristics that distinguish enlisted Navy men who at some time or other have been confined to the brig from those who have never been so disciplined. The subjects used in his study consisted of two groups of enlisted men. Group I, the experimental group, was composed of thirty men who were confined in the naval brig for violations of the Military Code of Justice and were awaiting court-martial. Except for two men who were involved in more serious difficulties, all were confined for being absent without leave (AWOL) on at least two occasions. All these men had a history of more or less serious delinquency before enlistment. Thus, all the men in the experimental group had difficulties in "social adjustment" both before and during military service. Group II, the control group, was composed of thirty enlisted men attending the various Navy service schools. None had a history of delinquency before enlistment, and none was disciplined in any way while in the Navy. The men in the experimental group were paired with men in the control group on the basis of age, General Classification Test score (which is the intelligence test used in the Navy), place of residence (whether city or country), and length of service.

All men were white. The mean age level for both experimental and control groups was 19.1 years. The mean General Classification Test (GCT) score was 53.5 for the experimental group and 54.2 for the control group. A score of 54 on the GCT approximates a Wechsler-Bellevue score of 106. In length of service, the brig population had a mean of 18.2 months and the service school personnel of 19 months. Since longer service means more time to get into trouble, the small difference in service is in favor of the experimental group.

Preliminary studies had shown that 12 TAT cards are sufficient to reveal an individual's motivational pattern. Accordingly, Petrauskas used a shortened version of the TAT, consisting of the most dramatic cards, namely, the cards that make storytelling easy. All these cards are included in the set used for men. To make sure that there would always be a clear majority of either positive or negative scores, Petrauskas used 13 cards (1, 2, 3, 4, 6, 7, 8, 11, 13, 14, 16, 17, 20, in that order). The men were shown these cards in sequence and given the standard instructions, emphasizing that they should tell stories with a plot and outcome. They worked in small groups and wrote down each story before being shown the next card. After finishing the set, they were given the Rosenzweig Picture-Frustration Test. The entire testing procedure took approximately an hour and thirty minutes. After the test, each man in the experimental group was interviewed to verify the reason for his confinement in the brig and to obtain his social history before enlistment.

When the test records for the thirty matched pairs were completed, ten pairs were selected at random to establish the scoring criteria. To get reliable differences between the two groups, Petrauskas felt that the scoring criteria would have to be more lenient than those for predicting high and low achievement or teaching effectiveness. It requires better motivation, a more constructive attitude, to reach a high level of achievement than merely to conform sufficiently to keep out of the brig. For this reason, he had to check the scoring criteria developed in McCandlish's earlier study against the actual imports of offenders and non-offenders.

The categories he employed were practically the same as those used by McCandlish and Burkard. They were: (1) attitude toward self and others; (2) attitude toward work and success; (3) attitude toward problems; (4) attitude toward external forces; (5) attitude toward duties and obligations. After working out the sequence analysis, each story in the sequence was scored according to these categories as either plus or minus. After the scoring criteria were defined in detail on the basis of the ten pairs of records, all identifying marks were removed, and they were mixed in with the other twenty pairs. Now all the protocols were coded numerically and scrambled.

All sixty records were now analyzed. After the sequence analyses were written out, the scoring criteria worked out before, now served as guide in scoring each import as plus or minus. When all sixty records had been scored by the experimenter, two copies of the sequence analyses of the sixty sets were typed on work sheets, together with the original stories and the scoring criteria, and submitted to two other psychologists for independent scoring. These scorers were instructed to refer to the original stories whenever they were in doubt. From the sixty records, one matched pair was removed before shuffling and used as an example of the scoring procedure for the two scorers who were unfamiliar with this group. This pair was not included in the statistical analysis of the differences between the two groups.

Interjudge reliability was determined by calculating the percentage of agreement between the three raters. In scoring the stories as positive or negative, rater *A* and rater *B* agreed on 82 percent or 616 stories; rater *A* and rater *C* agreed on 80 percent or 600 stories; raters *B* and *C* agreed on 607 or slightly in excess of 80 percent of the stories. All three raters agreed on the same sign for a story import in 70 percent of the cases. Contingency coefficients were calculated to measure the significance and extent of the relation between the ratings of the three judges. All of the chi-square values obtained in the computation of these coefficients (.54 for raters *A* and *B*, .51 for raters *A* and *C*, .52 for raters *B* and *C*) are significant well beyond the 1 percent level. The percent agreement among the raters, and the contingency coefficients reflect a moderate degree of reliability in scoring the story imports as plus and minus.

Applying the criteria established for this group, rater *A* scored all sixty records correctly, that is, he identified all offenders and non-offenders. Rater *B*, who had only one sample each of an offender's and a non-offender's record together with the description of the categories, but did not have the opportunity to practice by scoring the ten criterion pairs, identified 48 out of 58 records correctly. Rater *C*, with the same handicap as rater *B*, but a different pair of records as sample, identified 50 out of 58 records correctly. Thus, all three raters were successful far beyond chance in distinguishing the records of offenders from those of non-offenders.

Finally, Petrauskas used a composite rating of each sequence analysis; the sign (plus or minus) common to any two of the three raters was taken as the final score for a particular story import. When this was done, 27 out of the group of 29 offenders obtained more negative scores than the non-offenders. One of the remaining two offenders apparently had had a change of heart (before the TAT was given). In the interview that followed the test, he said he had learned his lesson and was going to do better from now on. His positive score on the TAT sequence analysis seems to be an indication that he was serious. For the composite rating the Wilcoxon matched-pairs signed-ranks statistical test yielded a *t* value of 6.5 which, when transformed, resulted in a *z* score of —4.47. The probability that

TABLE 4. *Distribution of plus and minus scores for thirty offenders and thirty non-offenders on 13 TAT stories*

		1	2	3	4	6	7	8	11	13	14	16	17	20
								TAT card #						
Offenders	+	2	8	4	3	4	4	6	3	1	7	7	7	5
	—	28	22	26	27	26	26	24	27	29	23	23	23	25
Non-offenders	+	21	25	21	25	23	26	24	16	13	16	24	26	18
	—	9	5	9	5	7	4	6	14	17	14	6	4	12

such an extreme score will occur by chance is .00003, and consequently can be disregarded for practical purposes. The accompanying Table 4 gives the distribution of plus and minus scores as derived from the judgment of rater *A* who possessed the most extensive experience with the method as applied to this particular group.

In considering this distribution, we must remember that the chances that a story will be scored plus is equal for any TAT card. There is no card which would compel or even incline a person to tell a positive story rather than a story which will be scored as minus. Even though the picture provides the story theme, the scoring depends not on the theme but on the storyteller's attitudes as revealed in the story imports. Instead of the equal distribution of scores among all the cards as found by Fagot (see Chapter 9), this distribution shows a decided drop in positive attitudes for card 13. Stories told about this card by non-offenders (the "high" group in this study) actually receive more minus than plus scores; and receive minus scores in the records of all but one of the offenders. This seems to indicate a rather prevalent negative motivation in sexual matters among this group: stories to card 13, particularly among this group, talk almost without exception about sexual themes; non-offenders also tell many negative stories to cards 11, 14, and 20 (stories to card 11 usually give some indication of a person's outlook on life; card 14 frequently reveals the story-teller's attitude to his daily tasks, and card 20 may betray his general expectations, i.e., what he is waiting for).* The fact that stories about card 11 earn almost as many negative as positive scores among the non-offenders may mean that this group does not have a very positive outlook on life. Apparently, they do not feel very positively about the daily routine (card 14) nor about their expectations (card 20). These rather frequent negative attitudes coupled with the fact that Petrauskas' positive scores were more lenient than the scoring used for other groups would suggest that the non-offenders in this group would not necessarily be high achievers.

Finally, Petrauskas compared the effectiveness of the TAT sequence analysis with that of the Rosenzweig Picture-Frustration (P-F) Test. When each offender was matched with a non-offender, 21 out of 29 offenders obtained a higher score on the P-F test (i.e., showed more "aggression") than the paired non-offenders. But, several of the offenders had a lower score than some of the non-offenders. When a cutoff point was established below which most of the men would conform to the rules (hence be non-offenders), 18 P-F scores exceeded the cutoff point, of which 14 belonged to offenders and 4 to non-offenders. Forty-two cases fell below the cutoff point, of which 26 belonged to non-offenders and 16 to offenders. While the differences between offenders and non-offenders on the P-F test

---

* Murray's description of these cards: 11. A road skirting a deep chasm between high cliffs. On the road in the distance are obscure figures. Protruding from the rock on one side is the long head and neck of a dragon; 13. A young man is standing with downcast head buried in his arm. Behind him is the figure of a woman lying in bed; 14. The silhouette of a man (or woman) against a bright window. The rest of the picture is totally black; 20. The dimly illuminated figure of a man (or woman) in the dead of night leaning against a lamppost.

are statistically significant at the .001 level, no more than 40 out of 60 cases could have been predicted correctly. In contrast, the best trained judge (*A*) predicted 40 out of 40 cases correctly from the scores of the sequence analyses, while the composite scores of all three judges predicted 54 out of 58 cases correctly. Since the P-F test is supposed to test aggression and there is no particular reason to suppose that going AWOL is exclusively the result of anger or aggression, this difference in predictive power is not unexpected.

Perhaps a word should be said about Petrauskas' scoring procedure. He used ten criterion pairs for determining which imports were to be scored plus and which minus. Imports derived from stories of the ten non-offenders were scored plus, and imports derived from stories of the ten offenders were scored minus. This made it necessary at least in some instances to make the rules for scoring *plus* less rigorous than those used for high achievers or effective teachers. This procedure is defensible if the only intention is to discriminate between two extremes, namely, the group of offenders and non-offenders. However, this change would account for the lower reliability of the two outside scorers who had been trained in the standard procedure. With only one pair of records to check their scoring and change it to accommodate the particular objective of this study, it is surprising that they did as well as they did. Today we would not recommend changing the scoring criteria to accommodate a particular group. Instead, we would recommend that all the records be scored according to the scoring criteria provided in the Appendix. Some groups may earn higher scores than others, but there should always be sufficient distance between the low and high members of that group to give a good discrimination. It is desirable, however, to score at least a few records of known high and low raters in groups that are markedly different from the groups we have tested thus far. In this way, the scorer will familiarize himself with the particular trends of attitudes in his group. One group, for instance, may give a high proportion of "Pollyanna" stories, as did Burkard's group (Chapter 10); another may tell many dialogue stories, as did one of Quinn's groups (see Chapter 13); still another group may go in for spoofing by telling outrageous stories, as did another of Quinn's groups.

If all records are scored according to the same scoring criteria, the scorer will soon develop a feeling for the nuances of the import and the scoring category where he can look up the import. Even more important, he will develop confidence in his scoring and will soon be able to score any record, coming from any group, with a high degree of accuracy.

12

MOTIVATION AND SCHOOL ACHIEVEMENT

Up to this point, the TAT sequence analysis had yielded predictions of high or low achievement in high school, and effectiveness and in teaching for elementary and secondary school teachers, *when the midrange was excluded.* This restriction of the total range was necessary to develop a system of scoring criteria that would clearly indicate positive and negative attitudes. But, now it seemed that the scoring criteria developed on the basis of records from the extreme ends of the distribution were consistent enough to try out on the total range.

COLLEGE STUDENTS

Accordingly, Garvin (1960) tested a group of seniors at two neighboring institutions, one a men's college, the other a women's college. A total of 50 men and 50 women were tested, but some of the records had to be discarded for one reason or another; mostly because the test was incomplete or the student had obviously misunderstood the instructions. This left a total of 46 men and 45 women. Thirteen cards from the set for men were used: 1, 2, 3, 4, 6, 7, 8, 10, 11, 13, 16, 18, 20, and projected via positive transparencies. Each story was written by the subject himself.

For the men, Garvin obtained the grade point average (GPA) for the first semester of their junior year; for the women, he worked out a quotient by dividing the number of semester hours accumulated during the three previous academic years by the number of honor points earned during that time. This quotient gives a figure analogous to a grade point average for each student. The two groups, men and women, were kept separate for all statistical calculations. As a measure of intelligence, Garvin used the American Council on Education intelligence test 1952 (ACE) scores for each student, whenever available. In this study, two positive and two negative scores instead of a simple minus or plus, were used for the first time. Since the total range was to be used rather than the upper and lower extremes, it was imperative to distinguish between imports that were barely positive or negative and those that were strongly so.

In this study, strongly negative imports were given a score of 1, mildly negative, a score of 2, while mildly positive imports were scored 3, and strongly positive imports, 4.* When the scores for all imports are added, and divided by the number of stories obtained, the raw score for the record will be a number between 1 and 4, with any score below 2 indicating negative, and any score above 2 indicating positive motivation. This manner of scoring was eventually abandoned because unscorable records could not be fitted into this scheme. If they are given a score of zero, it would make them more negative than stories that actually reveal strongly negative motivation—and that cannot be justified. If they were given a score of 2.5, as the score lying between negative and positive, they would actually be within the positive range. In Garvin's study, this difficulty was avoided by eliminating unscorable stories and dividing by the number of scorable stories; when a record contained more than two unscorable stories, it was discarded.

Results: Our method of scoring the TAT sequence analysis proved highly effective for the prediction of college achievement. The correlation coefficients between grade point average

---

* It is obvious that the scores of 1, 2, 3, and 4 used in this study represent the scores of −2, −1, +1, and +2, in that order.

(college achievement) and TAT scores (motivation) were .85 for men and .83 for women. They are considerably higher than the correlation between grade point average and intelligence (r .63 for men, r .50 for women). The multiple correlation of grade point average, TAT scores and intelligence test (ACE) scores adds little to the correlation obtained between grade point average and TAT scores (R .87 for men, R .84 for women). The coefficients obtained are shown in Table 5.

TABLE 5 *Coefficients of correlation between TAT scores, grade point averages and intelligence test (ACE) scores*

	GPA	ACE	GPA + ACE
TAT (college men)	.850	.582	.865
(college women)	.832	.470	.841
(seventh graders)	.750	.468	.835

By means of a multiple regression equation, the most likely grade point average for any combination of TAT and ACE scores obtained by each student can easily be predicted. Since the three factors are interrelated, an index number can be found that will show the amount of relationship between school achievement and the other two variables combined. This index cannot be simply the sum of the separate correlations but will be the coefficient of multiple correlation (see above). The percentage contributions of TAT scores to the predicted grade point average was calculated as 62.4 for men and 63.9 for women; of the ACE scores, as 12.4 for men, and 6.8 for women. By using the formula for the standard error of estimate from multiple predictions, Garvin found that the predicted grade point averages will deviate from those obtained in his sample by .22 for men, and by .21 for women. About two thirds of the obtained grade point averages will lie within .22 or .21 grade points of those predicted. This can now be expressed in graphic form (see Figure 1).

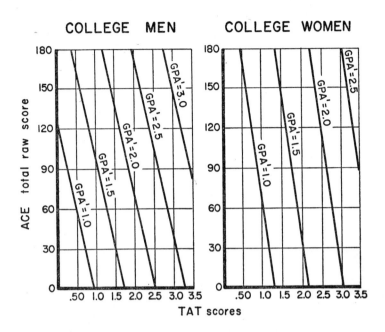

FIGURE 1. *Constant values of predicted Grade Point Average for different combinations of TAT and ACE score, with appropriate weights.*

Now let us see how these graphs can be used. If a male college student (in the same college) has an ACE score of 82 and a TAT score of 3.5 (according to Garvin's scoring), he is likely to have a grade point average of 3. If he has a TAT score of 3.5, he has strongly positive motivating attitudes and so could be counted on to obtain a grade well beyond the grades usually obtained by students of his intelligence level whose motivation is merely average. In contrast, an intelligent student with an ACE score of 140 would obtain a grade point average of only 1.5 if he has strongly negative attitudes, as represented by a TAT score of about 0.66. This combination of high intelligence and negative motivation may account for the poor performance of some bright students who obtain failing grades in college despite high test intelligence.

For the men studied here, a grade point average of 4 corresponds to an A average, a grade point average of 3, to a B. The letter grade of C corresponds to a grade point average of 2, and a grade of D, to a grade point average of 1. For the women students, a letter grade of A corresponds to a grade point average of 3, B corresponds to 2, and C, to 1. Since the two groups had different numerical means, the graphs had to be adjusted accordingly.

SEVENTH GRADE CHILDREN

To investigate the relation between school achievement, motivation, and intelligence at a lower level of schooling, we decided to test a class of seventh grade children (52), using cards 1, 2, 3BM, 4, 6BM, 7BM, 8, 11, 13B, 16, 14, in that order. We found that most of the children were able to write scorable stories, although a few of them left out one or the other story or started to write a few words and then went on to the next story. One record with several stories missing was discarded. This left 51 scorable records.

Since it might be interesting to compare the records of children with those of adult high and low achievers, we are quoting two children's records. We did not try to match them for intelligence because we would like to give an example of one of the best and one of the worst records.* The first record is that of a girl:

Record #19 (I.Q. 129, Grade point average 3.80)

[Card 1] I know a story of a poor boy who wanted badly to play the violin. His father thought it a waste of money but his mother finally helped the boy to change his father's mind. After he received his violin he worked hard and studied his music every day. He worked so long and so hard that his father was starting to

* Spelling and punctuation have been corrected but the word order is unchanged.

disapprove, for his father owned a grocery store. His father finally forbade it; well, the boy took it so hard that the father gave the violin back to the boy. As he grew older he began to become famous, and at the age of 25 he was playing at an opera house. He played so well, he was contracted for a large sum of money and he gave the money to his family to live on and they all lived together happily, father, mother, son, and violin.

[Card 2 was skipped because the child wanted to finish the first story, which apparently was close to her heart.]

[Card 3] A boy who was forced to protect his family from a group of Nazi soldiers in Hungary sits upon the floor sadly as he thinks of the soldier he shot at and killed. Although he is sad and he feels guilty of a death he still knows that it was a just killing and that he saved his family.

[Card 4] A young woman loves this one man and he, too, loves her, but he fears that once they get married that she will turn away from him after she finds out that once he was in prison for a robbery; although he was innocent he could not prove so. But she shows him she is and always will be faithful to him, and they marry and live together for many happy years.

[Card 6] A sad old woman stands there sadly as she watches her only son walking out of the house for good. Her son was always good and kind to her until he got involved with a gang of hoodlums. Now he is cold and she feels as if he were a stranger to her. But after he grows older, he will realize his fault and come back to his beloved mother.

[Card 7] An older bank owner who is now retired is helping his young successor with a grave problem of keeping the bank open, for the young man had made a very bad mistake, and he was now sorry, and he was paying a great debt for his wrong. But he will solve his own problem by praying, and he will surely pay his debt to humanity by his sorrow.

[Card 8] This young boy is standing in between two fields he loves, the field of medicine and he wants to serve his country as best as he can. Some day, though, he will study both fields thoroughly and will decide to become a doctor, and he will be a fine one.

[Card 11] Ten men, some old and some young, had dared to explore the Grand Canyon and the great Colorado River. These men will fight the rapids, the high and the low waters; some will lose their life, but those who survive will map and follow the river to its mouth, and they will some day all become famous.

[Card 13] During the days of log cabins, there was not much for young children to do. This little boy is dreaming of becoming a great frontiersman and of clearing the way for pioneers, and some day his dream will come true, for he will grow up to be Daniel Boone.

[Card 16] I can see a boy of about ten years old standing on a fence, trying to reach an apple which is hanging on the neighbor's tree. He is just about six inches too short, and he will not succeed. Instead, he will ask the neighbor man for an apple, and he will receive it, and right then he will learn, "Honesty is the best policy."

[Card 14] This is a picture of a young artist who is looking out the window and who can see down below him the trees and the flowers which seem to bounce at him as a reflection of the blue bright sky. As he watches he realizes the genius mind it took to create this most beautiful sight. Here he realizes that life is just another gift of God and that his life is to be God's. He is going to make his work God's work.

These are the imports:

1. When you have your heart set on an ideal, you work at it with such enthusiasm that you may get into trouble with those who do not understand. However, in the end you succeed and share your success with them.   [+2, I.B.1.a.]

2. (skipped)

3. In trying to do your duty, you may have to hurt others which makes you sad though you know you have done the right thing.   [+2, III.A.4.b.]

4. There is always the fear that others will turn away from you if they hear libelous stories about you; but you are innocent, and they will prove faithful.   [+2, III.A.2.a.]

6. Bad influence may estrange young people from those who love them. But as the young mature, they will realize their fault and return.   [+2, III.C.3.a.]

7. Young people may make a bad mistake but they are paying for it, and will make up for it with the help of those more experienced. [+2, II.A.1.a.]

8. When you are torn between two fields of interest, you will study both and then decide on one and do a fine job.

[+2, I.A.1.a.]

11. Men may have to struggle against difficulties, but those who survive will have done a good job and achieved fame as well. [+2, I.B.1.a.]

13. The young, however, who don't have much to do, can dream of achievement and one day their dream will come true. [—1, I.B.2.b.]

16. They will also learn that what they cannot achieve by dishonest effort, the kindness of others will provide for the asking. [+2, II.B.1.a.]

14. In the end they realize that life is just another gift of God and will make their work God's work. [+2, I.A.5.a.]

This child has a motivation index of 185 (on the basis of 10 stories, since one was omitted). A clinical evaluation shows immediately that even the one minus score does not detract from her entirely positive motivation. She accounts for the dream of achievement by saying that men can work—but children can only dream. Even at that, the little boy in the story dreams not of fame but of achievement. When we checked back with the teacher, she mentioned that this girl is the most reliable pupil in the class and can always be depended on to do something extra when needed.

The next record is that of a boy:

Record #20 (I.Q. 93, Grade point average 1.10)

[Card 1] He was thinking if he should take after his father or his grandfather. His father was a violinist and his grandfather was a great baseball player. I guess he'll take baseball.

[Card 2] I think they are going to a school in Asia or some place with the books and the lady is the teacher admiring the new schoolhouse being built and it was a success.

[Card 3] This boy looks like he killed one of his best friends or a parent by accident and he is crying and soon will get a doctor and everything will be O. K.

[Card 4] I think the man is married to the woman and he is trying to leave her but she don't want him to go but I think he will go.

[Card 6] I think the man is the lady's son and the man told his mother he was married and his mother didn't want him to get married and they made an agreement before he was married that he wouldn't get married until she died.

[Card 7] That man is staring at the boy as if he looked the same when he was a younger man.

[Card 8] The boy in the picture looks like it is one of his friends or parents getting operated on and won't get better.

[Card 11] It looks like a landslide and it fell on some people and killed them.

[Card 13] He is probably waiting for a friend to come over and play with him and he will be there any minute and he will come.

[Card 16] This is the family of the Joneses who live in Africa and there on the first floor somebody yelled "there is a fungus among us," and they ran on in the jungle and someone else said, "there's a rumble in the jungle," so they ran up in the attic and someone yelled, "there's a static in the attic" and they all went back to the United States and they lived happily ever after.

[Card 14] He looks like he is going to run away because he got punished but as he went he started to get hungry, so he started back for home, climbed back in the window and went to sleep and his mother didn't know it.

Here are the imports with their scoring:

1. You wonder whom to take as your model, the artist or the athlete, and you decide for the latter.   [—1, I.A.1.c.]

2. It is only the teachers who admire educational success.
          [—2, I.B.6.c.]

3. You can do nothing but cry when you destroy your friends by accident—though others will see to it that everything is O.K.
          [—2, IV.A.5.d.]

4. You owe them your loyalty but you turn away from them all the same; [—2, II.A.4.]

6. and though you have made an agreement, you can break it any time, [—2, II.A.4.]

7. knowing that others were like you when they were young. [—2, II.A.3.e.]

8. Your friends are doomed, [—2, III.F.2.b.]

11. Nature itself is destroying them; [—2, III.F.2.b.]

13. but when you want them, you only have to wait, they'll come. [—2, III.F.5.a.i.]

16. And when somebody cries havoc everywhere you go, you can always come back here and live happily ever after. [—1, IV.A.1.a.]

14. If you are punished, you may try running away—and when you need to, you can always come back with no one the wiser. [—2, II.C.1.c.]

This set of imports is almost a textbook example of the way a child who has a behavior disorder looks at the world. The boy has no notion of loyalty even to friends, who really seem more objects than people to him. He thinks they are doomed, anyway, but will come when he wants them. If he gets into trouble elsewhere, he can always come back home. The teacher, whom we consulted after this sequence analysis was done, said that this boy is very difficult in school and has to sit by himself because he disturbs the other children. In the teacher's opinion, he is cut out for a delinquent career. Unfortunately, there is little in the sequence analysis to disagree with her. The boy's M.I. is 9.

STATISTICAL RESULTS

Most of the story imports of these seventh grade children could be scored without difficulty on the basis of our scoring criteria (see Appendix A), though a few divisions had to be added. These additions, not found in adult records, are marked with an asterisk. The final (consistency) scores of these records were transformed into Motivation Index values according to the tables in Chapter 9.

The correlations we obtained are quite comparable to those reported by Garvin; we have added them to Garvin's coefficients in Table 5. Our grade point average was computed from the final grades for the year. Our correlation between M.I. (derived from TAT scores) and grade point average is .75, as compared with Garvin's correlations of .85 for college men and .83 for college women. The multiple correlation between grade point average, motivation (M.I.) and intelligence (Otis I.Q.) is .84 for the seventh grade children; Garvin's correlations are .87 for college men, .84 for college women. In spite of the fact that Garvin used average TAT scores as indicators of motivation and ACE scores as indicators of intelligence, the relative influence of these indicators on the grade point average is the same as of the indicators used by us.

When we attempted to predict * the grade point average of twelve individual children in our sample, using the formulae used by Garvin, we found an average error of .363 grade points. With a larger sample, it would seem possible to predict the grade points to be achieved by a child in a given school when the I.Q. and the M.I. are known. It would be easy to work out a graph which allows such prediction by inspection. But, it would seem preferable to do that for each school in which this prediction is to be used, so as to be sure that the basis of grading is the same.

INFLUENCE OF MOTIVATION ON SCHOOL ACHIEVEMENT

Though the combined influence of motivation and intelligence on school achievement remains the same from elementary school to college, the relative influence of motivation increases while the influence of intelligence decreases. When

---

* Or, rather, postdict.

motivation is held constant, the correlation between grade point average and intelligence is r .55 for seventh grade children, but drops to r .37 for college men and r .22 for college women. This is accounted for by the fact that the college population is highly selected for intelligence. Our selection procedures for admission to college are designed to select almost exclusively for intelligence. The college entrance examination is usually given more weight than the judgment of the high school teacher. One can hear complaints from high school teachers every day that the student with a high score on the college entrance examination is accepted even though he may be erratic in his work and may never finish what he starts; while the hard-working, highly motivated student who has a lower score is excluded. Perhaps now that a method is available to test motivation, it will be possible to select students who are not only intelligent but also highly motivated, which would raise college standards materially. What class would not progress at double the rate if every student were eager to learn?

RELATION BETWEEN INTELLIGENCE AND MOTIVATION

The relation between intelligence test scores and TAT scores does not change materially in the years between elementary school and college (seventh graders r .47, college men r .58, college women r .47). At first blush, this seems rather curious. Does not increasing maturity make it easier to realize what is an effective course of action? But on reflection we find that "maturity" is primarily a matter of positive motivation and only secondarily a matter of increasing mental age. We mean by maturity that the self-centered motivation of the child is gradually replaced by a more goal-oriented, more socialized set of motives; and these are precisely the positive motives we find in high achievers, whether these are children or adults.

In considering how to account for the moderate correlation

between intelligence and motivation it might seem plausible to say that the story imports also test intelligence, at least to some extent. Do not intelligent people tell better sories than people with low intelligence, and do not adults tell better stories than children? True though that is, a better story does not necessarily earn a higher score on the basis of our scoring criteria. Some of our highly intelligent adults with negative motivation tell literate and amusing stories yet reveal negative motivating attitudes. And, some of the children in our sample tell comparatively poor stories, yet obtain positive scores. It is much more likely that the correlation between intelligence tests and the story sequence analysis is accounted for by a psychological capacity or capacities needed for both tests.

To answer the questions posed in an intelligence test or to tell stories, obviously requires that we remember pertinent facts and experiences; and memory has long been known to have a positive but fairly low relation to intelligence. But, there is another human function that is vitally necessary for answering questions on intelligence tests and for telling stories; namely, imagination. To give a logical answer to even the simplest question and to tell even the shortest story with plot and outcome, we need not only memory but imagination. While memory can help us to solve a problem by recalling the answer to similar problems, we need imagination to solve this particular problem, because a new problem is always a little different from problems we have solved in the past. Without imagination, we would merely repeat the old answer without ever being able to adjust it to the changed conditions of the problem as it is presented here and now: we would never be able to learn and never be able to solve today's problem.

It would not be at all surprising if the common factor in intelligence and motivation were the facility and control of imagination (which actually includes the ability to recall relevant memory images). Perhaps it will be possible at some later date to work out a scoring method to test such imaginative adequacy on the basis of stories and story sequences. At the present time, our aim has been to score *what* is being imagined rather than *how well* the story plot and outcome has been constructed. It seems likely that a score that would reveal the adequacy or facility of imagination would have to be based on stories rather than on story imports. In the attempt to abstract the convictions and attitudes revealed in the story, the uniqueness of the story is often missed and the felicity of organization and expression is neglected. If it should be possible to develop a score for facility and control of imagination, such a score might suitably complement intelligence test scores, which test imagination only in so far as it is put in the service of problem-solving. Once we have such complementary tests of imagination, we might be able to detect the highly creative as well as the strictly manipulative intelligence measured by our present intelligence tests. Even then it will require the additional measurement of positive or negative motivating attitudes if we want to predict a person's success in school or in life.

13

MOTIVATION IN HIGHLY DEMANDING VOCATIONS

For a vocation that demands a radical change in a man's circumstances—for instance, that of a missionary or a member of a religious order—it is particularly important to devise selection procedures which will discover potential misfits. Of course, most of the potential neurotics or even psychotics who may be attracted to these professions can be excluded by a screening test like the Minnesota Multiphasic Personality Inventory (MMPI). But there are many applicants who are normal enough but are not willing or do not have the necessary persistence to make the sacrifices required, once their first enthusiasm is past.

A test that reveals a person's motivation seems the logical choice for the selection of candidates to such vocations. Quinn (1961) decided to test young men who had been members of a religious order for several years, to see whether the TAT sequence analysis would make it possible to predict their promise for religious life. He was hoping that the motivational pattern of young men who had been in the order for some time might then serve to guide the selection procedure for those who intended entering the Order. His most difficult task was to find an accurate measure of "promise for religious life." The best measure, of course, would be the actual success or failure of candidates in their early years of preparation in the novitiate, and later in their life as members of a religious community. This, however, would require years of follow-up after the initial testing. Since both the initial testing of candidates and the later follow-up would require that the Order be convinced of the value of such a procedure, Quinn decided on a preliminary study which would check the TAT scores against the judgment of superiors and fellow students.

Forty-five young men who had taken temporary vows but were still studying in the Scholasticate were given the TAT (20 cards, men's set) with the explicit instructions to write a story with plot and outcome. As his outside criterion, Quinn used ranking by superiors and ranking by fellow-scholastics. Superiors and fellow-students were asked "to evaluate the promise each [student] shows for future success in the Institute." By an ingenious method, each scholastic was assured complete anonymity, both in taking the test and in ranking his fellows. We quote this procedure, as outlined by Quinn (1961):

After a [student] had written his stories, he was given a stack of forty-nine cards that were perforated horizontally through the middle. Below the perforated line on each card there was a space indicated in which the subject could write his name; above the perforated line in the left hand corner of the card there was an identifying number printed on each card which was concealed by a removable plastic disc. Thus one [student] received a set of forty-nine cards with #17 printed in the upper left hand corner of each card. This number was, of course, neither visible to him nor to the investigator. Since each [student] actually drew his set of cards from a box containing all the sets, there was no way in which either the investigator or the individual [student] could know which number he had drawn on his set of cards.

Each [student] was instructed, after he had drawn his set of cards, to attach one of the cards to his set of TAT stories, to put one card in his pocket, and then to write his name on each of the other forty-seven cards. When he had done so, he gave the investigator his set of TAT stories and threw the forty-seven cards on which he had written his name into a box containing the cards from all the other subjects.

Once the investigator had received all of the TAT stories, he removed the seal from the card attached to each set of stories and wrote the concealed number on the corresponding set of stories. In this way each set of stories was marked with the author's identifying number. Then the investigator took all of the cards that had been thrown into the box by the subjects and which had a subject's name written on each of them, and rearranged them into forty-seven piles of forty-five cards. Each pile contained a card bearing the name of a different [student] who had taken the test [pp. 45-46].

Now two superiors and the forty-five students were instructed to select from his stack of forty-five names those nine students who should be retained by the Order under all circumstances and assign rank 5 to them; and the nine the Order could dispense with first, if necessary, and assign rank 1 to them. Next, he should select from the rest the nine least expendable (rank 4) and the nine most expendable (rank 2). In this way, a rank from 1 to 5 was assigned to each student, from most expendable to least expendable.

When the average ranks of the scholastics as given by their fellows were correlated with their scores on the TAT sequence analysis, a coefficient of .59 ± .10 was found; while their average rank as given by the superiors correlated with the TAT scores .61 ± .10. The correlation between the ranks given by superiors and the ranks given by fellow scholastics (r .65 ± .09) is not much higher than that obtained by correlating the TAT scores with the rankings given by either group. In spite of the fact that both the superiors and the fellow-scholastics were well acquainted with each student they ranked, the disagreement among them as to the rank to be assigned was quite marked. Most of the students complained that they had difficulties in assigning the middle ranks. We must realize, of course, that ranking for "promise in the Order" is not as easy (either for fellow-scholastics or for superiors) as assigning a grade to students on the basis of their actual performance in school or rating a teacher on the basis of her actual teaching.

To discover the reason for some of the discrepancies between the TAT scores and the rankings, Quinn was able to interview some of the students who had taken the test. This could be done because several scholastics were willing to identify their tests after the project had been completed. Among those that volunteered were three students (A, B, C), whose TAT scores placed them in the second highest rank, though they were actually ranked in the lowest group, by both peers and superiors; and student D, who was ranked high by both but scored low on the TAT sequence analysis.

Student A had left the Order six months after taking his TAT. From the sequence analysis, it was clear that he felt he was in the wrong place. Since the records were collected some months before they were analyzed and no clinical evaluation had been intended, this was not spotted at the time. Obviously, since the students had been promised anonymity, there was no point to a clinical evaluation of the records. This boy's record was given in full in Chapter 6 (record 13). Though it earned a positive score, the sequence analysis shows clearly that this student had been ill at ease for some time and wanted to go home to his old friends. Apparently, his dissatisfaction was sufficiently transparent to those who knew him that both his superiors and his fellow students detected it and gave him the lowest rank for "promise for religious life." However, his motivation is certainly positive. He shows willingness to work, decisiveness, positive attitudes toward others. His goal is not within the Order but outside it; but whatever his goal, his final score indicates that he will make an effort to strive for it.

Interestingly enough, the reformulated sequence has not materially changed the scoring, though it has made the clinical evaluation much easier. Quinn's final score is 3.05, which corresponds to a final score of +16 translated into our scoring. Most of the significant differences between his scores and ours (change of sign) are the result of inaccurate imports (e.g., 5, 7, 17). Our

final score according to the reformulated sequence analysis is
+10, which still is decidedly positive.

Scholastic B has many highly ambiguous stories in his record.
In these stories, the storyteller's attitude toward the hero's
action was in doubt much of the time. Many of the stories
could be interpreted either as mildly positive or mildly negative. In such cases, the trend of the imports is usually of help.
However, this record did not show much of a trend either.
Now that we have had more experience and have a fairly extensive set of criteria, we know that the very ambiguity of the
positive imports should have given the scorer a hint that all
was not well. There are a few imports that reveal the conviction: "Once you have taken on a job you better go through
with it"; and, "If you stick by your guns and do what is necessary you can help those that depend on you." But there are
more imports that say: "You can always take the easy way out";
or, "You might as well put off making an effort because something may happen that brings you what you want without it."
There are also imports that mention how often one's efforts
come to naught or are uncalled for. All these imports, when
evaluated clinically, would have indicated a man who may be
willing to do what he has to do, but only when absolutely
necessary—which does not reveal positive attitudes. In this case
also, the evaluation of fellow students and superiors was probably correct. If a clinical appraisal had been made at the time,
the ambiguity of the stories would immediately have been
noted and the candidate would have been asked for his comments. In the interview, the psychologist would have discovered
that the peculiar ambiguity of these stories may have been the
expression of a profound ambiguity in this student's outlook:
he wants to do what is necessary, but also take the easy way
out. Such lack of energy and decisiveness is not the mark of a
promising religious.

The third, *Scholastic C,* had been tested for Quinn's pilot study several years before the present test was given. In both cases, the TAT imports gave a uniformly favorable picture. In the four years between the two tests, several novices had left the Order but C had persevered. On looking over the earlier rankings, one of the superiors remarked that he had changed his mind about several scholastics and among them, about C. When other superiors and some of his fellow students were asked about him, they seemed to give rather superficial reasons for their unfavorable opinion: "He talks too fast, he is flippant, he is too fat, he has a slight lisp, etc." They readily admitted that in spite of these defects he might be promising as a member of the Order, might have high ideals and the courage to act upon them; and that they might have been prejudiced against him by his appearance and manner. In this case, the TAT probably gave a more valid picture of C than the rank assigned him by superiors and peers.

The same holds good for the record of *Scholastic D,* who scored low on the TAT sequence analysis but was ranked high by superiors and fellow students. Here most of the imports were clearly negative. Quinn comments that they repeatedly revealed "dependence on the direction of others, conformity to what others expect . . . a determination to escape [his] problems by unrealistic means, and . . . platitudes that are fundamentally meaningless for [him]" (p. 89). The superiors, when questioned, stressed the student's docility, obedience, tractability. He never gave any trouble and was easy to work with. They admitted that he probably had little initiative and would tend to wait for directions instead of acting on principle. While such passivity may give an appearance of fitting in with the customs and ideals of a community, it will become increasingly difficult to cope with as the young student grows up to become a man who has to take responsibility and make decisions. According to our records, it is not the quality of an outstanding student or teacher; we doubt that it is the quality that distinguishes an outstanding member of any religious Order. However, it is quite easy to mistake such passivity for agreement with the ideals of the Order, which probably accounts for the high rank assigned to this young man both by his superiors and his fellow students.

In the four cases investigated by Quinn, it seems that the judgment of superiors and peers was correct in two cases and that the TAT scoring gave a better appraisal in the other two. Even in the two cases where the scoring was misleading, a clinical evaluation would have corrected the mistaken impression immediately. The advantage of the story sequence analysis seems to lie in its concentration on the storyteller's attitudes and convictions, his principles of action, which is not influenced by personal impressions or unattractive appearance of the person to be evaluated.

14

MOTIVATING ATTITUDES OF EXECUTIVES

For several years, an Executive Development Program for federal executives has been carried on at the University of Chicago. In an attempt to examine the personal and professional characteristics of executives who enrolled in this program and those who did not, Steggert (1961) carried out an intensive program of testing.

Steggert's two main hypotheses stated that those executives who participated in the Executive Development Program, "as measured by informed opinion and psychological tests, tend to be 'better than average' employees"; and that they tend to be high achievers. According to Steggert, informed opinion confirmed the first hypothesis. Agency administrators described the participants in positive terms throughout, as able, ambitious, and energetic, with potential for greater responsibility; they also stated directly in answer to one of the questions on a questionnaire that these men were in fact better than average employees. In addition, the general job performance of all executives in one of the participating agencies was evaluated by three top level administrators; when their ratings of the participants in the program were later compared with their ratings of non-participants, it was found that the participants had been rated higher.

The psychological tests used to test the first hypothesis were the American Council on Education Psychological Examination (ACE) and the U. S. Civil Service Commission's Test No. 56 A.

These tests confirmed the hypothesis only partially. In those agencies where participation in the program was left to the executive's own initiative, participants had a significantly higher language ability score on the ACE test than non-partici-pants (at the 1 percent level of confidence), but mathematical ability was not significantly different. On the other hand, in agencies where the program was strongly sponsored by the administrations which paid the fees for the participants, there were no significant differences in ability between participants and non-participants.

Another test used to establish the superiority of participants in this program was Mandell's Administrative Judgment Test (AJT). The results were similar to those obtained from the intelligence tests. Executives who had to take the initiative in enrolling in the program and paid their own fees were su-perior to those who were assigned to the program by their agency.

To test the second hypothesis, that the executives participat-ing in the program would tend to be high achievers, Steggert used the TAT sequence analysis for a sample of ten participants and ten non-participants. He also tested fifteen participants and fifteen non-participants with Nelson's Survey of Manage-ment Perception (SMP) which, according to Nelson, is "a projective test built around pictures of problem situations and issues that are typical of everyday management experiences." The ten pictures in this test portray various office and factory scenes. The stories told about these pictures were abstracted into imports and combined into a sequence analysis which was scored according to our scoring criteria. In both tests, the two groups of participants and non-participants were equated for civil service grade, years in federal service, type of position, and education.

All the executives tested with the TAT and SMP came from agencies that left participation in the program up to the executive's own initiative. However, the two samples (executives tested with the TAT and those tested with the SMP) were not equal in other respects. Most of the SMP sample were at lower grade levels in the federal service and had fewer service years —and fewer of them had graduate degrees.

TAT SEQUENCE ANALYSIS

The TAT cards used included cards 1, 2, 3, 4, 6, 7, 8, 14, 17, 19, all taken from the set for men. This selection excluded all cards that might give offense. These men in senior executive positions were chary of psychological tests, particularly if they suspected that the psychologist might pry into private (and particularly sexual) matters. For this reason, the most innocuous pictures of the set were chosen. That the stories to these pictures gave as good results as the pictures used in other studies is proof, if proof is needed, that any sequence of stories about general human themes will reveal valid motivational patterns.

When the twenty records were scored after all identifying marks had been removed, it was found that nineteen of the twenty executives tested had positive scores. Steggert, like Quinn (see Chapter 13), scored strongly negative attitudes as 1; mildly negative ones as 2; mildly positive motivation was scored as 3; and strongly positive attitudes as 4. Since the final score in this system of scoring is the sum of individual scores divided by the number of stories obtained, any score over 2. is positive, and any score of 2. and under is negative. Those executives who had enrolled in the Executive Development Program obtained scores ranging from 3.33 to 3.80, all highly positive. Non-participants in the program, on the other hand, obtained scores ranging from 1.70 to 3.20. While only one of them obtained a definitely negative score (1.70), all of them obtained lower scores than the lowest of the program participants.

Since all the men tested have executive positions, we would

expect them to reveal positive motivation, for we have found in earlier studies that positive motivating attitudes indicate high achievement. All of them barring one actually did reveal positive motivation; but the ten who had been judged better than average employees, who were rated higher in a special assessment and had higher scores on the L scale of the ACE and on the AJT, also turned out to have a more positive attitude than the best of their lower-rated fellows. Here is an example of a record typical for program participants:

Record #21

[Card 1] A young man contemplates his violin as he mentally reviews the score of a violin sonata recently studied. He began the study of the violin at the age of four and is considered a musical genius. He will turn out to be a concert violinist.

[Card 2] A farm girl is returning home from school while her parents are busy in the field. She has just gotten off the school bus and has come out to greet her parents. She likes school very much and plans a career in nursing. She has great determination and will succeed in this venture.

[Card 3] A young woman sits despondently by the side of the bed after having attempted suicide and failing to accomplish it. The situation was brought about by unhappy marital relations and her husband's demand for a divorce. She was married too young and has not been able to adjust to maturity. She will remain unadjusted to her problems of life and will become a woman of loose moral character.

[Card 4] A wife pleads with her husband to change his way of life and stop running around with other women, gambling, etc. He has just returned in the morning from a night out. The situation will not improve, however, and she will leave him, get a job, and eventually get a divorce.

[Card 6] A young policeman has just informed an elderly kleptomaniac that she must accompany him to the police station again. She has been observed stealing or picking up various objects in a department store where she was a well-known character. She will eventually be sent to a detention home for it is believed that she is too old for rehabilitation.

[Card 7] Two law partners are discussing the case of a client in a court litigation of a civil suit. The case involves a dispute over a breach of contract, brought by the client of these two lawyers. The case will eventually be decided in favor of their client.

[Card 8] This involves the daydreams of a young boy who dreams of becoming a great surgeon some day when he is grown, and of how he will perform great operations on the battlefield, with only crude instruments and under primitive conditions. He will grow up to become a successful teacher—professor of sociology at a famous university.

[Card 14] A young man stands by an open window at night. It is too warm to sleep and he stands by the window in hopes of getting some cool air. He is leaning against the window casement with his arm against the wall, and considering some of the problems and decisions he will face at work tomorrow. As the night temperature begins to cool, he will return to his bed and go to sleep.

[Card 17] A circus aerial-trapeze performer is returning by rope to the group after a session of practice on the trapeze prior to the afternoon performance. He spends part of each day practicing new routines to improve his act. He will continue to be a circus performer, at the top of his profession for a year or two more, but is aging and will probably not be able to continue this strenuous work for long. He is training his young daughter in this work to take over after he retires.

[Card 19] Two hunters have come to a cabin in the north woods to do some hunting. Night is coming on. A storm is coming up. A heavy snow storm has covered the ground, and the storm will bring more snow. The cabin is well lighted by the use of lanterns and the light shines brightly through the windows. These conditions will not seriously affect the hunters as they are prepared for these weather conditions and the snow will enhance the hunting conditions. They will certainly have a very enjoyable week of hunting.

These are the imports, as given by Steggert:

1. One who begins to study at an early age will be recognized and will turn out to be very skilled. [+2, I.B.1.a.]

2. And, if he likes what he is doing very much and has great determination, he will have a successful career.   [+2, I.B.1.c.]

3. But if he acts too impulsively and in an immature way, he will fail. Despondent, he will remain maladjusted.

[+2, II.A.1.b.]

4. Pleas will not move him and eventually his impulsive actions will cause others to leave him.   [+2, III.B.1.b.]

6. When he has done wrong many times, he will be severely punished, for others will consider him to be hopeless.

[+2, II.A.1.a.]

7. Those who discuss a situation in advance will eventually have things work out to their advantage.   [−1, I.B.1.b.]

8. And one who dreams of becoming great and of performing great things in the face of adversity will go on to at least some sort of success.   [−2, I.A.2.c.]

14. He will think in advance of the problems and decisions facing him in his work.   [+1, I.B.1.a.]

17. When he reaches the top of his profession, he will still try each day to improve. When age and the strain of work may shortly force him to stop, he will start training someone younger to take his place.   [+2, I.A.1.a.]

19. And so, those who are prepared will enjoy what they have set out to do. Some adverse conditions may even help them achieve their goal.   [+2, I.B.1.b.]

While the sequence analysis could be improved upon, the scoring will remain the same. We have given the categories and subdivisions according to our scoring criteria to make it easier to check up. To show that the sequence analysis can tell a more connected story and one that seems to apply much more accurately to this individual's problem, without being less accurate and without changing the scoring, we offer this alternative:

1. When you start your training young, have talent, and re-

view your work as you go on, you will turn out to be outstanding in your job. [+2, I.B.1.a.]

2. When you like your work and have great determination, you will have a successful career. [+2, I.B.1.c.]

3. But, if a person is not able to adjust to maturity, he remains unadjusted and goes from bad to worse if he doesn't despair altogether. [+2, II.A.1.b.]

4. And, if it is your partner that indulges in impulsive actions, you can plead with him, but if the situation does not improve you will have to leave and make other arrangements. [+2, IV.A.1.a.]

6. He may be so set in his wrong ways that he has to be restrained. [+2, II.A.1.b.]

7. Since he has not fulfilled his obligations toward you, you can take legal action and gain redress. [+2, IV.A.1.a.]

8. When you grow up, glamorous dreams eventually make way for realistic achievement, [+1, I.C.1.a.]

14. and you take advantage of the circumstances at hand to consider the problems and decisions facing you in the future. [+1, I.B.3.a.ii.]

17. You continue to work for improvement in your profession, and when your age makes it advisable to retire, you prepare someone else who can carry on. [+2, I.A.1.a.]

19. Then you can engage in your favorite pastime for which you are prepared so that the winter (of life) yields additional gain. [+1, I.B.5.a.]

The main difference between this sequence and the original one is in the treatment of imports *3-7*. It does not seem likely that this part of the sequence refers to the same person to which the first and second imports refer. It is better to make that clear in the sequence analysis. While a storyteller always talks about his own situation, he does not always talk about himself. In this part of the sequence he seems to talk about someone close to him who is giving him trouble. It may be his wife, but could be a partner who has disappointed him. Since a clinical evaluation was not part of this study, it was impossible to check. This record is another example of the fact, mentioned in Chapter 6, that the sequence analysis provides clinical insights in addition to the quantitative scoring.

The above sequence analysis should be compared with record 15, Chapter 6, which is that of a non-participant in the executive development program. It is obvious in record 15 that the storyteller's negative attitudes effectively prevent him from participating in the program.

SURVEY OF MANAGEMENT PERCEPTION (SMP)

The imports derived from the SMP stories are formulated in the same way as those derived from TAT stories. However, the quantitative results are not nearly as clear cut. The scores of participants in the program ranged from 3. to 4. with a mean of 3.35, while the scores of non-participants ranged from 1.88 to 3.75 with a mean of 2.84. Consequently, the average of both groups reveals positive motivation; in fact, 28 out of 30 had a score over 2. Thus most of these executives, like the executives who took the TAT, reveal positive motivation, but there is considerable overlap within the range of positive scores. However, when we compare the motivating attitudes revealed in the two tests, we find an important difference. The TAT imports range over all four categories or areas covered in our scoring criteria, while various attitudes to work, achievement, or success are almost the only motives expressed in the SMP pictures. Though the pictures that are shown do not prescribe the kind of attitudes revealed in the stories (positive or negative), they do limit the topics about which stories will be told. In the SMP, the only topics are job situations. It is quite possible that a man may have positive attitudes to work and achievement, and negative attitudes everywhere else. This was exemplified, for instance, in record 15 quoted above. We also remember that Petrauskas's study of Navy men revealed markedly negative attitudes in their general outlook on life, their personal expectations, and particularly in the sexual sphere.

If a set of pictures is narrowly confined to one theme, that of work and achievement, we only tap a man's motivating attitudes in this one area. But, he is not influenced only by his motivation at work. Unwittingly but nevertheless effectively, his attitudes toward others, toward right and wrong, his habitual reaction to adversity of all kinds, will influence even his workaday life. The same executives who may be highly positive in the work and achievement area may have negative attitudes in other areas of life which prevent them from achieving as much or from showing as much initiative as they could. These attitudes may also prevent them from taking advantage of unusual opportunities, as, for instance, the Executive Development Program. It is perhaps significant that the reasons given by some of the high-scoring non-participants for their failure to enroll in the program (poor health, family responsibilities, commuting distance, overtime work, etc.) did not prevent others in the same circumstances from taking the course.

It may be instructive to give a record of stories told to the SMP.

Record #22

[Picture 1] A young and promising junior executive is working alone in the office after the rest of the staff have gone home. He is working on the report of a major project for which he alone is responsible. The project is extremely complex. It involves problems both of policy and procedure. The young man knows what he is going to do as far as the outcome of the project is concerned. He is only considering how best to phrase a particular key idea. The young man is a staff technician. He is trying to develop a particular personnel program which will be acceptable both to his superiors and to the operating officials who will be affected by the program. He is quite confident that he will be able to deal with the situation. After a thorough analysis of the problem, he finds he is "on the right track." He has broken through and the rest will be fairly simple. His report is completed before much longer. It is accepted by his superiors and praised highly by them.

[Picture 2] A young man is entering the office of a senior executive whom he has come to interview. He has with him a rather involved questionnaire which he hopes to have completed. He is somewhat concerned about the time this will require. The executive has asked him to come in but he has also indicated in a number of ways that he is very busy. The senior executive is prepared to cooperate but he has his own definition of cooperation. The young man is a professional researcher. He is cautiously confident. He feels he will get what he wants but he knows he will have to be careful. He handles the matter skillfully. He explains the significance of the interview so well that the senior executive forgets how busy he is and gives all the information needed.

[Picture 3] A production foreman has entered the plan manager's office. He is holding a broken machine part and has indicated that a major line is not operating because of a breakdown. The foreman wants to know what to do. No replacement part is available and none can be obtained until the next day. The plant manager has said that he will take care of things. While the foreman is quite excited, the plant manager has remained quite calm. He is a little perturbed that the other is so upset. The manager decides to divert the idle workers to other production lines. He calls the other foremen to tell them what to expect. He then makes sure that the needed part will be on hand the next day.

[Picture 4] An ambitious, hard-working young man has arrived home rather late. There are a few items he is trying to clear up for the next day. His son has been talking to him while his wife has been out. The young man has been carrying on a conversation with his son while checking some information. Fortunately, the work he is doing is quite routine. He is eager to get it out of the way. He is somewhat irritated by the fact that his wife has not returned as soon as he had expected. He does not, however, take it out on his son. Now that his wife is back, she takes over and gets the child ready for bed. The young man soon completes his work and is able to relax.

[Picture 5] The workers in a machine shop are standing off to the side while their foreman is angrily talking to a plant engineer. He is blaming a machine breakdown on the carelessness of one of the workers. The foreman is going on in this vein while the engineer is listening carefully. The workers are also talking about the situation. They do not feel that any careless action was involved. The engineer is paying little attention to the details of what the foreman is saying. He is thinking instead of the machine. When the foreman has talked himself out, the engineer suggests a method for repairing the machine temporarily. The next day he returns and suggests a machine attachment which will prevent further accidents of the type which caused the breakdown.

[Picture 6] A young mechanical engineer is supervising the installation of a new machine. The shop foreman and plant supervisor are standing in the background observing and talking. The engineer is working from his chart on a step-by-step basis. The worker installing the machine is not really listening. He is going ahead, relying on his knowledge of machines to guide him in what he is doing. The machine operator is dozing while he waits. He does not care how the machine is put together. His job is to operate the machine. The shirt-sleeved foreman in the background is talking about what the machine will do. When the installation is completed, the young engineer checks thoroughly to make sure everything is working. He returns periodically for spot-checks and the installation is successful. No complications develop.

[Picture 7] Four old-timers are sitting in the company cafeteria while another worker is sitting alone eating his lunch. He is reading the paper. The group is involved in run-of-the-mill company conversation. All five perform the same kind of stock work. The worker who is alone is not really conscious of the others. He is preoccupied with himself and his own interests. The four friends are aware of his presence. They do not dislike him but they rather distrust his serious manner and habits. Nothing immediately significant happens. In later years, however, the serious and aloof worker is promoted a number of times. The other workers continue as stock men.

[Picture 10] A young man is sitting in his office trying to clean up a host of details before leaving on a business trip. Some of the matters with which he is concerned must be taken care of. Others are not too significant. The young man is systematically working through the day item by item. He is somewhat concerned because some things will have to be postponed until he returns from his trip. He decides to take some work with him. By the end of the day, he has completed all the significant matters and some of the miscellaneous things. He has organized the remainder well and completes it without too much difficulty during the course of his trip.

These are Steggert's imports:

1. When working alone at a complex task, you may be quite confident that you know what to do, but you will still have to consider the best approach to your problem. Your thorough analysis will allow you to complete the job most successfully.

[+2, I.B.1.a.]

2. Although you are confident that you can solve a problem, you realize that you have to be careful when dealing with people, but your skill in handling a touchy situation leads to success.   [+2, I.B.1.b.]

3. If you remain calm—particularly when others are excited —and act logically, you will decide a problem satisfactorily.

[+2, I.B.1.d.]

4. Sometimes there will be irritations but, if you control yourself, you will finish your work and be able to relax.

[+2, I.B.1.d.]

5. If you concentrate upon the basic problem and ignore irrelevant details, you will be able to deal with a difficult situation.   [+2, I.B.1.d.]

6. Though others may not be interested, you can still attain your goal by care, thoroughness, and checking in doing your own job.   [+2, I.B.1.c.]

7. Your fellow workers may not trust you, but if you are serious about your work you will succeed in the long run while they fail.   [+2, I.B.1.a.]

10. It's all a matter of work, system and organization. If you organize your work and complete it satisfactorily, you will have little difficulty. [+2, I.B.1.d.]

Compared with the many TAT records we have analyzed and discussed, this is a dismally monotonous set of stories. While the sequence analysis is accurate and reveals highly positive motivation, it does not let us see the person behind the positive attitudes, as the two earlier records allowed us to do. While the other two records of executives included imports in every scoring category, this set contains only imports falling into Category I (Achievement). This is true for most of the records of the SMP. Obviously, such a set of imports is severely restricted and does not reveal motivation in other than the work and achievement area. Instead of making it easier to interpret a person's motivation in a particular job, which obviously was the intention of the originator, such highly specialized pictures make it harder. There is a deadly sameness about these stories that obliterates individual differences instead of uncovering them. These stories are easy to score, but the price for such convenience is far too high. A man does not live by work alone. His outlook on life, his reaction to adversity, his attitude toward others, his willingness to cooperate are at least as important—even for success in his job.

The fact that only achievement motivation is tapped in this series seems to explain why many of these executives revealed high positive motivation yet did not show the necessary initiative to enroll in the Executive Development Program. It would be interesting to see whether the same executives, given a set of pictures of more general interest, would score differently. We would venture to predict that a set of any ten TAT pictures which portray human situations rather than job scenes would be far more revealing; the sequence analyses derived from these stories might distinguish the executives participating in the program from those who did not, as effectively as

the TAT sequence analysis distinguished the two groups in
the earlier study.*

* There are two other factors that might have contributed to the indecisive
results. The executives were shown only 8 SMP pictures (*versus* 10 TAT pictures) and were given story outline sheets with four headings: Setting, Character,
Plot, Outcome. Under each heading was one of the following statements: "Describe what's going on in this picture." "Describe the characters and their occupations. What are they thinking and feeling?" "How are they dealing with the
situation? What are they feeling and doing?" "How does the story come out?"
These questions probably contributed to the monotony of the stories but they
could not have influenced the type of attitude revealed (negative or positive).
The smaller number and homogeneous nature of the pictures actually increased
consistency. Of the SMP records, 75 percent had high scores between 3 and 4;
while only 55 percent of the TAT sequence analyses were scored that high.

15

IMPLICATIONS

In these pages a method of scoring and interpreting story-telling tests has been demonstrated which can be used to predict a man's performance in a variety of situations. Though it is not possible to offer exact figures on the comparative validity of story sequences of different lengths, it seems advisable to publish the evidence obtained so as to encourage others to use the method and so obtain larger numbers of sequence analyses. Eventually, as such studies accumulate, it may become feasible to work out standard scores in place of the ratio values of the Motivation Index. In the meantime, this Index will provide a rough comparison.

Perhaps it should be emphasized once more that the scoring categories for use with the sequence analysis are not a priori judgments but have been worked out empirically. Each statement scored plus under any of these categories is an abstracted import which has been actually found among high achievers, well-adjusted Navy men, good teachers, ambitious executives; those scored minus were found among low achievers, Navy offenders, poor teachers, less ambitious executives. These imports reveal the attitudes and motives of actual storytellers. They are not based on scorers' judgments of how success can be achieved or adversity overcome, of what is right and wrong, but embody the storytellers' own convictions.

These scoring criteria have a high scorer reliability and will be found adequate for scoring story imports obtained from normal people. There is only a limited number of ways in which a positive or negative outlook can be revealed in stories. In any culture there is a limited number of ways in which a situation can be faced. Not all of these ways may have been catalogued in the scoring categories, but the alternatives given, at least approach a vanishing point of possibilities. In the course of collecting additional records, the scoring criteria will be expanded and revised. In addition, imports characteristic for various abnormal groups (schizophrenics, patients with personality disorders, alcoholics, and the like) are now being collected and will be presented at a later date. It is also hoped that records from other countries and other cultures will supplement the scoring criteria derived from a comparatively small segment of the United States population.

In taking stock of the evidence presented thus far, we find (in well over 500 cases, counting clinical records) a decisive difference in motivation between people who have achieved a measure of excellence and those who have not. In this sample, high achievers in whatever area—from elementary school to college, from the lowly Navy recruit to high-powered executives—reveal a set of principles that are close to the ethical principles of our traditional Western culture. They are sharply opposed to the dog-eat-dog ethic characteristic for the extreme low achiever. Our studies confirm the observations recorded by Peck, Havighurst, *et al.* (1960), after years of careful clinical study, that there are desirable and undesirable character types. Of the five types these authors list (the amoral, expedient, conforming, irrational-conscientious, and rational-altruistic) only the rational-altruistic type would correspond to our high achievers with strongly positive motivation. Indeed, the method of story sequence analysis demonstrated here provides a continuum from extremely negative to extremely positive motivation, which includes these five types at different points. As the rational-altruistic character would be at the extreme positive end of the scale, so the amoral character would be at its negative extreme. From both a psychological and a measurement point of view, it is preferable to have a continuum rather than a collection of isolated types. Our studies completely agree with the dictum of Peck and his associates that "these ethical imperatives are not just one among many, equally plausible ways of life. Instead, they seem more and more to represent some basic, crucial facts about human nature, if it is to be maximally developed and gratified" (p. 199).

To substantiate this claim, let us look at the convictions that are revealed in our empirically derived scoring criteria. Imports of high achievers reveal the conviction that, by and large, success and happiness follow actions for ethical, well-intentioned, rational, religious motives, while omitting to act for such motives results in failure and unhappiness. We find that positively motivated storytellers reveal a preference for altruistic, ethical, rational, religious values, as against material, expedient, irrational values; that they are optimistic and willing to back up their optimism with constructive action; and finally, that they have an active personal relationship to God.*
In contrast, negative imports reveal that the storytellers have either no goal or one that is shifting, uncertain; that they believe success is the result of ill-intentioned or selfish motives, or can be had by omitting ethical or well-intentioned actions; that success is doubtful, and failure much more likely; that success, if it does come, is a matter of luck, chance, or fate.

There is a similarly striking difference in the means high achievers believe to be essential for achievement, as against those used or advocated by low achievers. High achievers insist that success comes through active effort which includes control of emotions, reasonable action, even self-denial; while

---

* Comparatively few imports directly mention God or prayer. But of those that do, the imports of high achievers speak of God as creator, father, and the like, or express readiness to do His will. Imports of low achievers express passive dependence (e.g., by prayer) without active effort.

failure follows when these means are omitted. They may also
see the reason for failure in impulsive, irrational action or
personal inadequacy. They are positively oriented toward
work; they do it cheerfully and find that it offers intrinsic rewards, while work done reluctantly or unenthusiastically reaps
only moderate success. Not so the low achiever. For him, success comes in fantasy rather than being the fruit of active effort.
He favors the long shot, pretends that reality makes no demands, or revels in Love written large that is better than any
achievement. He is convinced that success can be had by using
force, devious or dishonest means, or that it comes despite
lack of interest in work and despite devoting his time to play
and recreation. He shuns effort because he is afraid he would
fail and feel frustrated and unhappy; when he does fail, he
does not admit it, blames it on everybody and everything but
himself or passes it off as of no account. He has a negative attitude toward work and often even toward play: work is distasteful, harmful, degrading; and play may be exhausting or
not worth the effort.

A man who is positively motivated believes that failure can
be overcome by personal effort and initiative, by controlling
his emotion, by acting reasonably. His negatively motivated
fellow believes that failure must be overcome by illegitimate
means or ends in despair, unless fate comes to his aid.

The attitudes of high achievers, as sketched here and derived
from our Category I (Achievement, success, happiness, active
effort [or lack of it]), are often called idealistic, impractical,
unsuited to our workaday world, while some of the attitudes
characteristic of the low achiever seem to be condoned if not
advocated by hard-headed, practical people. How often do we
not hear that success is a matter of chance or pull, that the
only effective motive is self-interest? Does it not seem that
some practices in business and industry, both in management
and among labor organizations, are based on such convictions?

We need only think of the ruthless competition in the name of self-interest, the price fixing and collusion among respected firms; and among labor unions, of the violence often connected with strikes, the featherbedding among workers, the doubtful practices among union bosses that have brought them in conflict with the law. Does it not seem that they subscribe to the creed of the low achiever who despises work and believes that success requires devious or dishonest means, or can be had by force?

At least, the attitudes of the high achiever to work and achievement are recognized as desirable by individual men and women, including social scientists. Indeed, these attitudes still form our ethical convictions as a nation and are acknowledged even among those who think them impractical. It should provide food for thought that these impractical attitudes are found among high achievers, men and women who in their own sphere, whether that is school or life, are doing well and are, in fact, outstandingly successful. In contrast, the doubtful practices condoned by practical men are found in stories of low achievers, people who do not use their talents, though these may be considerable, or do not use them constructively. Perhaps if our criterion of success were the amount of money or power a man achieves, the picture would be different. But, as long as our criterion is a judgment of performance by those in a position to know, the outstanding people will be people like our high achievers, no matter how impractical, idealistic and high-minded they may sound.

While the low achiever's attitudes toward achievement are well recognized as undesirable, it is rather different with his attitudes toward right and wrong (Scoring Category II). For the low achiever, wrongdoing is a matter of personal relations or social conventions. At worst, it gets him into trouble, but this can often be avoided by simply admitting his fault or saying he is sorry. In fact, it may be covered up by those who love him, is forgiven by them because they love him, or is forgiven when he begins to succeed. He thinks he can avoid punishment altogether or can avoid it if he is a big enough personage. He is convinced that wrongdoing is caused by external factors: bad environment, poor upbringing, poor heredity, or simply the rascality of others. In fact, wrongdoing is justified, he thinks, when right action would conflict with his selfish interest or when means are needed for something worthwhile. He is sure that punishment has undesirable consequences: it does no good, arouses resentment, may lead to despair. At best, the culprit resolves not to be caught again.

Some of these attitudes are not immediately recognized as undesirable today. In fact, they have an uncomfortable resemblance to some of the principles advocated in recent years by social scientists. Since psychotherapists base their theories on their observations of disturbed people, it is not really surprising that they should have adopted the convictions of their patients as the norm for everybody. It is much more surprising that there has been so little opposition to such a low estimate of human aspirations. We have been told with increasing assurance that right and wrong are strictly a matter of social conventions; that wrongdoing is the result of bad environment or poor childhood training; that punishment does no good because it leads to resentment, and that the wrongdoer should be treated psychiatrically instead of being punished. This latter conviction has an ironical counterpart in the imports of many low achievers who insist that wrongdoers can be "straightened out" by others even though they may show no evidence of repentance nor make any attempt at restitution. Low achievers, like some social science devotees, also like to predict that a person will do the right thing because of good upbringing or because he comes from a good home or desirable environment.

Compared to this easy tolerance of wrongdoing and the

wrongdoer, the high achievers are quite uncompromising. They say in their imports that right action depends on a man's choice or will; that wrongdoing deserves punishment and should not only be admitted but repented, amended. They have a lively concern with injustice of all kinds and are willing to demand justice, work and even fight for it. At the same time, when injustice must be suffered, they advocate overcoming resentment and other negative emotions. They hold that vices and negative emotions harm oneself and others. They do not believe that revenge is ever justified and believe that ill intentions will be frustrated in the end. They also insist that any temptation to wrongdoing must be actively resisted.

A similar discrepancy between some of the attitudes of high achievers and the attitudes advocated by social scientists is found in the field of human relations (Category III). It is only low achievers who think that lack of love or affection, either in childhood or later, leads to failure, difficulties, or unhappiness—and so do many clinical psychologists for whom parental "rejection" is the main and often the only cause of later troubles! Low achievers also believe, in common with many clinical psychologists, that rejection by others has exaggerated effects. They think it undermines confidence, causes failure. For this reason one's actions should conform to others' opinions: one should yield for the sake of peace or for social reasons. They also believe that a man is doomed to failure unless others help him, even before he himself has made much of an effort. Low achievers hold that love solves everything; and when there is no love, they support blind rebellion against authority.

In contrast, high achievers make a sharp distinction between legitimate pressure from those in authority to which they are ready to yield, and illegitimate pressure, which they resist. This is a far cry from the notion, found in some social science writings, that "authoritarianism" is always bad. High achievers also insist that unfavorable environment or the bad influence of others can be overcome or avoided by one's own determined efforts. Their actions seem not to be dictated by the opinions of others. On the contrary, reasonable actions are carried out despite objections, disagreements, or the negative attitudes of others. While they are ready to ask or follow reasonable advice, high achievers insist that a man must choose his own work or course in life. They are independent, yet willing to seek or ask for professional help when they have problems that require it. Finally, they see themselves as having a positive influence on others. They succeed in comforting, amusing, or inspiring others, or in persuading them to be reasonable. They contribute actively to other people's happiness or success, enlist their co-operation in well-intentioned enterprises, and successfully reconcile them to their own (the high achievers') reasonable course in life. They know that adversity can be overcome by positive, self-determined action, either alone or in cooperation with others. If it cannot be overcome, it must be suffered in a positive way, by working, helping others, overcoming negative emotions, and the like.

NEGATIVE PATTERNS

While high achievers differ among themselves mainly in the degree of positive effort they reveal, low achievers seem to exhibit different patterns of negative attitudes. For instance, there is the pattern revealing sheer passivity, an unwillingness to make a positive effort. A man with this pattern has either no goal or relinquishes it as soon as the going gets rough. He may hope for success or dream about it; but if it comes, it is brought about by sheer patient waiting, by fate or chance which make the dream come true. He finds work too demanding or altogether exhausting and gives up striving—if he ever started—because he sees difficulties or unpleasantness ahead. He depends on the sympathy and advice of others and basks in the success of his family, group, or country, to which he has contributed nothing. When others do not advise or help him, he is resigned to failure, tries to be happy in spite of it, escapes into dream or fantasy, or hopes that chance or Providence will transform failure into success. He consoles himself that success often brings out undesirable attitudes or is the result of doubtful practices. He believes that wrongdoing is caused by unfavorable environment, bad heredity, poor upbringing; but if the wrongdoer simply admits his mistake he is forgiven without more ado. The passive low achiever is no rebel. He is willing to conform, willing to yield to pressure of any kind, just for the sake of peace. He does not act impulsively and lacks the courage for wrongdoing. For him, good relations with others come about by chance or sheer passage of time. They are pleasant but may be disturbed accidentally and later restored by chance or fate. In the same way, bad relations are caused by external circumstances. The passive low achiever cannot influence others; for one thing, because he does not try and, for another, because he believes that his advice may turn out to be wrong. So he is helplessly dependent on others. If they are kindly disposed toward him, he may fall into an easy optimism and depend on routine and the continued support of others for his happiness. When he encounters difficulties of any kind, he again depends on others for help and hopes that things will straighten out. Accident, Providence, or fate serve to explain adversity.

This basic passivity may lead to paralyzing fear and numbing anxiety if a man with such attitudes is in a definitely unfavorable situation. Without support and help from others, he reveals a general pessimism. He feels that difficulties with others poison his life indefinitely and that rejection or lack of love and understanding are bound to result in failure and unhappiness. He no longer expects help, but is convinced that without it he is doomed. He expects failure, even if there is initial success. Eventually, everything becomes a source of worry and bewilderment. Adversity cannot be overcome, any positive effort is useless or impossible. He sees difficulties everywhere: they follow harmless or well-intentioned action, and danger lurks even in legitimate pleasures or recreation.

Some low achievers reveal a self-centered or self-seeking motivational pattern. A self-centered person believes that success demands that he work to please others or to achieve fame and recognition. He tries to impress others with his ability and is sure of success because of the kind of person he is. Failure, he thinks, results from lack of ability, aptitude, or opportunities; it may also be the result of interference by others. The self-centered low achiever works when he has to but dislikes effort without recognition or reward. He tries to achieve success by manipulating others, playing on their weakness, or even deceiving them. He believes that favors must be repaid by favors and often blames his failure on the ineptness or downright malice of others. He expects success without putting himself out or committing himself to a definite course of action. In his opinion, obligations or duties can be evaded if they conflict with self-interest, and he is indignant if this attitude gets him into trouble. He is willing to establish and maintain good relations with others if he gets something out of them, if others give in to him and do what he wants. When friendships or partnerships end in disagreement or separation, it is the fault of others, who are expected to make up for his shortcomings. The self-centered low achiever will conform when it is in his interest to do so. He is unwilling to care for others who depend on him, but always expects that they will be considerate and take care of him; but at worst, he feels, attention or care can always be bought. While such a man sees others as troublesome and self-seeking, he is convinced that he and his group are of prime importance; he is willing, however, to tolerate others if things go his way. Adversity he blames on others; he expects help from them and uses them to compensate for his loss.

Beside the passive, the fearful, and the self-seeking low achiever, we could describe several other "types," all of which can be found in the scoring criteria: the indecisive low achiever; the heedless or impulsive person who wants his own way and does not care who gets hurt; the chronic pessimist who is convinced that his efforts are bound to fail and who sometimes reveals a paranoid tinge in his conviction that his best intentions are misunderstood and frustrated by others.

Finally, there is the malicious low achiever with a straight —2 scoring. He is determined to do what he wants and thinks he can get away with it if he is clever. When caught and punished, he coolly justifies his wrongdoing and promises himself not to be caught again. If he is in love, this "love" overrides principles and the legitimate interest of others, though he is likely to fall in and out of love without much caring, and to break off a relationship without compunction. When such a man does not get along with others, he becomes angry, insults them, fights them, or tries to get back at them in some other way. He has no scruples in deceiving or destroying others, or in refusing to help even those who depend on him. He finds it natural to gloat over his rivals or brag about his success. He does not listen to advice, for he is sure it is wrong or will lead to trouble. When he gets into serious difficulties, he becomes desperate and may destroy others or even himself.

There are other kinds of negative patterns that could be isolated from the scoring criteria and can actually be found in some of the records. Most of the time, of course, strongly negative and mildly negative attitudes exist side by side or may even alternate with positive attitudes. Compared to these varied negative patterns, people with positive motivation seem to have a singularly uncomplicated pattern. Reasonable, ethical, well-intentioned action and intention apparently reveal themselves in very similar ways. Constructive action seems to be simple, direct, without great variation. In contrast, the wrong kind of action can apparently be done in a hundred different ways.

IMPLICATIONS FOR THEORIES OF PERSONALITY

It has often been said in recent years that some of our most influential theories of personality have been derived from clinical experience with abnormal people. Those who are inclined to regret this fact are usually silenced by the dictum that normal people have the same characteristics and attitudes that are revealed in much more vivid colors in those we call abnormal. Could it be that this is a generalization that could be disproved? It is perhaps a sign of great honesty that psychotherapists have always seemed to recognize their own shortcomings in the patients they treat—but have they perhaps mistaken their emotional tendencies for deliberate intentions? Or temporary upsets that barely disturb the even tenor of their lives, for chronic disturbances that make a patient incapable of carrying on a normal life?

In recent years, two prominent theorists have attempted to correct the notion that normality is simply a less spectacular form of abnormality. Maslow (1954) has shown that "self-realizers" are decisively different from the run-of-the-mill personality and still more so from neurotics and psychotics. He calls them "healthy personalities" and thinks of them as having radiant mental health rather than being merely free from complaints. His insistence is a step in the right direction. However, the term "healthy" suggests that their enviable state is more the result of a robust constitution and fortunate early satisfaction of their needs than the outcome of sober planning or willing self-discipline.

Mowrer (1961) takes the opposite point of view. For him, mental disorder, particularly neurosis, is a man's own fault

and own responsibility: it is the result of "sin." While Maslow
underestimates the individual's responsibility, Mowrer patently
overestimates it. No man can be guilty, still less can he sin,
unless he recognizes that he is breaking a law he is bound to
obey (see Arnold, 1961, II., Chapter 10). Though everyone may
have broken an important moral law at one time or another in
his life, not everyone is neurotic. Sin, surely, is not a sufficient
condition for developing mental disorders, nor is it a necessary
condition. There are cases of childhood psychoses and traumatic neuroses that develop before the child can be held
responsible for his actions, that is, before he can recognize that
some of his actions go against a universally valid law. If sin
is neither a necessary nor a sufficient condition for developing
a neurosis, it cannot be sin that is responsible for neurosis.
One sinner may become seriously disturbed over his sin and
guilt, and so develop a neurosis. Another may sincerely regret
what he has done, make amends, and be forgiven—and he will
no longer be troubled and will be free from any kind of disturbance.

Instead of calling people with outstandingly positive motivation "healthy," or "self-realizers," and calling people whose
disturbance prevents achievement and drives them to a clinic
"sinners," it seems rather more reasonable to acknowledge that
man is responsible for his motives, his intentions, and actions;
but he is not responsible for his emotions. He may be so
frightened by an early traumatic experience that it would require superhuman fortitude to act courageously in a similar
situation. If his motives are positive and constructive, he may
nevertheless find ways of controlling his emotion or overcoming
it by a corrective experience (see Arnold and Gasson, 1954,
p. 92 f.).

Men who are positively motivated do not have the same
attitudes as those negatively motivated. According to our studies, a man who has positive motives does not merely mind work

and effort less than his negatively motivated fellow. He finds work interesting, valuable, rewarding, he is willing to expend great effort to achieve something worthwhile. He is not merely less pessimistic, less distrustful, less selfish. He is optimistic, full of confidence, likes people and trusts them, is willing to deny himself and make sacrifices for the common good. Whether others deserve such sacrifices, objectively speaking, is not the point. A man who is friendly, outgoing, glad to be with others, who is interested and interesting, is also good company and finds friends everywhere. Seeing the best in people makes it possible for him to act vigorously, confidently, and so to succeed, while withdrawing in fear and distrust saps a man's effort and means courting failure.

Stories freely told, we have seen, reveal a man's preoccupation, his motivating attitudes, and convictions. If these are positive, they promote vigorous and constructive action. If they are negative, they reduce his constructive effort or urge him to downright antisocial conduct. A man's attitudes are acquired by his own experiences and reflections and so can be influenced for good or ill. Perhaps it is time we became concerned over the effect of personality theories that are derived from observations of abnormal and disturbed people. Do we really know what forces we may have unleashed by giving scientific sanction to the convictions of negatively motivated people? They are not helped by assuring them that they are not responsible for their motives or actions, or that right and wrong are a matter of personal relations and social conventions. Neither are they helped by reinforcing their conviction that punishment does no good and that they should be "straightened out" by others (social workers, psychiatrists, or psychologists). These notions of behavioral scientists may seriously harm young people who are still in the process of forming their motives and who may easily be swayed by them. Unfortunately, it is easier to sway people in the direction of letting go, relinquishing responsibility, forsaking discipline, work, and effort for the easy spoils of violence and deceit. Social scientists did not intend these effects, but they are inevitable once man's self-determination and responsibility are questioned. Social scientists dethroned ideals in the name of reality, forgetting that once ideals are gone, reality becomes unbearable. Edith Weisskopf-Joelson (1961) remarks that "the psychological terminology for 'helping the patient develop an idealistic ideology' is 'strengthening his defenses.' Materialistic ideologies are labeled as 'facing reality,' 'lifting repression,' and the like. The former have a pathological connotation, while the latter are surrounded by an aura of virtue and health" (p. 21). She suggests that this bias has considerably retarded the progress of psychotherapy. We might add that it has had an incalculable and altogether adverse effect on the average man's outlook on life, for psychological science is the ideology of sophisticated modern man.

Once we realize that it is possible to devise methods of personality study that sample a man's motives which *do* determine his conduct rather than probing his emotional impulses and his childhood impressions which do not, we may begin to do justice to men and women with positive motivation and cease to interpret what they do by norms derived from the negative attitudes of those who fill our mental health clinics and prisons. Perhaps we could help at least some people to keep out of both kinds of institution by providing scientific support for their intuitive knowledge that it is possible to conquer temptation, to strive for excellence and succeed, and that goodness and truth are not social conventions but the basic requirements for human achievement and happiness.

The following scoring categories are intended as a help for the scorer in deciding on the correct score. They consist of summarized imports that are ordered into divisions fitting into subheadings, and these in turn are ordered into headings which fit into categories. The import to be scored must not be interpreted with the help of extraneous considerations to fit the score, any more than the stories can be so interpreted in the formulation of imports. Rather, the meaning of the story is abstracted into an import, and the import is compared with the summarized imports in the scoring categories until the subheading and division are found that correspond to it.

To find the correct score, each import to be scored should first be examined as to its general *theme:* does it talk about achievement or active effort, about right and wrong actions or intentions, about reactions to adversity? Or simply about various kinds of human relationships? These four main themes are embodied in the four *categories.*

Once the category is decided on, find the *heading* that *specifies the theme.* For instance, an import may read: "Whatever you do, you will fail." This import implies efforts to achieve and so will be found under *Category I. Achievement, etc.* Since many things have been tried, according to the import, the means taken are not important; rather, it is the purpose (achievement) that is emphasized. Accordingly, the import will be found under the heading *A. Goals, purposes* (see list of categories and headings, p. 226).

Next, turn to the *subheadings.* These show the way in which, quite generally, the situation set in the theme is to be *resolved.* This is, as it were, the lesson the import teaches, albeit unwittingly. In the above example, every effort leads to failure; we find this type of resolution under score −2, under the subheading *4. Failure as outcome* (see list of individual scores, p. 229).

The divisions under the various subheadings now *specify possible solutions* or state how the solution is to be brought about. In our example, we find under score −2, I.A.4. the subdivision *a. failure is expected.* This is the solution this particular individual has reached: he expects that every effort will end in failure—which is implied in the actual import: "Whatever you do, you will fail."

Since the solution actually chosen determines the positive or negative score, it is desirable to select a score before looking for the subheadings and divisions. This is the efficient way to go about it, though it is possible, of course, to read every subheading under every score until the right one is found. This preliminary decision takes practice and close study of Chapters 5 to 8 and the scoring system; but eventually, it is possible to find the correct score, subheading, and division almost immediately.

NOTE FOR SCORERS

The divisions a., b., c., d., etc., are abstracted imports; the subheadings 1., 2., 3., etc., classify these abstracted imports within a given score; and the headings A., B., C., etc., represent an ordering of these headings within a given category.

To score a given import correctly, it should be matched at least with the subheading (1., 2., 3., etc.) and, if possible, with the appropriate division (a., b., c., d., etc.). It should match in the sense that a similar meaning as indicated by the division or subheading is carried by the import to be scored. It is *not permissible* to *interpret* the meaning of the import on the basis of what it might imply according to dynamic principles.

Some imports (marked with †) were found principally or exclusively in children's records thus far.

SCORING SYSTEM: Categories and Headings

I. ACHIEVEMENT, SUCCESS, HAPPINESS, ACTIVE EFFORT (OR LACK OF IT)
  A. Goals, purposes, pp. 227-29
  B. Means taken toward goal, pp. 230-35
  C. Adaptability as to goals and means, p. 236
  D. Influence of others on success, achievement, etc., pp. 237-40
  E. Consequences of success (failure), pp. 241-43
  F. Attitudes connected with success (failure), pp. 244-45

II. RIGHT AND WRONG (Well-intentioned, reasonable, responsible action *versus* ill-intentioned, impulsive, harmful, irresponsible action)
  A. Actions, pp. 246-49
  B. Intentions, attitudes, emotions, pp. 250-51
  C. Effects (consequences) of punishment, pp. 252-53

III. HUMAN RELATIONSHIPS
  A. Good (friendly) relations (including friendship, love, marriage), pp. 254-58
  B. Bad relations (including quarrels, enmity, etc.), pp. 258-59
  C. Influence of others, pp. 260-63
  D. Influence of others on success, achievement, etc., pp. 264; 237-40
  E. Influence on others, pp. 264-65
  F. Attitudes (toward people and things, God, Nature, Life, etc.), pp. 266-68
  G. Attitudes connected with success, achievement, or lack of it, p. 268; 244-45

IV. REACTION TO ADVERSITY
  A. Loss, harm, danger, terror, separation, disappointment, difficulties, pp. 269-71

SCORING SYSTEM: Individual Scores

I. ACHIEVEMENT, SUCCESS, HAPPINESS, ACTIVE EFFORT (OR LACK OF IT)

A. Goals, purposes

+2

1. Success is reached when goals are reasonable; it follows upon
   a. action for ethical, religious, well-intentioned motives
   b. action dictated by prudence, experience, etc.
2. Failure, no achievement, when goals are unreasonable or self-centered; it follows upon
   a. action for ill-intentioned, imprudent motives
   b. failure to act for ethical, religious, well-intentioned, prudent motives
   c. action undertaken to impress others

When the import indicates neither success nor failure, look for evidence of:

3. Preference for immaterial values, as against material, expedient, irrational values; preferences for values that are
   a. ethical   b. religious   c. spiritual   d. altruistic
4. Optimism, implying
   a. constructive action (e.g., life is responsible, constructive, worthwhile; compromise on principles leads to disaster, harm, penalty, etc.
5. Imports exemplifying an active personal relation to God
   a. God is seen as creator, father, sustainer of life
   b. readiness is expressed to do His will

I. ACHIEVEMENT, SUCCESS ... *A. Goals,* +1, —1

+1

1. Goals are minor, or achievement is yet uncertain:
    a. success when goals are modest (e.g., you may not become famous but you'll do well)
    b. success with some failure along the way
    c. goals striven for but outcome not certain
When the import indicates neither success nor failure, score for:
2. Imports embodying (constructive) principles (e.g., freedom must not be sacrificed for strength)
3. Optimistic imports:
    a. with reasons given, but not implying action (e.g., in nature, good times follow after hard times)
    b. implying that pessimism is undesirable (e.g., a dim outlook makes things seem worse)
4. Imports appreciating immaterial values (e.g., education, learning, etc., is valuable)

—1

1. Lesser goals are preferable; because they
    a. require less effort   b. do not affect personal worth
    c. are best
2. Two conflicting goals can be reached:
    a. with the help of others   b. by chance, fate
3. Success follows action for extraneous motives:
    a. for the approval of others
        i. simply to please others
        ii. to please others by delaying one's action
    b. for fame or recognition
    c. for the sake of conformity
    d. for self-centered motives (e.g., you succeed if you look after your own interests)
4. Success is foretold if character should try, persevere, etc.
When no indication of success or failure, score for evidence of:
5. Optimism without good reason ("Pollyanna" stories)
    a. success comes as eternal reward (no action)
6. Heroics, phoniness of every kind

I. ACHIEVEMENT, SUCCESS . . . *A. Goals,* —2

—2

1. Success follows upon action for negative motives
    a. involving ill-intentioned or self-seeking goals
    b. failing to act for ethical or well-intentioned motives
    c. delaying when immediate action is called for
    d. acting to impress others (e.g., showing off)
2. Success is possible:
    a. is uncertain, a mirage
    b. is hoped for oneself or others
    c. is dreamed about or thought about
    d. comes in unexpected guises (e.g., you dream of one thing, become another)
    e. is expected but failure is experienced instead
3. Success is foretold from the manner or look of the character (e.g., I can tell he'll be successful from his determined look)
4. Failure as outcome; failure is:
    a. expected
    b. experienced, just happens, etc.
    c. not admitted (e.g., everything will turn out well—when story indicates failure)
    d. caused by other people or things
    e. result of chance, fate, etc.

When the import indicates neither success nor failure, score for evidence that

5. Goal is not firmly pursued:
    a. it seems foolish, unrealistic
    b. is relinquished because of pain, danger, etc.
    c. becomes more difficult to reach
    d. is wondered about
6. No goal is indicated
7. Pessimistic imports (e.g., when destruction is general, you may just be able to save yourself, but there is no help even for the man next to you)

B. Means taken toward goal

   +2

1. Success comes through active effort or adequate means;
    through
    a. personal effort, work
    b. personal initiative
    c. positive attitudes (e.g., persistence, perseverance, cour-
        age, etc.)
    d. control of emotion, and reasonable action
    e. altruism (facing danger, making sacrifices for others)
        i. because it is the right thing to do
        ii. for ethical, religious reasons
        iii. for love of someone
2. No achievement or failure follows neglect of active effort,
    or adequate means; lack of
    a. personal effort, work (e.g., refusal to work results in
        loss of job)
    b. personal initiative
    c. positive attitudes (e.g., perseverance, courage, etc.)
    d. emotional control
    e. reasonable action
3. No achievement or failure follows ineffective action:
    a. impulsive, imprudent action
    b. lack of application
When there is no indication of success or failure score for:
4. Positive attitude toward work; it
    a. is liked, is seen as valuable
    b. creates new interest
    c. brings reward
    d. brings only moderate success when done mechanically,
        or out of sheer obedience
    e. is continued †
    f. is done cheerfully †
    g. is done to get back to play †

I. ACHIEVEMENT, SUCCESS . . . *B. Means,* +1

+1

1. Success follows when fairly adequate means are chosen:
   a. planning rather than acting
   b. good management (e.g., sufficient sleep, appropriate work schedule)
   c. taking risks
   d. work or active effort with some undesirable side effects (e.g., you succeed but regret missing childhood play)
   e. eternal reward despite present failure *if appropriate action is taken*
2. No success, or failure, follows upon omitting fairly adequate means. Failure follows
   a. lack of planning
   b. poor management of affairs (e.g., insufficient sleep)
   c. negative attitudes (e.g., carelessness, laziness, etc.)
   d. making the wrong choice
   e. putting off work or active effort

When the import indicates neither success nor failure, score for evidence of:

3. Possibility of success; import shows
   a. resolution to achieve
      i. with recognition of difficulties
      ii. with deliberation and planning
   b. active effort
      i. with the hope of achievement
      ii. because there is nothing to do †
   c. there is no use wondering about the future
4. Mildly positive attitude toward work; it is
   a. done reluctantly, mechanically
   b. difficult but is done
   c. difficult but brings reward
   d. done because it is right but with reluctance
   e. rewarded but has bad side effects or consequences
   f. advantageous; idleness has disadvantages
5. Positive attitudes toward rest, recreation, sleep; they are
   a. deserved after work   b. a prelude to more work
   c. accompanied by vigilance   d. important for success

I. ACHIEVEMENT, SUCCESS . . . *B. Means, o, —1*

o

1. Rest after work (e.g., after work, you rest)

—1

1. Success because of extraneous factors:
   a. fate, chance, miracle
   b. passage of time without evident cause
   c. external circumstances (e.g., race, nationality, heredity, possessions, etc.)
   d. ability, aptitude, type of person
   e. passive dependence on the help of others
   f. change of circumstances (e.g., leaving home)
2. Success follows upon vague means toward goal without indication of active effort:
   a. wishing, hoping, thinking of goal
   b. dream becoming reality
   c. prayer
   d. weeping, wondering, worrying and similar emotions
   e. positive but passive attitudes (e.g., patience, tolerance of frustrations, etc.)
   f. decision or resolution without action or planning
3. Low achievement, no achievement, or outright failure follows reasonable or thoughtful approach; upon
   a. constructive planning ⎫
   b. thinking and planning ⎬ without action
   c. prudent management
   d. positive attitudes
   e. not putting off work or active effort
4. Low achievement, no achievement, failure or unhappiness are caused by extraneous factors: by
   a. accident, frustration by God, life, fate, etc.
   b. unavoidable circumstances (e.g., sickness)
   c. lack of ability, aptitude, opportunities
   d. habit

I. ACHIEVEMENT, SUCCESS . . . *B. Means,* —1 *(cont.)*

When the import indicates neither success nor failure, score for evidence of:

    5. Possibility of success; import indicates
       a. thinking or hoping to do or achieve something
       b. resolving to achieve (no planning, no active effort)
       c. giving thought to problem
       d. hoping or knowing dreams of success will come true
    6. Negative attitude toward work; work is
       a. difficult, boring, exhausting, depressing
       b. done under constraint
       c. distasteful when work is hard and rewards are slight
       d. increased after temporary escape
       e. put off
    7. Undesirable attitude toward rest, recreation:
       a. rest is made necessary by exhausting work
       b. rest, recreation, sleep, are indulged in or enjoyed for their own sake
    8. Action without reason; it is
       a. predicted because of type of person one is
       b. taken out of curiosity
    9. Heroics, phoniness of every kind (e.g., in bravely facing a necessary task you make a heroic contribution to the well-being of others)

—2

1. Success when fantasy and emotion is substituted for active effort; import indicates success
    a. by magic or highly unlikely means
    b. by pretending reality is not as it is, to avoid meeting its demands
    c. when there is "love" (e.g., love solves everything; love substitutes for achievement)
    d. by planning, only when given the means
    e. as heavenly reward satisfying earthly wishes (no action)
2. Success despite antisocial or ineffective means:
    a. by using force or the threat of force
    b. by dishonest means, or the manipulation of others
    c. despite lack of interest
    d. despite playing, sleeping, dreaming, etc., instead of active effort
3. Despite active effort, failure follows in the form of
    a. giving up
    b. frustration by others, God, life, fate
    c. despair, desperation, destruction
    d. disappointment, unhappiness
4. Failure is met by negative attitudes:
    a. is blamed on other people or things
    b. is not admitted (e.g., everything will turn out well in spite of failure)
    c. just happens, does not matter
    d. is expected

I. ACHIEVEMENT, SUCCESS . . . *B. Means,* —2 *(cont.)*

When the import indicates neither success nor failure, score for evidence of:

    5. Absence of active effort because of personal preference or external circumstances; because of:
       a. laziness, daydreaming, etc.
       b. difficulties or unpleasantness
       c. opportunity for rest or play
    6. Negative attitude toward work; work is
       a. distasteful, harmful, degrading
       b. too much; no reason to work so hard
       c. for some people, not others
       d. not necessary and can be evaded by fussing, moping, sulking, etc.
    7. Negative attitude toward recreation, play; play is
       a. exhausting, harmful
       b. not worth the effort
    8. Imports embodying non-constructive principles:
       a. overconfidence brings harm
       b. favors must be repaid by favors
       c. undesirable attitudes
          i. are overcome by circumstances, chance, fate, etc.
          ii. produce withdrawal
    9. Wondering
       a. what will happen †
       b. what to do †

I. ACHIEVEMENT, SUCCESS . . . *(cont.)*

C. Adaptability as to goals and Means

+2

1. Success follows when goals or means are readily adaptable:
   a. when unrealistic goals or means are modified realistically
   b. when goals are modified according to circumstances
2. Failure follows when goals or means are not adaptable; they are
   a. not adapted to reality
   b. not modified according to circumstances

+1

1. Success follows when goals or means are modified conditionally:
   a. with increasing maturity
   b. when biding one's time until circumstances are right
2. Failure follows upon refusing to defer action until circumstances are right

—1

1. Success follows when goals or means are not adaptable; when they are
   a. modified unrealistically
   b. practically unchanged despite changing circumstances

—2

1. Success follows upon rigidly refusing to modify (unrealistic) goals to fit circumstances
2. Failure follows when goals are modified in accordance with circumstances

I. ACHIEVEMENT, SUCCESS ... (*cont.*)

D. Influence of others on achievement, success, etc.

$+2$

1. Success or happiness follows upon positive reasonable actions:
   a. acting positively with the help of others *after* having done all one can
   b. actively seeking professional help for problems that need it
   c. actively listening to the advice of another (even though it was not actively sought)
   d. insisting on the right to determine one's own course of action and doing so (e.g., work, profession, marriage, etc.)
   e. yielding to legitimate pressure but also doing other work that is interesting
2. Failure or unhappiness follows upon blind dependence or rebellion
   a. acting blindly on the advice of others without judging it on its own merits
   b. refusing to seek advice for problems that really require it
   c. refusing to follow reasonable advice or legitimate authority
3. Failure in spite of effort can be corrected or prevented by special (professional) help

I. ACHIEVEMENT, SUCCESS . . . *D. Influence,* $+1$

$+1$

1. Success follows reasonable action with some dependence on others; upon
   a. actively seeking (professional) help as a substitute for doing one's own thinking
   b. seeking advice before having done all one can, but judging advice on its merits and then acting
   c. acting positively when stimulated by
      i. understanding and sympathy from others
      ii. thought of loved ones
   d. acting positively at the *legitimate* command or influence of another
   e. trying to think things out, finding it difficult, and actively seeking help
   f. determining one's own reasonable work or course in life
      i. with misgivings and hesitations
      ii. by deciding or planning
      iii. by making use of a fortunate chance
2. No success, failure or difficulties follow because of exaggerated independence:
   a. refusing to pay attention to reasonable advice

When import indicates neither success nor failure, score for evidence of:

3. Active effort which is undertaken despite
   a. lack of appreciation by others
   b. negative attitude of others

I. ACHIEVEMENT, SUCCESS ... *D. Influence,* —1

—1

1. Success follows upon reluctant action, upon
   a. waiting for another's approval or permission for doing
      something one has the right to do
   b. doing what one is legitimately commanded but resent-
      fully or reluctantly
   c. refraining from ill-intentioned actions *only* because
      another intervenes
   d. passively depending on
      i. advice or help from others
      ii. others' acceptance and understanding
   e. help coming from others while remaining inert
      oneself
   f. acting constructively when forced by another's pleading
   g. making use of chance occurrences instigated by another
2. Success or self-satisfaction though one has taken no positive action; when
   a. accepting advice passively
   b. belonging to a successful group
   c. another achieves something which one approves
3. No success, failure, or unhappiness follows through
   others' fault; when they
   a. do not help, advise, cooperate
   b. have made a mistake
*When the import indicates neither success nor failure, score for
evidence of:*
4. Lack of regard for others:
   a. decision to follow own work or course in life
      i. puts burden on others
      ii. harms others
5. Work brings commendation
   a. because it is the first attempt
   b. because of good intention, despite lack of success or
      mediocre success
6. Heroics, phoniness of every kind

I. ACHIEVEMENT, SUCCESS . . . *D. Influence,* —2

—2

1. Success follows upon blind dependence or rebellion; upon
   a. "love" which solves everything or is romanticized as escape, inspiration
   b. refusal to listen to another's reasonable advice
   c. refusal to seek advice for problems that require it
   d. blind following of others' advice to work or achieve (e.g., others suggest you make something of yourself, and you do)
   e. humiliation by others (for failure, etc.)
2. Through the fault of others, positive action results in failure, unhappiness, lack of success:
   a. when one's best efforts are misunderstood by others
   b. when active effort is frustrated by others and so wasted
   c. upon actively seeking (professional) help for problems that need it
   d. upon actively listening to another's advice though not seeking it
   e. when obeying legitimate commands
   f. when one has experienced lack of love either in the past or the present
3. No success, failure, or unhappiness follows positive action
   a. which has the help or cooperation of others
   b. which is intended to help others
   c. when helping others
   d. as a result of helping others
   e. when actively determining one's work or course in life

When the import indicates neither success nor failure, score for evidence of:

4. Passive dependence on others:
   a. asking for help (no action either by others or self)
   b. getting help, advice
   c. being reminded of things to be done
5. Hoping for others' success

I. ACHIEVEMENT, SUCCESS . . . (*cont.*)

E. Consequences of success or failure

$+2$

1. Failure is overcome by active effort or adequate means, implying
    a. personal effort
    b. personal initiative
    c. positive attitudes (persistence, courage, etc.)
    d. emotional control
    e. reasonable action

$+1$

1. Failure is overcome by active effort, aided by incidental factors:
    a. with another chance
    b. by changing to another (more realistic) goal
    c. through learning from mistakes
    d. by drawing good from evil
    e. for the sake of others or with their help
2. Failure brings punishment and increased work
    a. but some encouragement for having done the right thing
3. Work is appreciated but has undesirable side effects; it
    a. is rewarded
    b. has advantages; idleness has disadvantages

I. ACHIEVEMENT, SUCCESS . . . *E. Consequences,* —1

—1

1. Failure is overcome with little or no positive action:
   a. by the efforts or prayers of others
   b. by making less than the required effort
2. Failure is not overcome; but is tolerated by
   a. making the best of it, being resigned to it, doing nothing
   b. just hoping; hoping to do better
   c. consoling oneself with having tried
   d. quickly forgetting failure
   e. trying to be happy in spite of failure
   f. superiors who decide one is failing (though one feels he is improving)
3. Success is followed by undesirable attitudes or events:
   a. worries continue
   b. success is hollow, it fails to bring satisfaction
   c. failure or loss recurs
   d. others are culpably neglected

I. ACHIEVEMENT, SUCCESS . . . *E. Consequences,* —2

—2

1. Failure is overcome by unlikely and/or harmful means;
   by
   a. a long shot, accident, providence, etc.
   b. awakening to find it was only a dream
   c. finding it was not real because of mistaken judgment
   d. positive action which leads to harm
2. Failure is not overcome and leads to undesirable consequences; it
   a. leads to despair, desperate action
   b. ends in emotion (dejection, worry, tears, etc.)
   c. results in pretense, deceit
   d. leads to escape, actually or in dreams, sleep, etc.
   e. paralyzes all action or hinders it
3. Failure is followed by negative attitudes; it is
   a. not admitted
   b. blamed on others
   c. met with indifference
   d. a prelude to more failure
4. Success, achievement, work, routine, etc., is undesirable
   or of little importance; it
   a. leads to fatigue, boredom, harm, impulsive action
   b. is relinquished for "love"
5. Failure, lack of effort, has desirable consequences:
   a. refusal to work brings rewards
   b. failure brings comfort from others

I. ACHIEVEMENT, SUCCESS ... (*cont.*)

F. Attitudes connected with success or failure (See also III. F. Attitudes toward people and things)

+2

1. Negative attitudes lead to harm:
   a. though coupled with competence, they lead to failure, punishment, etc.
   b. though coupled with success, they are punished (e.g., bragging, gloating)
2. Interest in work is approved; it leads to
   a. success
   b. failure or little achievement if interest is lacking
3. Blaming own failure on others is disapproved: it
   a. leads to punishment

+1

1. Disapproving attitudes of others have mild and temporary effects on oneself; they
   a. make one sad, depressed, etc., but work goes on
2. Success compensates for difficulties; it
   a. makes one forget minor annoyances

I. ACHIEVEMENT, SUCCESS . . . *F. Attitudes,* —1, —2

—1

1. Negative attitudes can lead to achievement:
   a. lackluster performance can inspire others
   b. success is achieved despite lack of interest
2. Success or active effort is not really desirable:
   a. success, etc., bring negative attitudes (e.g., gloating, bragging, etc.)
   b. negative attitudes can be prevented by omitting active effort, by avoiding work, achievement, etc. (e.g., dissension connected with work is avoided by not working)

—2

1. Attitudes that belittle success or successful people:
   a. success comes to unworthy men (e.g., bad men can be great; mean, contriving people succeed)
   b. men of superior achievement are impractical, gullible, etc. (e.g., great men are easily duped)
2. Success, achievement serve antisocial or unethical purposes; they
   a. can be used to annoy others
3. Feelings of inadequacy:
   a. knowledge, preparation, etc., are not adequate, or no longer adequate

II. RIGHT AND WRONG (Well-intentioned, reasonable, responsible action *versus* ill-intentioned, impulsive, harmful, irresponsible action) *

A. Actions

+2

1. Wrongdoing, ill-intentioned, imprudent action is positively disapproved: it
   a. brings punishment, penalty (the import indicates that this is recognized as just, deserved)
   b. ends in destruction
   c. is followed by a resolve to give oneself up
   d. results in repentance, amendment, restitution
   e. is followed by forgiveness (with position action)
   f. is made good by making restitution for others
2. Injustice is *overcome* by positive action; by
   a. fighting for freedom
   b. demanding and working for justice
   c. escaping from injustice
3. Injustice is *suffered* by positive action; by
   a. consulting professionals (e.g., lawyer, clergy, etc.)
   b. overcoming resentment and other negative emotions
4. Well-intentioned, prudent, responsible action is approved and chosen; it
   a. brings commendation, recognition, etc.
   b. depends on own choice, self-determination
5. Neglect of duties, obligations leads to punishment, penalty:
   a. refusal to work leads to loss of job, demotion, etc.
6. Accidentally harmful action is corrected by
   a. giving help, going for help, etc.
   b. attempting to give relief to others

* Ordinarily, *well-intentioned, reasonable, responsible action* will be found under Category I. It is scored in Category II. only when the import is concerned with the ethical or social aspect of action or its personal consequences rather than the goal, the means to the goal, or possible success.

II. RIGHT AND WRONG, *A. Actions*, +1

+1

1. Wrongdoing is disapproved for extraneous reasons: it
   a. leads to satiation, boredom
   b. makes others mad, breaks their heart †
   c. leads to restitution, but
      i. only at the insistence of others
      ii. is followed by quarrels, litigation, etc.
   d. is forbidden
2. Right action (duty) is done for extraneous reasons: it is
   a. done out of obedience, loyalty, etc.
   b. done without conviction
   c. made easy by others' compliance
3. Injustice is suffered by positive attitudes; with
   a. hope and resignation
   b. prayer, etc.
4. Accidentally harmful action is regretted; it
   a. is not punished (if no evidence of careless action)
   b. is corrected by others' help, skill, etc.
   c. arouses sorrow, concern, etc., when help is not possible

II. RIGHT AND WRONG, *A. Actions,* —1

—1

1. Wrongdoing is a matter of personal relations or social conventions; it
   a. is prevented by others' suspicion or vigilance
   b. is followed by forgiveness out of "love" (no repentance, restitution, etc.)
   c. is forgiven when culprit becomes great
   d. is compensated by admission or apology
   e. is covered up by others
   f. gets culprit into trouble (no realization that punishment is deserved or just)
   g. brings scolding †
2. Wrongdoing is followed by inappropriate reactions; by
   a. platitudinous resolutions
   b. despair
3. Right action is done for extraneous reasons:
   a. it brings reward
   b. omitting it brings discomfort
   c. others insist that it be done
4. Right action is of doubtful value; it
   a. is suspect
   b. brings harm, penalty, which is turned aside by "love," prayer, etc.
5. Punishment is disproportionate:
   a. neglect of small obligation leads to big penalty
   b. accidentally harmful action is imputed to the doer; it is
      i. punished (no evidence of careless action)
      ii. punished as crime (evidence of some carelessness)

II. RIGHT AND WRONG, *A. Actions,* —2

—2

1. Wrongdoing does not have undesirable consequences; it
   a. is followed neither by punishment nor repentance and restitution
   b. is not admitted, or is covered up
   c. is not punished when offender is important (e.g., big scoundrels escape)
   d. succeeds if one is clever; fails if one is inept
   e. escapes penalty, which is turned aside by "love"
2. Wrongdoing is caused by extraneous factors; by
   a. bad environment, poor upbringing, bad heredity, etc.
   b. another's wrongdoing which must be avenged
3. Wrongdoing or impulsive action is justified; it
   a. is worth it
   b. provides means for good actions
   c. can turn out well if others do their share
   d. brings desirable results (freedom, friends, etc.)
   e. is justified in fantasy
   f. is defended when right action conflicts with self-interest
4. Obligations, duties, etc., can be escaped without punishment
5. Wrongdoer is "straightened out"
   a. by punishment (no evidence of repentance)
   b. by prayers of others
6. Injustice is inescapable;
   a. defense against it brings harm

II. RIGHT AND WRONG (*cont.*)

B. Intentions, attitudes, emotions

$+2$

1. Ill intentions are prevented by
   a. fate (e.g., in pursuing revenge, you come to harm)
   b. other people (e.g., discovering your plot, others jail you)
   c. goodness or innocence of another
2. Vices, negative emotions and attitudes are harmful; they
   a. make men impotent, helpless
   b. harm self or others
3. Wrong attitudes are disapproved;
   a. though coupled with competence, they lead to failure, harm, punishment
   b. though coupled with success, they are punished (e.g., bragging, gloating brings disapproval, ridicule)
4. Temptation is actively resisted when
   a. one realizes that contemplated action is wrong
   b. ill intent is conquered through love
5. Revenge is disapproved; it
   a. should not be planned
   b. is not right (e.g., revenge is not the way to combat injustice)

II. RIGHT AND WRONG, *B. Intentions,* +1, −1, −2

+1

1. Wrong intentions are not carried out because
   a. consequences are realized in time
   b. other's prayer or pleas are answered
   c. one becomes disgusted
2. Temptation is resisted but some disturbance continues

−1

1. Wrong intentions are not carried out for extraneous reasons; because of
   a. reluctance to cause incidental harm to loved ones
2. Temptation is overcome for extraneous reasons:
   a. when opportunity is gone
   b. because of "love" which is romanticized
   c. because reason for it was unfounded
3. Unacceptable intentions turn out to be acceptable
   a. through fortuitous circumstances
4. Unethical attitudes accompany something desirable; they
   a. can lead to achievement   b. are the result of success

−2

1. Wrong intentions are not carried out for extraneous reasons; because
   a. one lacks courage
   b. something or somebody interfered
   c. the opportunity is gone
   d. the intentions are discovered by others (e.g., your victim discovers your plot and gets away)
   e. an accident serves the purpose (e.g., before you can take revenge an accident destroys your enemy)
2. Resistance to temptation, etc., is *predicted* from "look" of person
3. Right action is *predicted* because of extraneous factors:
   a. good upbringing (e.g., high ideals taught in childhood)
   b. nationality, race, sex, heredity, etc.

II. RIGHT AND WRONG (*cont.*)

C. Effects (consequences) of punishment (includes penalties, legal punishment, scolding, etc.)

+2

1. Punishment has desirable effects; it
   a. is accepted (either immediately or after consideration)
   b. can profit the culprit
   c. can help others
   d. will prevent further wrongdoing if taken in right spirit

+1

1. Unjust punishment is revoked
   a. immediately or later
   b. with the help of others
2. Just punishment is accepted, though slowly;
   a. with the hope that it will be revoked

II. RIGHT AND WRONG, *C. Effects,* —1, —2

—1

1. Punishment has undesirable consequences; it
   a. is resented
   b. is followed by disgrace
   c. brings disappointment to friends
2. Punishment arouses irrelevant or inappropriate reactions; it
   a. brings respect, esteem for good men
   b. leads to exaggerated promises (e.g., culprit resolves to lead blameless life and so will his children)
   c. leads to worry on the part of others (e.g., culprit sulks and later finds that others are worried about him)
3. Punishment cannot be avoided; escape
   a. is frustrated
   b. brings additional punishment

—2

1. Punishment has very undesirable consequences; it
   a. does no good
   b. leads to despair
   c. results in negative attitudes (sulking, brooding, etc.)
   d. arouses the intention not to be caught again
2. Punishment is considered unjust because
   a. wrongdoer is a good man (e.g., culprit tries to live a good life but is caught and sentenced)
3. Punishment has exaggerated effects:
   a. it "straightens out" the wrongdoer (without his doing anything)
4. Phony, goody-goody reactions (e.g., unjust punishment, if met with a smile, leads to happiness)

III. HUMAN RELATIONSHIPS

A. Good (friendly) relations (including friendship, love, marriage)

+2

1. Good relations result (or are expressed) in positive action; in
   a. acting unselfishly
   b. cooperating with others
   c. resisting impulsive action
   d. being considerate and making sacrifices for others
   e. overcoming one's feelings
   f. rejoicing over another's success or good fortune
   g. giving gifts
2. Good relations are enduring, helpful; they are
   a. proved in adversity (e.g., standing by friends; praying for them if no other action is possible)
   b. a mainstay in work and hardship (e.g., hard work with love is better than easy work without love)
3. Good relations are deepened through a common enterprise; through
   a. common work, effort
   b. life in common
   c. common suffering
4. Good relations are subordinated to duty; they must be
   a. sacrificed for a higher motive (e.g., you must leave those you love when your country needs you)
   b. subordinated to conscience (e.g., you may have to hurt those you love for the sake of conscience)
5. Deliberately endangering good relations is condemned; it
   a. results in difficulties
   b. brings harm, punishment

III. HUMAN RELATIONSHIPS, *A. Good,* +1

$+1$

1. Good relations are desirable; they endure; they
    a. are not upset or disturbed by small imperfections, mishaps, jokes, hardships
    b. withstand separation
    c. allow for individual interests
    d. make hardships bearable (e.g., love consoles the exile)
    e. are valuable
2. Good relations are deepened by positive attitudes
    a. during enforced absence
    b. by understanding of others' mistakes
3. Good relations are disturbed but later restored by positive actions or attitudes; by
    a. friendly action
    b. common suffering
    c. repentance
    d. positive emotions (e.g., pity, sympathy, etc.)
    e. making use of a chance happening
When import indicates no outcome, look for evidence of:
4. Positive attitudes toward implied human relationships (e.g., good training is valuable, brings reward, recognition; a home is valuable, even when love is lacking)

For Positive Attitudes toward others see III.F.5. (score +1)

III. HUMAN RELATIONSHIPS, *A. Good,* —1

—1

1. Good relations are *not* established or maintained by outgoing affection or good will. They are
   a. developed from subservient, fearful motives
   b. the result of fortuitous happenings
   c. the result of waiting and praying
   d. based on platitudinous resolves with no real action
   e. the result of gifts, parties, etc.†
   f. dependent on reward (e.g., devotion requires recom-
      pense)
2. Good relations are not very durable; they are
   a. upset by rumor, interference from others
   b. disturbed without good cause
   c. superficial, sentimental, or romanticized as "love"
3. Good relations are disturbed but later restored without
   taking positive action:
   a. by sheer passage of time, chance or fate
   b. by prayer alone
4. People and things bring pleasure:
   a. love, friendship, thought of loved ones, innocence, etc.,
      are beautiful, pleasant
   b. thought or expectation of marriage or a child is pleas-
      ant †
   c. love, etc., brings happiness (e.g., happiness proves one's
      love)
   d. sudden reunion (by accident, chance, or after legitimate
      punishment) brings joy
   e. separation is hard, sad; is avoided because hard
   f. lack of love, friendship, etc., is sad †
5. Good relations are expressed in emotions, not actions; by
   a. assurances of loyalty
   b. displays of affection
   c. professions of devotion
6. Heroics, phoniness of every kind

III. HUMAN RELATIONSHIPS, *A. Good*, —2

—2

1. Good relations have undesirable consequences, or con-
comitants:
   a. love overrides principles
   b. love overrides urgent and legitimate self-interest
   c. love overrides legitimate interests of others
   d. good relations mean giving in to another; or mean
   another's giving in to one's wishes
   e. good relations are accompanied by undesirable attitudes
   f. good relations are established or maintained for selfish reasons (e.g., people are liked for what you can get
   out of them)
2. Good relations are not durable; they
   a. end in separation, serious disagreement, disaster
      i. because of own fault
      ii. by fate, chance, accident
      iii. for no reason
   b. are broken by independent action
      i. without any reason (e.g., because it is better so)
      ii. without any effort at reconciliation
      iii. for selfish reasons
   c. are broken because of own fault
      i. without apology or effort at reconciliation
      ii. with apology possible or in the future
3. Good relations improve or deteriorate capriciously:
   a. separation
      i. ends love
      ii. increases love (no reason given)
      iii. increases love because separation brings physical
      discomfort (e.g., man comes to appreciate wife
      during her absence because he has nobody to cook
      for him)
      iv. gives inspiration, perfects understanding (without
      saying how)
   b. near-tragedy increases love (e.g., serious accident makes
   you care)
   c. love comes and goes capriciously

III. HUMAN RELATIONSHIPS, *A. Good,* −2 *(cont.) B. Bad,* +2, +1, −1

  4. Good relations have exaggerated effects:
    a. lack of love leads to later failure, unhappiness
    b. sheer presence of others produces unselfishness
  5. Good relations bring assurance of favorable outcome:
    a. hoping or knowing that loved ones will do well

B. Bad relations (includes quarrels, enmity, etc.)

  +2

  1. Bad relations are condemned: they
    a. end in disaster
    b. lead to difficulties or punishment
    c. can be prevented or corrected by positive action
  2. Undesirable emotions and attitudes (e.g., disloyalty, infidelity, anger, vindictiveness) mar human relations

  +1

  1. Bad relations can be corrected; they are
    a. prevented or corrected by others (e.g., others clear up a misunderstanding)
    b. resolved by separation when no obligation is involved (e.g., friends separate when not good for each other)

  −1

  1. Bad relations have prolonged ill effects; they
    a. poison others' lives indefinitely
  2. Bad relations can be corrected by extraneous factors; they are bettered
    a. just by passage of time, by fate, by chance
    b. *suddenly,* and shortcomings are suddenly conquered
    c. *suddenly,* by conquering emotions (anger, etc.) offhand
    d. by others' pleading
    e. when being advised to talk things over
    f. after a close shave
  3. Pollyanna endings (e.g., everything ends well)

III. HUMAN RELATIONSHIPS, *B. Bad,* —2

—2

1. Bad relations have no ill effects: they
   a. go unpunished
   b. lead to no real problems or difficulties
   c. end in separation (when obligations are involved) without ill effects (e.g., marital quarrels end in walking out)
   d. end in conflict with no attempt at resolution
2. Bad relations are caused by undesirable actions or attitudes (no outcome): by
   a. neglect
   b. aggressive action (not punished)
   c. negative emotions (anger, suspicion, etc.)
   d. envy of others' achievement, success, etc.
   e. fate, circumstances, etc. (e.g., some nice people can't get along)
3. Bad relations are expressed in undesirable ways; in
   a. insults which must be avenged
   b. angry words or actions (unpunished)
4. Bad relations are caused by external circumstances; they
   a. are caused by differences in race, heritage, interest, etc. (e.g., people who are different cannot understand each other)
   b. can be prevented or corrected by change in external circumstances (e.g., familiar places prevent misunderstanding)
5. Bad relations have exaggerated effects:
   a. lack of love, affection, understanding, etc., leads later to failure, unhappiness

For Negative Attitudes toward others see III.F.1 (score —1)

III. HUMAN RELATIONSHIPS (*cont.*)

C. Influence of others

+2

1. Reasonable actions are not unduly influenced by others' opinions:
    a. carrying out reasonable actions despite others' objections, disagreements, etc.
    b. resisting illegitimate pressure
    c. not resisting illegitimate pressure leads to difficulties, penalties, etc.
    d. insisting on one's right to choose one's course in life, and acting accordingly; this choice is accepted by others
        i. immediately
        ii. after some time but without anger or persisting conflict
2. Others serve as example or warning; this is
    a. followed resolutely
    b. not followed and leads to difficulties
3. Bad influence can be overcome; it can be
    a. prevented or corrected by own determined effort
    b. avoided by separating from bad companions
4. Reasonable advice (warning) is desirable; it is
    a. asked for and heeded
    b. not asked for but is heeded
    c. not heeded; this results in harm, punishment, etc.
5. Others help when one's own effort is not sufficient:
    a. professional help is sought for problems that require it
    b. failure in spite of effort is corrected (prevented) by professional help
6. Imports state constructive principles (e.g., discipline is necessary)
7. Imports acknowledge a positive relationship to God:
    a. God is seen as creator, father, sustainer of life
    b. readiness is expressed to do His will
    c. God is seen as merciful and pardoning

III. HUMAN RELATIONSHIPS, *C. Influence of others,* +1

+1

1. Positive actions are somewhat influenced by others' opinion, etc.; such actions
   a. require cooperation, sympathy, understanding
   b. depend on following reasonable advice or commands
   c. imply resisting illegitimate pressure
      i. slowly
      ii. with misgivings
      iii. by passive waiting
   d. succeed when done upon legitimate commands
   e. mean taking some risk in following one's course in life (e.g., job might bring temptation)
   f. when emotional, are restrained by others' influence
   g. when reasonable, may be hindered but not prevented by negative attitude of others
2. Others are helpful:
   a. their (good or warning) example is followed
   b. their help succeeds (when one is unable to act oneself)
   c. bad influence can be overcome or corrected through effort of others (e.g., when bad companions persuade a boy to join in wrongdoing, parents help him find other friends)
3. Reasonable advice is followed with hesitation or misgivings; it is
   a. neither admitted nor acknowledged
   b. considered, taking action later
   c. resented, but one is grateful later
4. Positive decisions are not influenced by others' negative attitude; they imply
   a. choosing one's own work or course in life

III. HUMAN RELATIONSHIPS, *C. Influence of others,* —1

—1

1. Heavy reliance on outside influence for one's opinions and actions; they
   a. depend on understanding, acceptance, sympathy
   b. are put off to please others
   c. are influenced by others (no reason given)
2. Refusal to depend on or comply with others:
   a. acting in complete disregard of others
      i. despite others' opposition
      ii. without any attempt at reasoning
   b. refusing to comply until compliance is forced by one's need
   c. feeling that others interfere (e.g., others' suspicions or criticism spoils best intentions)
3. Blind dependence on others:
   a. help from others saves from despair
   b. others are good example or warning (no action)
   c. others compensate for one's defects (e.g., exhaustion, incompetence, poverty, loneliness)
   d. resisting illegitimate pressure leads to enduring difficulties
   e. insisting on the right to choose one's course in life leads to failure or difficulties
4. Heroics, phoniness of every kind

—2

1. Actions are dictated by others' opinion:
   a. illegitimate pressure is yielded to
      i. for the sake of peace
      ii. for social reasons
      iii. for selfish reasons
2. Negative attitude of others toward self has exaggerated effects:
   a. lack of understanding or love causes failure
   b. rejection by others results in own failure
   c. rejection is cause for revenge
   d. refusal of help results in failure
3. Help from others is ineffective; it
   a. is not offered
   b. does not succeed
   c. is impossible
   d. harms the helper
   e. is not appreciated though successful
   f. is refused by others, which dooms to failure
4. Bad influence prevails
   a. in spite of active effort (e.g., you try to break away from bad company but they won't let you)
   b. unless stopped by desperate action
5. Advice or commands from others are not heeded:
   a. reasonable advice is disregarded without penalty
   b. obeying legitimate commands leads to
      i. wrong action (e.g., fighting one's own people)
      ii. failure, unhappiness

III. HUMAN RELATIONSHIPS *(cont.)*

D. Influence of others on success, achievement, etc.
   See I.D. Influence of others on success, achievement, etc.

E. Influence on others

   $+2$

1. Exerting positive influence on others; one is *successful* in
   a. amusing, or inspiring others
   b. persuading others to be reasonable
   c. persuading others to correct undesirable attitudes
2. Contributing to others' happiness, success, etc.; by
   a. work or active effort
   b. encouragement, help, etc.
3. Enlisting others' cooperation
   a. by acting for well-intentioned, ethical, religious motives (e.g., goodness, generosity, etc., bring out the best in people)
4. Reconciling others to one's own course in life; their distrust, disappointment is conquered by
   a. success, happiness
   b. friendly action

   $+1$

1. Attempt at exerting positive influence on others is fairly successful; it is
   a. successful in amusing, inspiring others, with undesirable side effects
   b. unsuccessful in making others see reason, but effort continues
   c. successful by making use of a fortunate chance
When the import indicates neither success nor failure, score for evidence of:
2. Attempt at exerting positive influence on others; by
   a. imparting information

III. HUMAN RELATIONSHIPS, *E. Influence on others,* —1, —2

—1

1. Attempt at exerting positive influence on others is at
   least partially unsuccessful; the attempt to inspire, amuse,
   comfort, warn others
   a. fails
   b. succeeds
      i. only after a long time (no reason given)
      ii. only after disaster strikes
2. Exerting negative influence on others:
   a. fooling others   b. trying to fool others (no outcome)
3. Failure to help others:
   a. resolving to help others (no action)
   b. giving advice which turns out to be wrong
4. Negative attitude toward others:
   a. their action is approved only after one's advice turns
      out to be wrong
   b. others appreciate us only after we help them
   c. one is surprised over the incompetence of others
5. Heroics, phoniness of every kind (e.g., you experience
   vicariously other people's feelings and so can help them
   and improve yourself)

—2

1. Attempt at exerting positive influence on others is unsuccessful; it fails to
   a. keep others from wrongdoing
   b. persuade others to see reason
   c. persuade others to change undesirable attitudes
2. Exerting very negative influence: by
   a. manipulating others (even for a good cause)
   b. becoming emotional until others give in (e.g., when you
      fuss or mope, others will let you off work)
   c. deceiving others   d. destroying others
3. Failure to help others:
   a. refusing to help or procure help
   b. being unwilling to take care of others who need it

III. HUMAN RELATIONSHIPS *(Cont.)*

F. Attitudes (toward people and things, God, Nature, Life, etc.)

+2

1. Imports acknowledging man's active personal relation to God:
   a. God is seen as creator, father, sustainer of life
   b. God is seen as merciful, pardoning
   c. readiness to do His will is expressed
2. Optimistic imports implying constructive action:
   a. life must be responsible, constructive
   b. life is worthwhile
   c. life is seen realistically
   d. material values are subordinate to immaterial values
   e. compromise on principles leads to disaster, harm, etc.

+1

1. Optimistic imports
   a. giving reasons but not implying action (e.g., in nature, good times follow after hard times)
   b. implying that pessimism is undesirable (e.g., a dim outlook makes things seem worse)
2. Imports embodying constructive principles (e.g., freedom must not be sacrificed for strength)
3. Imports appreciating immaterial values (e.g., education, learning, etc., is valuable)
4. Negative attitudes toward others are undesirable:
   a. impatience, snobbery, bigotry, etc., deserve a penalty
   b. withdrawing from people leads to difficulties
5. Positive attitudes toward others; people are
   a. good, helpful
   b. forgiving (after repentance, restitution, etc.)
   c. trustful when one repents after having done something wrong
   d. loyal and true
   e. upright; they act according to principles

III. HUMAN RELATIONSHIPS, *F. Attitudes,* —1

—1

1. Negative attitudes toward others; they
   a. are inept, incompetent
   b. appreciate us only after we help them
   c. can be bought
   d. have undesirable attitudes from which one withdraws
2. Optimism without reason; sheer enjoyment of nature, God, religion, children, etc.; they
   a. are beautiful
   b. are appreciated, cause elation
   c. should be kept beautiful, innocent, etc.
3. Imports embodying (non-constructive) principles:
   a. overconfidence brings harm
   b. laziness, intolerance, etc., can be overcome by fortuitous circumstances
   c. self-will leads to success
4. Heroices, phoniness of all kinds (e.g., though everybody else rests after exertion, your work is to carry the torch, to hold it high)

III. HUMAN RELATIONSHIPS, *F. Attitudes*, —2

—2

1. Negative attitudes toward others:
   a. others are troublesome, malicious, self-seeking
   b. self and one's group are the most important factors
   c. others can be tolerated if things go your way
   d. only the weak live by convention
2. Pessimistic imports:
   a. life, people, things, are sources of worry, bewilderment, annoyance, etc.
   b. time, war, nature, etc., produce destruction (e.g., eat and be eaten is the law of nature)
   c. life, nature, is insensitive (e.g., you live and die alone)
   d. when expecting something nice, something bad happens instead
3. Undesirable attitudes are justified:
   a. bragging, intolerance, cavalier disregard, etc., are normal under certain circumstances (e.g., when you succeed you have reason to gloat over your rival)
4. Passive dependence on extraneous factors; on
   a. routine (e.g., routine brings happiness)
   b. the support of others
   c. environment, training, etc. (e.g., you become what your environment has made you)
5. Sheer passivity:
   a. waiting *
      i. for somebody   ii. for something to happen
      iii. for loved ones †   iv. for food †
   b. remembering the past
   c. wondering
      i. about things   ii. what will happen
   d. being uncertain about the future

G. Attitudes connected with success, achievement, or lack of it
   See under I.F. Attitudes connected with success, achievement, etc., or lack of it

* When waiting is successful, look under success by positive but passive attitudes (score —1, I.B.2.e.).

IV. REACTION TO ADVERSITY

A. Loss, harm, danger, terror, separation, disappointment, difficulties

$+2$

1. Adversity is overcome by self-determined action; by
   a. positive action (either now or in the past)
   b. action that is helped by thought of others, happy emotion, etc.
2. Adversity is not overcome but faced by positive action or attitude:
   a. suffered by positive action (e.g., working, helping others, overcoming negative emotions, etc.)
   b. suffered by positive attitude or prayer when action impossible (e.g., seeing constructive effects)
   c. avoided by positive action

$+1$

1. Adversity is overcome by positive action or attitude; by
   a. forced action
   b. decision not to give in (no action)
   c. some positive action after *sudden* decision to resist
   d. positive attitudes though not by positive action
   e. some positive action
      i. but emphasis on worry or waiting
      ii. but followed by regret
      iii. though impeded by negative attitude of others
   f. seeking professional help
2. Adversity is not overcome, but faced by positive action or attitude:
   a. accepted with hope and resignation (no depression)
   b. avoided rather than actively overcome (when problem is relatively unimportant and does not involve obligations, responsibility)
   c. remains a source of worry despite success or adequacy
   d. brings resolution to get professional help
   e. arouses emotion together with constructive intention

IV. REACTION TO ADVERSITY, *A. Loss* . . . —1

—1

1. Adversity is overcome through external circumstances:
   a. through other people or things (e.g., others rescue you; you are saved because sheltered in a safe place)
   b. by fate, chance, coincidence (no action)
   c. by passage of time
   d. without evident cause
2. Adversity is overcome despite failure to act when action is possible; by
   a. prayer alone   b. prayer and others' efforts
3. Adversity is overcome through ineffective response; by
   a. deciding it was a bad dream, had not really happened
   b. clowning or joking
   c. becoming indifferent
   d. imitating others' behavior
   e. compensating others through a sense of remorse
4. Adversity is not overcome but tolerated with the help of others; by
   a. people or things compensating for it (without acting oneself)
   b. appealing to others for help if help is possible (no action by self or others)
   c. receiving help from others
5. Adversity is not overcome but avoided or fled: it is
   a. avoided
       i. either passively or with undue emotion, though responsibility demands positive action
       ii. by refusal to believe it has happened
   b. escaped through dream, sleep, fantasy
6. Adversity is accepted:
   a. passively, though action is possible
   b. with vague hope for good outcome
   c. after prayer, sleep, passage of time, talk to friends; these make you feel better
7. Adversity cannot be overcome; it
   a. pursues into dream, sleep   b. is never forgotten
8. Heroics, phoniness of every kind

IV. REACTION TO ADVERSITY, *A. Loss* . . . —2

—2

1. Adversity is overcome because it was unreal:
   a. awakening to find it was only a dream
   b. finding it was not real because of a mistaken judgment
2. Adversity is overcome by accidental, unlikely means or harmful action; by
   a. altogether unlikely means, a long shot
   b. accident, providence, vow, etc.
   c. positive action which leads to harm (e.g., you escape from danger but hurt yourself doing so)
3. Adversity is not overcome but evaded; by
   a. escape
   b. cavalier disregard (e.g., you can go back to your earlier love because your wife doesn't care anyway)
   c. giving in to impulses that led to original harm
4. Adversity cannot be overcome; action is
   a. useless   b. impossible (e.g., because shock paralyzes)
   c. hindered   d. followed by greater adversity
   e. incomplete and has no outcome
5. Adversity leads to undesirable actions or attitudes; it
   a. arouses impulsive or desperate action
   b. ends in emotion, despair or destruction (whether adversity is real or not)
   c. is blamed on others
   d. has no outcome but a good one is wished, prayed for
   e. leads to avoidance of harmless action that had caused adversity
6. Adversity is caused or accompanied by
   a. harmless action   b. virtuous action
   c. supernatural action
   d. legitimate pleasure or recreation
   e. accident   f. malice (no reason or outcome)
7. Adversity is imagined or relived in memory; by
   a. thinking about it   b. remembering it
   c. being relieved or grateful that it is over

APPENDIX B

Chapter 5, *Record #4,* Card 1. +1, I.A.1.a.
                                  8. +2, I.B.1.a. *and* I.B.1.c.
                                  3. +2, II.A.1.a.
Chapter 5, *Record #5,* Card 1. —1, I.B.2.b.
                                  8. —1, I.B.5.d.
                                  3. —1, I.B.6.a.
Chapter 5, *Record #6,* Card 4. —2, III.B.1.c.
Chapter 5, *Record #7,* Card 4. +2, III.B.1.c.
Chapter 5, *Record #8,* Card 4. +2, II.A.1.b.
Chapter 5, *Record #9,* Card 4. —2, IV.A.5.b.
Chapter 5, *Record #10,* Card 8. +1, IV.A.2.e.
                              11. —1, IV.A.6.a. *or* I.B.6.a.
Chapter 5, *Record #11,* Card 8. —1, I.B.4.a.
                              9.)—2, II.A.1.a. *or* II.A.6.a.
                          10.(—2, IV.A.4.e.
Chapter 5, *Record #12,* Card 5.(+2,) I.B.1.d.
                           6.)+2,)
Chapter 6, *Record #13,* Card 1. +1, I.D.1.d.
                              2. +2, III.C.1.d.ii.
                              3. +1, I.E.1.e.
                              4. +2, II.B.4.b.
                              5. —2, IV.A.5.a.
                              6. +2, III.A.4.b.
                              7. +1, II.C.2.a.
                              8. +2, I.D.1.b.
                              9. —1, I.B.6.a.
                            10. +1, II.A.2.c.
                            12. +2, IV.A.1.a.

13. —2, II.A.3.d.
14. +2, I.B.1.a.
15. —1, IV.A.1.b.
16. —1, III.C.3.a.
17. —1, III.A.4.a.
18. —1, I.B.2.b.
19. +2, I.B.1.a.
20. +2, III.C.1.a.
11. —1, I.E.2.a.   (final score +10)

Chapter 6, *Record #14*, Card 1. —1, I.B.6.b.
2. —2, III.A.3.c. (not scored under I.D. because of capricious rejection and acceptance)
3. —2, III.A.4.a. *or* IV.A.5.b.
4. —2, I.B.2.a.
5. —2, I.B.2.a.
6. —2, IV.A.3.b.
7. —1, III.B.2.e.
8. —2, IV.A.7.c.
9. —2, II.A.1.d.
10. —2, III.F.3.a.
11. —2,$\Big\}$ III.E.2.a
12. —2,
13. —2, IV.A.5.a. *or* III.B.3.b.
14. —1,$\Big\}$ I.B.4.c.
15. —1,
16. —2, I.D.1.d.
17. —2, III.F.1.a.
18. —2, I.B.2.a.
19. —2,$\Big\}$ IV.A.3.b. (final score —36)
20. —2,

Chapter 6, *Record #15*, Card 1. +1, I.B.4.a.
2. +2, I.D.1.d.
3. —1, III.B.2.a.
4. —2, III.B.3.b.
6. —2, III.B.1.d.
7. —1, I.B.4.b.
8. —1, IV.A.7.b.
14. —1, I.B.5.d.
17. —2, I.A.2.c.
19. —1, IV.A.1.a.   (final score —8)

REFERENCES

Allport, G. W. 1937. Personality: a psychological interpretation. New York, Holt.

Amatora, M. 1950. A diagnostic teacher-rating scale. J. Psychol. 30:396-99.

—— 1954. Teacher rating by younger pupils. J. Teacher Educ. 5:149-52.

Arnold, M. B. 1960. Emotion and personality. 2 vols. New York, Columbia University Press.

Arnold, M. B., and J. A. Gasson, eds. 1954. The human person: an approach to an integral theory of personality. New York, Ronald.

Atkinson, J. W. 1961. Discussion of Dr. Lazarus' paper. In: J. Kagan and G. S. Lesser, eds. Contemporary issues in thematic appercep- tive methods. Springfield, Thomas.

Atkinson, J. W., ed. 1958. Motives in fantasy, action and society. New York, Van Nostrand.

Atkinson, J. W., and D. C. McClelland. 1948. The projective ex- pression of needs: II. The effect of different intensities of the hunger drive on thematic apperception. J. Exp. Psychol. 38:643-58.

Ayalla, Z. 1957. Personal communication.

Barton, A. 1961. Measuring the values of individuals. Religious Education (in press).

Beecher, D. E. 1949. The evaluation of teaching backgrounds and concepts. Syracuse University Press.

Beigel, H. 1959. Mental processes during the production of dreams. J. Psychol. 43:171-87.

Brown, J. E. 1953. Personality dynamics of high and low academic achievers in high school; a modified Thematic Apperception Test reliability study. M.A. thesis, St. Louis University, St. Louis.

Brozek, J., H. Guetzkow, and M. V. Baldwin. 1951. A quantitative study of perception and association in experimental semistarvation. J. Pers. 19:245-64.

Bryan, R. C. 1937. Pupil ratings of secondary-school teachers. New York, Teachers College. Contrib. to education, No. 708.

Burkard, M. I. 1958. Characteristic differences, determined by TAT sequential analysis, between teachers rated by their pupils at the extremes in teaching efficiency. Ph.D. dissertation, Loyola University, Chicago.

Bush, R. N. 1954. Teacher-pupil relationship. New York, Prentice-Hall.

Campbell, D. T. 1950. The indirect assessment of social attitudes. Psychol. Bull. 47:15-38.

Clark, R. A. 1952. The projective measurement of experimentally induced levels of sexual motivation. J. Exp. Psychol. 44:391-99.

Cronbach, L. J. 1960. Essentials of psychological testing. 2d ed. New York, Harper.

Davis, C. O. 1924. The high school as judged by students. Proc. N. Central Assn. of Coll. and Sec. Schools, 1:120-21.

Dement, W. 1960. The effect of dream deprivation. Science, 131:1705-7.

Dement, W., and N. Kleitman. 1957. The relation of eye movements during sleep to dream activity: an objective method for the study of dreaming. J. Exp. Psychol. 53:339-46.

Dodd, S. A. 1951. On classifying human values. Am. Sociol. Rev. 16:645-53.

Edwards, A. L. 1957. Techniques of attitude scale construction. New York, Appleton-Century-Crofts.

Ennis, M. A. 1961. Personal communication.

Eron, L. 1951. Chapter 7 in: E. S. Shneidman *et al.*, eds. Thematic test analysis. New York, Grune & Stratton.

Fagot, H. J. 1961. Personal communication.

Farrell, W. L. 1961. Personal communication.

Feshbach, S. 1961. The influence of drive arousal and conflict upon fantasy behavior. In: J. Kagan and G. S. Lesser, eds. Contemporary issues in thematic apperceptive methods. Springfield, Thomas.

French, E. G. 1955. Some characteristics of achievement motivation. J. Exp. Psychol. 50:232-36.

Freud, S. 1953. The relation of the poet to daydreaming. Coll. papers, vol. IV. London, Hogarth.

Garvin, J. A. 1960. A Thematic Apperception Test study of non-intellective factors related to academic success on the college level. Ph.D. dissertation, Loyola University, Chicago.

Gasson, J. A. 1954. Personality theory: a formulation of general principles. In: M. B. Arnold and J. A. Gasson, eds. The human person. New York, Ronald.

Getzels, J. W. 1955. Necessity and innovation in the selection and training of teachers. Elem. School J. 55:427.

Goldsen, R. K., M. Rosenberg, R. M. Williams, Jr., and E. A. Suchman. 1960. What college students think. New York, Van Nostrand.

Green, B. F. 1954. Attitude measurement. In: G. Lindzey, ed. Handbook of social psychology. Cambridge, Addison-Wesley.

Hart, F. W. 1934. Teachers and teaching. New York, Macmillan.

Hartman, A. A. 1951. Chapter 9 in: E. S. Shneidman *et al.*, eds. Thematic test analysis. New York, Grune & Stratton.

Henry, W. E. 1961. Discussion of Dr. Veroff's paper. In: J. Kagan and G. S. Lesser, eds. Contemporary issues in thematic appercep- tive methods. Springfield, Thomas.

Hokanson, J. E., and Gordon, J. E. 1958. The expression and inhi- bition of hostility in imaginative and overt behavior. J. Abnorm. Soc. Psychol. 57:327-33.

Holt, R. R. 1961. The nature of TAT stories as cognitive products: a psychoanalytic approach. In: J. Kagan and G. S. Lesser, eds. Contemporary issues in thematic apperceptive methods. Spring- field, Thomas.

Jones, A. W. 1941. Life, liberty and property. Philadelphia, Lippincott.

Kagan, J. 1961. Stylistic variables in fantasy behavior: the ascrip- tion of affect states to social stimuli. In: J. Kagan and G. S. Lesser, eds. Contemporary issues in thematic apperceptive methods. Springfield, Thomas.

Kagan, J., and G. S. Lesser, eds. 1961. Contemporary issues in thematic apperceptive methods. Springfield, Thomas.

Kelly, E. L., and D. W. Fiske. 1951. The prediction of performance in clinical psychology. Ann Arbor, University of Michigan Press.

Kenny, D. T. 1961. A theoretical and research appraisal of stimulus factors in the TAT. In: J. Kagan and G. S. Lesser, eds. Contemporary issues in thematic apperceptive methods. Springfield, Thomas.

Kluckhohn, C. 1951. Values and value-orientations in the theory of action: an exploration in definition and classification. In: T. Parsons and E. Shils, eds. Toward a general theory of action. Cambridge, Harvard University Press.

LaPiere, R. T. 1934. Attitudes vs. actions. Soc. Forces, 13:230-37.

Lazarus, R. S. 1961. A substitutive-defensive conception of apperceptive fantasy. In: J. Kagan and G. S. Lesser, eds. Contemporary issues in thematic apperceptive methods. Springfield, Thomas.

Lazarus, R. S., H. Yousem, and D. Arenberg. 1953. Hunger and perception. J. Pers. 21:312-28.

Levine, R., I. Chein, and G. Murphy. 1942. The relation of the intensity of a need to the amount of perceptual distortion. J. Psychol. 13:282-93.

McCandlish, L. A. 1958. An investigation of a new method of TAT analysis, by a prediction study of high and low academic achievers. Ph.D. dissertation, Loyola University, Chicago.

McClelland, D. C., and J. W. Atkinson. 1948. The projective expression of needs: I. The effect of different intensities of the hunger drive on perception. J. Psychol. 25:205-22.

McClelland, D. C., J. W. Atkinson, R. A. Clark, and E. L. Lowell. 1953. The achievement motive. New York, Appleton-Century-Crofts.

Mandell, M. M. 1950. The administrative judgment test. J. Appl. Psychol. 34:145-47.

Maslow, A. H. 1954. Motivation and personality. New York, Harper.

Miner, J. B. 1960. The concurrent validity of the PAT in the selection of tabulating machine operators. J. Proj. Techn. 24:409-18.

—— 1961. The validity of the PAT in the selection of tabulating machine operators: an analysis of predictive power. J. Proj. Techn. 25:330-33.

Morgan, C. D., and H. A. Murray. 1935. A method for investigating fantasy. The Thematic Apperception Test. Arch. Neurol. Psychiat. 34:289-306.

Mowrer, O. H. 1961. The crisis in psychiatry and religion. Princeton, Van Nostrand.

Murray, H. A. 1943. Thematic Apperception Test manual. Cambridge, Harvard University Press.

Murstein, B. I. 1961. The role of the stimulus in the manfestation of fantasy. In: J. Kagan and G. S. Lesser, eds. Contemporary issues in thematic apperceptive methods. Springfield, Thomas.

Mussen, P. H., and M. K. Naylor. 1954. The relationships between overt and fantasy aggression. J. Abnorm. Soc. Psychol. 49:235-40.

Nelson, C. W. 1959. A look at some of the basic organizational forces that affect leadership attitudes and may cause management development course to fail. Paper presented at Midwestern Psychol. Assn. Meeting.

Peck, R. F., R. Havighurst, and others. 1960. The psychology of character development. New York, Wiley.

Petrauskas, F. B. 1958. A TAT and Picture-Frustration study of naval offenders and non-offenders. Ph.D. dissertation, Loyola University, Chicago.

Piotrowski, Z. 1950. A new evaluation of the Thematic Apperception Test. Psychoanal. Rev. 37:101-27.

Quinn, T. L. 1961. Differences in motivational patterns of college student brothers as revealed in the TAT, the ratings of their peers and the ratings of their superiors: a validation study. Ph.D. dissertation, Loyola University, Chicago.

Roe, A. 1961. The psychology of the scientist. Science, 134:456-59.

Ryans, D. G. 1953. The investigation of teacher characteristics. Educ. Record, 34:371-96.

Sanford, R. N. 1936. The effect of abstinence from food upon imaginal processes: a preliminary experiment. J. Psychol. 2:129-36.

——— 1937. The effect of abstinence from food upon imaginal processes: a further experiment. J. Psychol. 3:145-59.

Sanford, R. N., M. M. Adkins, R. B. Miller, E. A. Cobb, and others. 1943. Physique, personality and scholarship. Monogr. Soc. Res. Child Dev. vol. 8, No. 1 (Serial No. 34).

Shneidman, E. S., W. J. Joel, and K. B. Little, eds. 1951. Thematic test analysis. New York, Grune & Stratton.

Snider, L. B. 1954. A research method validating self-determination. In: M. B. Arnold and J. A. Gasson, eds. The human person. New York, Ronald.

Steggert, F. X. 1961. An analysis of some personal and executive characteristics of participants in a university program of executive development for federal personnel. Ph.D. dissertation, Loyola University, Chicago.

Tiedeman, S. C. 1942. A study of pupil-teacher relationship. J. Educ. Res. 35:657-64.

Tomkins, S. S. 1947. The Thematic Apperception Test. New York, Grune & Stratton.

Tomkins, S. S., and J. B. Miner. 1957. The Tomkins-Horn Picture Arrangement Test. New York, Springer.

Vassiliou, V. 1961. Personal communication.

—— 1962. Motivational patterns of two clinical groups as revealed by TAT sequence analysis. Ph.D. dissertation, Loyola University, Chicago.

Veroff, J. 1961. Thematic apperception in a nationwide sample survey. In: J. Kagan and G. S. Lesser, eds. Contemporary issues in thematic apperceptive methods. Springfield, Thomas.

Weisskopf-Joelson, E. 1961. Psychotherapy: an ideological problem. Mimeo.

Witty, P. A. 1950. Some characteristics of the effective teacher. Educ. Admin. Superv. 36:193-208.

Wyatt, F. A. 1958. A principle for the interpretation of fantasy. J. Proj. Techn. 22:229-45.

Wyatt, F., and J. B. Veroff. 1956. Thematic apperception and fantasy tests. Progr. Clin. Psychol. 2:32-57.

INDEX

Achievement, 5-6, 9, 55-60 *passim*, 67-75 *passim;* correlation with motivation, 5, 176, 184-85; and TAT, 11-12, 38-39; and scoring, 101-3, 105, 107-8, 207; correlation with intelligence, 116, 184-7; school, 174-87; of federal executives, 195-208; and ethics, 210; scoring category, 226, 227-45; *see also* High Achievers; Low Achievers

Action, story, 12-14; origins of, 18-19; and motives, 32-33, 34; and values, 36, 37-42; and attitudes, 42-44; and imports, 51, 76; ethical significance of, and scoring, 105; right and wrong scoring category, 226, 246-49

Active effort, scoring of, 105; scoring category, 223, 226, 227-45

Adaptability, in scoring, 226, 236

Adaptive processes, and TAT, 10

Administrative Judgment Test (AJT), 196, 198

Adversity, and scoring, 106, 127, 226, 269-71; and low achiever, 217-18

Affects, and TAT, 10-12 *passim*

Affiliation, McClelland's scoring category, 11-12

Aggression, 4-5

Allport, G. W., quoted, 42

Amatora, M., 156

Ambiguity, of picture, 10-11

American Council on Education (ACE), Psychological Examination Intelligence Test *1952*, 175, 176, 184, 195-96, 198

Amygdalar pathway, 20

Anonymity, of Quinn's subjects, 189-90

Anxiety, 9-10, 12

Appetitive functions, 19, 22

Appraisal, 19, 33

Arnold, M. B., 14, 17, 27, 221

Atkinson, J. W., 4, 9-10, 31

Attitudes, 23-25 *passim*, 29, 70, 221-23; and motives and values, 31-46 *passim;* evaluative *vs.* motivating, 42-44; verbal and action, 43; and success, 80-81, 89, 211-13, 226, 244-45; teachers', 162; executives', 195-208; high achievers', 210-12; low achievers', 211-12; and right and wrong, 213-15; scoring of, 226, 244-45, 250-51, 266-68; *see also* Negative imports; Positive imports

Autobiographical stories, 25

Ayalla, Z., 22

Barton, A., 36, 38

Behavior, and TAT, 3-4, 9-10, 12-13; and need imagery, 8; disorder, sample records, 52-55, 181-83

Beigel, H., 22

Blacky pictures, 49-50

Brown, J. E., 101, 155

Brozek, J., 4, 8

Burkard, M. I., 149, 150, 155-65 *passim*, 168, 173

Campbell, D. T., 42

Categories, scoring, 105-14, 224-71

Character types, 210-11

Chein, I., 4

Chicago, University of, 195

Children's records, 178-85

Civil Service Commission Test No. 56A, U.S., 195-96

Clark, R. A., 8

Clinical evaluation, of story sequence analysis, 80-98, 202; and personality theory, 220-23